MONASTIC WISDOM SERIES: NUMBER THIRTY-FOUR

Augustine Roberts, OCSO

Finding the Treasure

Letters from a Global Monk

MONASTIC WISDOM SERIES: NUMBER THIRTY-FOUR

Finding the Treasure

Letters from a Global Monk

by

Augustine Roberts, OCSO

Cistercian Publications
www.cistercianpublications.org

LITURGICAL PRESS
Collegeville, Minnesota
www.litpress.org

A Cistercian Publications title published by Liturgical Press

Cistercian Publications
Editorial Offices
Abbey of Gethsemani
3642 Monks Road
Trappist, Kentucky 40051
www.cistercianpublications.org

1 2 3 4 5 6 7 8 9

Library of Congress Cataloging-in-Publication Data

Roberts, Augustine, 1932–
Finding the treasure : letters from a global monk / by Augustine Roberts.
p. cm. — (Monastic wisdom series ; no. 34)
"A Cistercian Publications title published by Liturgical Press"—T.p. verso.
ISBN 978-0-87907-034-2 — ISBN 978-0-87907-206-3 (e-book)
1. Roberts, Augustine, 1932– 2. Monks—Biography. 3. Trappists. I. Title.

BX4705.R5795A3 2011
271'.78092—dc23 2011025899
[B]

The kingdom of heaven
is like treasure hidden in a field,
which someone found and hid;
then in his joy he goes and sells all that he has
and buys that field.

(Matthew 13:44)

The Lord Jesus, when praying to the Father
"that they may all be one . . . even as we are one,"
has opened up new horizons closed to human reason
by indicating that there is a certain similarity between
the union existing among the divine persons
and the union of God's children in truth and love.
It follows, then, that if human beings
are the only creatures on earth
that God has wanted for their own sake,
they can fully discover their true selves
only in sincere self-giving.

(Gaudium et Spes, 24)

CONTENTS

Editor's Note ix

First Letter 1
China
Missionaries • Beijing • Departure

Second Letter 19
New England
Valley Falls • Mount Hermon • A Highway in the Heart • New Haven

Third Letter 46
But Where?
Two Concerns • Fruits of Prayer • The Plunge

Fourth Letter 62
First Formation
Postulancy • Novitiate • Father Thomas • Inner Formation • Profession and Prayer • Life with the Professed • Theology • Lost and Found

Fifth Letter 103
Expansion
Profession and Ordination • To Rome • Change of Abbots • End and New Beginning

Sixth Letter 125
Life at Azul
New Circumstances • The Novitiate and Vatican II • The Heart • Communal Autonomy • The Cistercian Order • Growth in Prayer

Seventh Letter 154
Called Back
Seeds of Change • Poverty and Wealth • Passages • Constitutions • Contacts • The Clergy • The Servant • Africa • What Next?

Eighth Letter 188
Viale Africa
What to Do? • Scourmont • Roman Secretary • Traveling with Bernardo • Procurator General • Troubleshooting • Called Once More

Ninth Letter 218
Taken
Kenosis and Integration • Past and Present • "Glory of Thy People Israel" • Two Popes • Spousal Love

Appendix I 241
Text by Dorothy Roberts
It Took Sixty Years • Deo Gratias

Appendix II 255
Text on Church Unity
Searched for by Unity

EDITOR'S NOTE

Born in China while his father, an Episcopalian bishop, was on mission there, Dom Augustine Roberts has been a Trappist monk since the early 1950s. After serving as abbot of St. Joseph's Abbey in Spencer, Massachusetts, he became Procurator General of the Cistercian Order of the Strict Observance. In the 1960s he was one of the founders of the first abbey of his order in South America in Azul, Argentina, later serving as its abbot.

Finding the Treasure tells of Dom Augustine's conversion to the Catholic Church while attending Yale and of his remarkably varied monastic experience during the turbulent years of Church renewal following Vatican II. Today he is a much sought-after guide, called to help many communities, mostly Benedictine and Cistercian, in the delicate task of adapting the perennial monastic way of life to the needs of the 21st century.

These letters from a "global monk" will not disappoint anyone fascinated by the paradox of a monk who, rooted by vow to his monastery, nevertheless becomes a world-trotter precisely out of deep obedience. Augustine Roberts is a New England Yankee, transplanted by circumstance first to Argentina and then to Rome, from where frequent travel took him to nearly every part of the globe. The historical era into which he was born, so fraught with personal and communal soul-searching, also made him wrestle, from the unique perspective of a monk based in Rome, with all the tensions of the contemporary Church and world.

Despite his own intentions to live as a pure contemplative, Dom Augustine has come to embody in a wholly unexpected way Thomas Merton's favorite definition of a monk: someone who belongs everywhere and to everyone precisely because he does not, in the usual sense, belong anywhere or to anyone in particular.

Brother Simeon Leiva, ocso

Letter 1

CHINA

1948

Azul, Argentina

August 15, 2009

Dear Eddie,

Both you and José[1], here at Azul, have encouraged me to write something about my life, perhaps because it is not the typical history of a Trappist monk. In fact it's not the typical life story of anybody. On the other hand, no one is a complete model for anyone else, but I can understand how one or another phase or incident in my life might help, encourage or warn someone in a similar condition. I hope so. I will try to avoid going into too many details, so as to bring out the central lines of my story, which is what counts. I hope it's what you had in mind. As you can see, what follows appears in the form of a series of letters to you, each about a different phase of my life, perhaps highlighting the joys and discoveries more than the aches and pains, since the discoveries are much more important. Besides, you know enough about my sins and pains from having accompanied me in the spirit for many years, sometimes even walking together physically.

Probably the best place to start is not so much with my birth, which I don't remember anyway. They say it took place in the ancient walled city of Nanjing, in east-central China, shortly after midnight one Sunday morning in 1932. It would be more to the

1. "Eddie" is Father Edward Steriti, a monk of Saint Joseph's Abbey, Spencer, MA, and "José" is Padre José Otero, a monk of Our Lady of the Angels Abbey, Azul, Argentina. [Note of the editor.]

point to start with my experiences during a trip I made 16 years later, traveling between two other Chinese cities, Shanghai and Beijing. But maybe I should first explain the general situation of my family and how I came to be born and brought up in China.

Missionaries

My parents were Christian missionaries of the Protestant Episcopal Church, which is the American branch of the Anglican Communion of Churches. My father, William Payne Roberts, and my mother, Dorothy Mills, had volunteered, each on their own, to go to China under the ægis of the Episcopal Church soon after graduating from college. My father, whom we always called "Daddy," had been born in 1888 near Staunton, Virginia, the home of his mother's family. Her father—my great-grandfather—was a Presbyterian minister in different Virginia towns before, during and after the Civil War. Daddy, however, grew up in Brooklyn, New York, where his father, who had emigrated from England in the 1870s, worked in an export-import firm and met his future wife a few years later. Daddy went to Yale University, in New Haven, Connecticut, where he was on the track and field team as a pole-vaulter.

He probably was thinking, even then, about becoming a minister, because he majored in Greek and passed immediately from Yale to the Episcopal Theological School in Cambridge, Massachusetts, from which he graduated in 1912, a good-looking, well-educated minister, a keen athlete, an even better pianist and a very eligible bachelor. He immediately volunteered for foreign missionary work, probably inspired to do so during his three years in Cambridge.

My mother was born the same year as my father, in Newton Upper Highlands, an outer suburb of Boston. Her father was an Episcopal minister, although the previous generations had been Congregationalists, descended from John Adams, the country's second president, whose ancestors had come from England in the 1500s on the second trip of the *Mayflower*. Soon after my mother's birth, her father accepted ministering to a country parish in the state of Kansas, taking his wife and two young daughters with him.

Grandpa's wife, Mother's mother, was one of the first graduates of Wellesley College outside Boston, and evidently found this radical move out West very difficult to handle. Her geographic isolation was probably compounded by the subservient role expected of a minister's wife and, in a particular way, by the fact that her second daughter, my mother, was born strongly cross-eyed. Little Dorothy's face was not pleasant to look at, as I realized when I saw one of her early photographs. To make the story short, soon after my grandmother arrived in Kansas she committed suicide by poisoning herself and, before doing so, tried to poison her cross-eyed, two-year-old daughter. Little Dorothy survived, the first sign of her strong constitution that was to last her 94 more years, but her mother did not.

My grandmother's family in Massachusetts came to the rescue at once and an aunt cared for the two young girls until my grandfather remarried. My mother, of course, did not remember all this tragedy, at least on an intellectual level, and never complained about her childhood. It seems that her relationship with her stepmother, whom I never knew, was a good one. Mother graduated from Wellesley College in 1911 and did social work for two years among the Italian immigrants in Boston's North End, before asking for more permanent work in China, putting into practice the slogan of a student movement she had belonged to at Wellesley: "The World for Christ in the Twentieth Century."

During her two years of work in Boston she consulted a doctor about her cross-eyed condition. He explained that it could be corrected, but the operation would be purely cosmetic, that is, it would not improve her vision and only bring both eyes closer to their normal parallel condition. Without much hesitation, Mother decided to go ahead with the cosmetic operation. Was she thinking—or had she been told—that this would improve her chances of getting married? Or, as seems more probable, did she believe that her witness and message as a missionary would be better accepted? Whatever her underlying motives might have been, the operation was successful and during those same months she was briefly introduced to my father at a meeting in Boston for future missionaries.

Daddy was a young, newly-arrived Episcopal minister in Shanghai when Mother disembarked there in 1913. Since he was the only person on hand who knew her, he was asked to meet her again on the Shanghai wharf and bring her to Saint John's University, an institution run by the Episcopal Church on the outskirts of the city. After a week or two, Mother left for her assignment at a girls' school hundreds of miles up the Yangtze River, in Wuchang, while Daddy went to work in a church in Suzhou, a city only 50 miles inland from Shanghai. They met again a year or so later, when Mother returned to Shanghai en route back to the USA on a brief furlough. It seems to have been a significant meeting for them, since Daddy wrote her soon afterwards, while she was in the States, to propose marriage, saying that if she accepted she should cable him with a single word, the name of any city, so as to keep their secret from prying eyes. She replied immediately: "Springfield." When she handed this one-word message to the telegraph clerk at the Western Union office, the lady read the message, looked up at Mother with a wry smile and asked, "What does this mean? I'll marry you in June?"

Their engagement lasted almost four years, until 1918, just before the end of the First World War, when they were married in Winchester, outside of Boston, by Mother's father, back now in Massachusetts. After a honeymoon on Nantucket Island, where Daddy's family used to spend their summers, they returned to China together. Daddy's assignment was soon changed from Suzhou to Shanghai for three years, then to Nanjing, where he served for 15 years as pastor of Saint Paul's Episcopal Church. Their five children would be born in these three cities.

Thanks to his first years in Suzhou, Daddy had learned Chinese according to the Shanghai dialect. He could speak it correctly and could read the Bible and the local newspapers, though he had never studied the Chinese classics as such. His was the functional vocabulary of a normal 20th-century missionary, preacher and diocesan pastor. When, in 1936, he was chosen to be Bishop of the Episcopal diocese of Jiangsu, which embraced both Shanghai and Nanjing, he was prepared for this new service by his working knowledge of both the Shanghai dialect and the markedly different Nanjing Mandarin. Above all, he was aware of the cultural contrasts between these two large, very different cities, which represented the two poles of his diocese, each of which contained a mixture of American Episcopal missionaries—of both sexes—and Chinese ministers and laity. Since our family belonged to what was called the "Low Church" in the Anglican Communion, we did not call these ordained ministers "priests."

As a young boy, I first learned to speak in Nanjing Mandarin from the Chinese family who lived with us, probably because they could not understand English, whereas all our family at least understood Chinese. My very first memories are from that period, but I have been told that one of the first crises in my life—which seems to have been so disastrous that I do not remember it—occurred when I was three. Our family returned to the United States that year, 1936, on Daddy's regular furlough, which came every four or five years. On my first meeting with my grandmother, I was so distraught that I ran in tears to my mother and sobbed, "*Lao nai-nai bu shuo zhong guo hua!*" (Grandma can't speak Chinese!) So I was forced to learn English, especially when our family moved to Shanghai later that year and my new playmates spoke either English or the Shanghai dialect, which I did not understand. So I soon forgot my Mandarin and had to relearn it imperfectly as a teenager, but the little episode with my grandmother may be one reason why my relationship with my grandparents was never a warm one, as compared with what I enjoyed with other relatives.

My four siblings—Edith, Helen, Bill and John—returned to the States at different times between 1937 and 1940, either to start their college education or to finish their secondary schooling. Since I was younger, I returned to the USA with my parents on their furlough in 1940 and remained in the Boston area with Mother, while Daddy returned to Shanghai alone, because even then, a full year before the Japanese attack on Pearl Harbor, the U.S. State Department had warned women and children not to stay in the Far East for fear of armed violence. So from 1941 to

1946, that is, during the Second World War and for a year afterwards, Mother and I lived together in Auburndale, outside of Boston, while I attended the Newton public schools. My siblings would visit us there during their vacations.

One Sunday afternoon, December 7, 1941, in our little rented house on Commonwealth Avenue, Mother and I were listening on the radio to the New York Philharmonic Symphony Orchestra, because my siblings were all away at their respective schools or colleges. The broadcast was suddenly interrupted by an announcement that the Japanese Navy had attacked Pearl Harbor in the Hawaiian Islands, sunk several ships, and President Roosevelt was convening Congress the next day, to declare war on Japan. Mother was not unused to this type of situation, due to the long Japanese occupation of mainland China with its occasional air raids and shelling. In fact one of my childhood recollections was watching the Japanese soldiers drill together and march in the streets of Shanghai during the late 1930s. But this time, Daddy and Mother were separated and halfway around the world from each other. Mother, clearly distressed, immediately phoned her older sister, Aunt Margaret, and my two sisters.

Daddy, along with all British, Canadian and American citizens throughout the Far East, spent most of the war years as an interned civilian in a detention camp under Japanese guards. His camp was located outside of Shanghai and was featured many years later in the movie *Empire of the Sun*. He and most other American citizens were repatriated in 1944, in exchange for Japanese civilians similarly detained in California.

For Mother, who was in her early fifties, these four and a half years of separation from her husband were not easy. Financially, the Episcopal Church always took good care of her, but there were very few letters from her husband, since it was long before anything like faxes or the Internet. We only gradually learned about his detention and that his life in the camp was austere and strictly controlled, but peaceful. When he returned in 1944, Mother went to New York to meet him as he got off the boat. I stayed in Auburndale and remember how impressed I was as I ran up to hug this pale, gaunt, peacefully affectionate and smiling middle-aged man who stepped off the train. It was really from then on, as a young adolescent, that I began to know my father, since I had last seen him when I was only seven.

Daddy served for eight or nine months as assistant to the Episcopal bishop of Philadelphia, before returning to Shanghai soon after the war ended in August 1945. Mother and I were with him in West Philly, where I went to Friends' Select School downtown. The two of us returned to Auburndale for a year before joining my father again in Shanghai, in September of the following year. Commercial airplane travel was only just beginning at that time, so we all took the cross-continental trains to San Francisco, then the two-or three-week transpacific boat trip. Mother and I arrived in September 1946, in time for me to start my freshman year of high school in the newly reopened Shanghai American School, a 20-minute bicycle ride, which an American neighbor of my age, Ben Gilson, and I made each day, back and forth, rain or shine.

Two years later, when I made my plane trip with Mother to Beijing, I was about to start my third year at S.A.S. as a high school junior. By that time my oldest sister, Edith, had graduated from Wellesley with honors in her Music major. After two years of graduate school, she had turned down a teaching position and moved to California to help the Japanese civilians who had been herded into detention camps during the War, perhaps thinking of our father's similar situation across the Pacific. In 1948 she was at Palo Alto with her husband, bringing up the first three of their 12 children.

Helen, the second oldest of my siblings, had attended Wheelock College in Boston, worked during and after the Second World War as an assistant army nurse, and was now teaching in the Greater Boston public schools. Both Bill and John, who was three years younger than Bill, had graduated from Hotchkiss School in Connecticut and had entered Yale. Bill left Yale after two years, in 1942, because he refused to be drafted into the armed forces, in protest against America's participation in the Second World War. It was a federal offense and he spent most of the War in different federal prisons, though for a time he was on parole for good behavior and worked as an orderly in Massachusetts

General Hospital. He finished his three-year prison sentence soon after the War and, in 1947, entered as a novice in a Trappist monastery in Rhode Island, thus becoming a Roman Catholic monk. Bill was clearly the "black sheep" of the family, though especially loved—perhaps even secretly admired—by us all.

John was my closest sibling, 7 years my senior, while Bill was 10 years older than me. After graduating from Hotchkiss, John, who did not share the anti-war convictions of his older brother, entered the Army Air Force, did his basic training and was on his furlough before going overseas when the War ended. Thanks to the G.I. Bill, he enrolled at Yale and, by 1948, was finishing his premedical studies, had been accepted at the Yale Medical School, and had married Kate, the daughter of a close friend of the family, Lloyd Craighill, the Episcopal bishop of Wuhu, in China, a short journey up the Yangtze River from Nanjing.

Beijing

At the time of my trip to Beijing, I was not particularly aware of the imminent victory of the Communist army under Mao Zedong over the increasingly weak and corrupt nationalist regime headed by Chiang Kaishek. My parents seem to have foreseen such a victory, however, and to have decided to give me the widest possible experience of China during the summer vacation of 1948, in case it would be my last year in the country, as indeed it was. The summer months coincided with the time of the Lambeth Conference, the meeting in England every ten years of all bishops of the Anglican Communion of Churches—in this case the first such meeting since World War II. This meant that my father was away almost all summer. In fact he was going around the world by plane: Shanghai to London, then to the USA to visit my brothers and sisters, and back to Shanghai in September.

After seeing my father off to England in late June, Mother and I prepared for our trip to Beijing. She would leave our house in Shanghai in the hands of our trusted Chinese cook and his family. We would be going with my Aunt Frances, a missionary professor of English literature at Saint John's University, the large Episcopal educational center on the outskirts of Shanghai, and with two of her children, Mary and Harley, my cousins. Aunt Frances was married to Uncle Donald, my father's younger brother, history professor at Saint John's. Both Aunt Frances and Uncle Donald, of course, lectured in English.

All commercial planes in those days were propeller-driven and the trip to Beijing took three hours, almost entirely over the fertile valleys of the Yangtze and the Huang He, the Yellow River further to the North. The relatively slower speed and lower altitude of the flight made it possible to appreciate the almost infinite succession of rice paddies in all directions of the horizon, with periodic villages of a few peasant huts, all interconnected by an endless spiderweb of brown footpaths separating the greener paddies. It was—and to a great extent still is—the inner heart of China.

The scenery changed radically during the last half hour of the trip as we approached the airport and someone told me to look out the window. My thoughts had turned to the city of Beijing and our arrival, but I glanced out the window and there on the right side of the plane, perhaps a third of the distance between us and the dry, rocky horizon of the Western Beijing Hills, was the vision: a dazzling city of gold! What's more, this golden city was set in the middle of brown aridity, like a treasure trove in the desert. The sun reflecting off this collection of golden roofs, surrounded as they were by the austere bleakness of the dry landscape, came up to the plane as a message of transcendental glory, as if it were a holy city. At the time, I did not even try to find words to express it. It was too otherworldly, literally ineffable. Almost immediately the plane banked for its approach into the airport and the vision disappeared from sight. Only later, after visiting Beijing's famous "Forbidden City," used by China's successive emperors and their court, did I realize that what I had seen from the plane was the sun reflecting off the gold-painted roofs of this conglomeration of imperial palaces. The rest of the city of Beijing, which is now a showplace of modern office buildings and skyscrapers, was in 1948 relatively nondescript, at least from the air.

While Aunt Frances and her children stayed at a university compound on one side of the city, Mother and I used as our home base the unpretentious residence of Bishop T. Arnold Scott, the Anglican Archbishop of Beijing, a personal friend of my father's who, for reasons that escaped me at the time, had not gone to the Lambeth Conference. His decision not to attend the meeting might have been due to the cost of the trip, since it was clear that he and his English missionary companions lived in an austere simplicity unfamiliar to the American members of the Anglican Communion further to the south. However, the more likely reason for the archbishop's presence at that time was the threat of a Communist takeover in the coming weeks or months, since their army had practically surrounded the city by then. Unknown to me, the Communists had already, the previous year, captured, tortured and dispersed the flourishing community of Trappist monks of the Abbey of Our Lady of Consolation at Yang Jia Ping, over 100 miles to the north. In the innocence of my adolescence, I was more interested in the Olympic Games going on at that time in London than in either the Lambeth Conference or the imminent Communist victory in China.

Despite the desperate military and political situation of the place, life for American visitors to Beijing continued relatively undisturbed. We made the usual train trip to the Great Wall, admired the Ming Tombs, enjoyed the lake and park of the emperors' Summer Palace, walked around the Altar of Peace and through the large Tiananmen Square, 40 years before the massive student uprising that would take place there in 1988. I do not remember anyone's portrait overlooking the square, since Mao Zedong's face would appear there only a few months later. One day, with both of us exhausted from walking around the city in the summer heat, Mother took me to an ice cream parlor, where I enjoyed for the first time in my life—and I think the last—a banana split, an unforgettable memory! With her connivance, I also bought some bubble gum, which she encouraged me to chew in the presence of our very discreet English hosts. I did so the next morning at the end of the usual breakfast of rice porridge, stewed apricots and tea. Just as we had foreseen, the good lady missionaries were disconcerted by the sticky, pinkish blob that came out of my mouth. They laughed, embarrassed, but made no really negative comment, perhaps hesitant to offend a bishop's wife and son.

Looking back at this last episode, I think it reveals a character trait of my mother probably inherited by most of her children: a vein that could be called iconoclastic, a willingness to break with traditional ways for the sake of truth and justice. It perhaps explains why none of our family, except my father and despite his deep personal goodness, remained practicing Episcopalians throughout our adult life. Daddy's sincere dedication to accepted standards of behavior and Mother's equally strong convictions on the personal search for truth naturally influenced all their children, though in differing proportions and degrees. Probably I turned out more like my father temperamentally, but intellectually and spiritually more influenced by my mother.

I was not aware that, at the time of our trip to Beijing, a deep struggle was taking place in Mother's heart and soul about a key religious question: should she or should she not become a Roman Catholic? From what I now know, the outcome had already been decided in the depths of her spiritual judgment. In her later years, she shared with me what had happened. Bill had sent some books on Catholic spirituality to my parents, in order to explain something of why he had become a monk. They included the autobiography of the French Carmelite nun, St. Thérèse of Lisieux, and a well-written description of Trappist history and spirituality, by an English Trappistine sister: *La Trappe in England*.

To supplement these books, Mother visited a few Catholic churches and convents in the city of Shanghai, starting with the big Catholic cathedral. Unfortunately, most of the priests and sisters she met at these places were French-speaking, but one of them was able to direct her to a city parish run by the American Jesuits from California. So, like most persons in Chinese cities, she rode her bicycle there one afternoon, probably a Sunday when there would be less traffic, and happened to arrive during Benediction of the Blessed Sacrament. The pews were full of people looking at the altar, each one singing with all their heart. She was caught up in their devotion and intuited two similar realities: that there was something divine here, something sacred, and that this massive congregation surpassed anything she had experienced in her 59 years as a fervent Protestant. Somewhat stunned, she got up, left and pedaled home. She returned on another day and looked for a priest to talk to. One of them, Father Gatz, heard her story, answered her questions very objectively but warned her how difficult it would be to become a Catholic in her situation as the wife of an Episcopal bishop. She should go very slowly. That was where she was at the time of our trip to Beijing.

My mother's increasing interest in Catholicism explains why, toward the end of our Beijing stay, she took me to the Roman Catholic Cathedral, which remains such to this day. She invited me to stay outside in the large square, which I did very gladly, while she went inside. I thought her intention was just to pray and see the building, but actually she had a talk with a Father Morin, probably a Canadian missionary, about her own situation. When she came out of the Cathedral, we went together to a small dairy, tucked into an inside corner of the ancient city walls and run by the small group of Trappist monks who had survived the ordeal of their community at Yang Jia Ping and had been able to escape into the safety of the city. Somehow my mother and I got it across in our broken Mandarin that we were the mother and brother of a Trappist monk in the United States. The monk who spoke with us was most simple and gracious. In fact he seemed sincerely pleased that we came.

This was not my first contact with Trappist monks, although perhaps the most poignant, since a French monk had visited our home in Shanghai a few months before. He was Father Benoît Morvan, the former abbot of the first Trappist monastery in Japan and, at the time he visited us, the special pastoral visitor of the six or seven Trappist monasteries then existing in Japan and China. He had visited my brother's monastery in Rhode Island, met Bill and wished to greet his parents. My father invited him to supper one evening during his stopover in Shanghai and, despite the language barrier, his gentle kindness had impressed me. It was this same impression that I received from the Chinese monk in the Beijing dairy. Despite the stark austerity of almost no furniture and a room full of buzzing flies, he gave us a cup of sweetened tea and showed us what he could of this provisional monastery. Only many years later I read that the dairy continued for another five or six years before being closed by the Communist government in the mid 1950s. A few days after our visit there, Mother and I, with Aunt Frances and my cousins, returned to Shanghai.

Departure

It was only one or two weeks later, at the beginning of August, that the two of us set off again, this time by an overnight train to the traditional mountain resort of Culing. I had often heard of this place from different members of the family. In fact I had vague personal memories of being there in the summer of 1937, when I was four years old, especially the excitement of covering the windows with blankets at night so as not to be spotted by Japanese planes during their air raids. It was the start of the Sino-Japanese War and my father was forced to leave Culing by himself in the middle of a torrential rainstorm, making the hazardous trip down the mountain on foot, then back to Shanghai so as to be with his diocese during the war. This present visit, eleven years later, coincided with that of several of my schoolmates from S.A.S., so it was a real vacation among friends. At that time there were no automobile roads in Culing. Everything was brought up the mountain on foot or on the backs of donkeys and all communication was done on foot, which meant a lot of walking up and down hills, and much healthy exercise. The younger element would meet every afternoon at the public swimming pool. My mother would slip off now and then, without me or anyone else knowing about it, to attend Mass at a small Catholic church she had discovered.

We returned to Shanghai on a river steamer going downstream on the Yangtze, an overnight trip that would have taken three days in the opposite direction, which explains why we took the train up and the boat back. Only a few days later, Daddy returned from his long trip to England and the United States. After a few days of rest, he had to make an overnight pastoral visit to Suzhou, the city where he and Mother had lived the first years after their marriage.

He made the trip by car, that is, in the U.S. Army jeep that he had obtained from the American troops stationed in Shanghai, so he asked if I would like to go with him, which of course I did. It was only a two-hour ride, but it gave me a chance to see the farmland surrounding Shanghai.

On our return from Suzhou the next day, we passed a small Buddhist monastery on the side of the road. Daddy stopped to look and we were greeted cordially by two young monks, who invited us to look around. There was something about them, and about this peaceful place of meditation in the middle of a series of ordinary rice paddies, that appealed to me. It was my first visit to a real monastery, as distinct from the temporary Trappist refuge in Beijing that Mother and I had visited only a month before. Reflecting on it now, many years later, it is clear that God had planted in my heart a monastic seed even in my early teens, a seed which first expressed itself by feeling at home with these special persons I happened to meet at that time: the Anglican missionary nuns who would visit us, Father Benoît Morvan, then the Trappist monk in the Beijing dairy, and now these two Buddhist monks. Nevertheless, if someone had asked me at that time if I wanted to become a monk, I almost certainly would have replied that it would be an interesting experience for a few weeks or months, but not for one's whole life.

Meanwhile, school had begun again, my junior year at S.A.S., and with it the classes and football practice. One morning at school in early October, I broke out with a fever and returned home early with what turned out to be a case of contagious hepatitis, that is, jaundice perhaps caused by the food on that river ferry down the Yangtze. During my convalescence, which involved a kind of quarantine at home, word arrived that several large cities north of Shanghai had fallen to the Communists and Beijing could fall at any moment. The U.S. State Department urged women and children to leave China as soon as possible and my parents thought it best for me to return to the States, to finish high school there. Mother decided to stay at the side of my father.

Once again I think that they had talked things over and had concluded, for reasons unknown to me, that Hotchkiss would not be the best school for me. Perhaps it was the economic factor, but more probably some religious reasons intervened. My parents asked me what I thought about Mount Hermon School in northwest Massachusetts, a more explicitly Christian, nondenominational boarding school where several missionary families we knew had sent their children: the boys to Mount Hermon, the girls to Northfield School, on the other side of the Connecticut River. I felt comfortable with that and my father, covering over my quarantine for jaundice, cabled Mount Hermon, asking for my midterm admittance with my "record and health excellent." Within a week the reply came back: "Bruce accepted."

I was basically happy to return to the States. It was a clear step toward growing up and I looked forward to seeing my brothers and sisters again. Besides, there was really not much choice, since most of the students at the S.A.S. were doing the same. I have kept in touch with two of them over the years. Ben Gilson was my closest buddy and neighbor. We bicycled together to school every morning, then returned home in the afternoon through the back streets of the city. He later went to Dartmouth, became a naval surgeon and was intensely involved in the Vietnam War, stationed onboard a hospital ship anchored offshore, where he operated day and night on the battle casualties that were constantly flown in by helicopter.

Carl Scovel, on the other hand, was a border at S.A.S. We played together as linemen on the school football team. After graduating from Oberlin and Harvard Divinity School, he became the long-term, deeply respected pastor of King's Chapel, the Unitarian church in downtown Boston. S.A.S. sputtered on for another year after the Communist army entered Shanghai four months after most of us left, but it was soon taken over to become a Naval Academy. The school reopened, however, in the early 1980s and is now bigger than ever in two new locations on the outskirts of the city, though without the dominant presence of us "missionary kids."

It was only a few weeks after recovering from my jaundice that I left Shanghai, together with about 15 other students from S.A.S. and a similar number of adult missionaries, on the U.S.

Navy troopship, *General Breckinridge*. The vessel was by no means a luxury liner, but the officers' quarters were comfortable enough, especially compared with the cramped bunks of the troop transport *Marine Lynx*, in which my mother and I had arrived three years before. It was especially interesting to get back to American cooking, after three years of more Chinese style.

My mother accompanied me as I boarded the ship and we went together to the cabin which I was to share with three other passengers. She and I were alone there and, as we said goodbye, she put a little book into my hands, saying simply, "You might like to look at this. It is about the Catholic Church, which is really wonderful." We hugged discreetly, as was our family custom, before she turned around and went alone up to the deck. I looked at the little book: *Father Peyton's Rosary Book, Special Edition for the U.S. Military*. It was the first time that Mother had revealed so openly where she was headed or had tried to influence me so directly. I was not totally surprised, much less shocked, by this revelation, perhaps because there had always been, between my parents and us children, a deep spirit of reciprocal trust. No matter what we did, their love and their respect for our decisions would remain, and they tacitly expected the same from us.

This family attitude had been expressed by my father on another occasion that was significant in the light of where I was to end up. It was during my last two years in Shanghai. Every morning after waking up—and after my parents would fill their bathtub with cold water and plunge in and out, first my father then my mother—the family would meet before breakfast in the living room, read a section from the New Testament, and have a short prayer. The whole meeting seldom lasted more than five or six minutes. The children were invited and I usually assisted, though passively, since, frankly, my interests were elsewhere. My father used a monthly pamphlet from the Episcopal Church, *Forward Day by Day*, with readings and prayers. There was hardly ever any shared reflection among those who assisted, since my father was not the preachy type. One morning it was the section of the Gospel where Jesus says, "I have come to set a man against his father, and a daughter against her mother. . . . Whoever loves father or mother more than me is not worthy of me; and whoever loves son or daughter more than me is not worthy of me."[2] I must have heard these words before, but they hit me with special violence that morning, "How could Jesus say such a thing?"

My inner questioning must have showed on my face, because my father broke through his customary reserve, looked directly at me and said, "What Jesus says is true. You must follow him in all things, even when it might be different from what Mother and I do or like." This episode explains why I thank God that I was born into a Protestant family, because if my parents had been Catholic, my father would probably have been a priest, and my mother almost certainly would have been a nun, and then where would I be?

Back in my cabin of the *General Breckinridge*, I pocketed the little prayer book, then went up to wave goodbye to my parents and to most of the S.A.S. student body that had come to see us off, since there were about a dozen of us students leaving on the same ship. The *General Breckinridge* pulled out of Shanghai on January 1, 1949, slowly moved out of the Yangtze River delta and went due north, up to the U.S. Navy base at Qindao.

We had a full day there and I decided to brave the bitter cold in order to see the city, without thinking of any particular destination. Walking along the shore road, I could see that the city was built on a sloping hill, close to the top of which was a large Christian church. I walked uphill to get a better look and saw that it might be a Roman Catholic church, though I wasn't sure what the Chinese characters said, because it seemed different from the Protestant churches I was familiar with. I stepped inside, partly to get out of the cold and partly out of curiosity, and found that I had entered the side door. There were a few small red candles flickering in different places and about a dozen people kneeling in silent prayer, scattered among the benches in the central part. No one paid any attention to me. Later I would learn that the red candles are called "vigil lights" and symbolize the prayer of

2. Mt 10:35-37. All biblical quotations are from the *New Revised Standard Version*, except the Psalm verses, which will be from the *Grail Psalter*.

the persons who light them even when they cannot be physically present in church.

I stood near the side door for five or ten minutes, neither questioning nor feeling uncomfortable: simply taking it in. At that time I did not connect what I was looking at with what my mother had given me a few days before. Although I had never been inside a Catholic church, I suspected that this was one of them, mainly because I had never experienced such a presence of silent prayer and reverence in a Protestant church, especially when there was no service going on. I left, walked back out into the biting cold wind, and hurried to return to the shelter of the warm ship. That night we cast off for another Navy base far to the south on the island of Guam, before making the long trip east across the International Date Line into the port of San Francisco. But I'll tell you about that in another letter.

Letter 2

NEW ENGLAND

1949–1951

Dear Eddie,

That long trip across the Pacific ended peacefully early one morning toward the end of January 1949, when the *General Breckinridge* passed under the Golden Gate Bridge and into the San Francisco harbor. It had been, in fact, a leisurely three-week passage from the first part of my life to whatever was coming. I would soon discover what.

After visiting my sister Edith in Palo Alto, I flew to the East Coast and finally arrived at what would be my home address for the next few years, my brother John's temporary residence in the village of Quonset huts built for married war veterans studying under the G.I. Bill, near the Yale Bowl in western New Haven, Connecticut. Helen came down from Boston to see me and after a few days, during which John helped me buy my first dark dress suit, I started my trip to Mount Hermon.

Valley Falls

The first stop was Valley Falls, north of Providence, Rhode Island, where Bill's monastery was located: the Trappist Abbey of Our Lady of the Valley. The abbey buildings themselves were impressive, at the end of a long entrance road lined with old oak trees. One of the brothers at the guest house showed me my room, which I shared with a young man who turned out to be a seminarian. When I returned to the entrance hall, there was my brother, now called "Brother Luke." I knew that he would have a beard, but was not prepared for such a long, bushy, dark one, since I myself am blonder. In fact I had never really met anyone like this before. He greeted me very affectionately and we spoke together for several hours in the parlor, about the family, my trip, the monastery, his experiences. It was clear that he was happy, communicative, and at peace, which made me feel the same.

Toward the end of our conversation, there was a knock on the door and a large, middle-aged monk entered. He was full of beaming energy, had a friendly face, white hair, no beard. A cross was hanging around his neck, for he was the abbot, "Dom Edmund" or simply "Reverend Father," as the monks called him. He immediately smothered me with the warmest of embraces, which made me feel most welcome, yet embarrassed, since neither my father nor my mother had ever embraced me this way.

This first meeting with Bill as a monk was at the end of January 1949. I would visit him twice more that year and on each occasion I would stay about two days in the guest house, enough to get a feel for the life of the brothers yet not enough so as to get tired or bored. On one of these visits, I was even allowed to go out to work with the brother novices, peeling the bark off pinewood poles to be used as fence posts. Bill worked elsewhere, in the large carpentry shop.

What most impressed me, however, was the chanting in choir, seen and heard from the guest tribune at the back of the big church, just a few steps from my bedroom. The view from this tribune, the ceremonies, the chanting of the Psalms and singing of the hymns in Latin were totally new to me and fascinating in their mysterious solemnity. I was especially struck by the solemn bows, which did not exist in the Protestant services I was familiar with. I had studied Latin at S.A.S., so understood the phrase *Gloria Patri et Filio et Spiritui Sancto*—"Glory to the Father, to the Son and to the Holy Spirit"—and could see why all would bow when singing these words, but I puzzled over the final phrase *per omnia sæcula sæculorum*. From its context, it seemed to take the place of the Anglican phrase, "world without end," but the Latin word that I had learned for "world" was *mundus*. Only later I learned that *mundus* refers to the world of human interaction, whereas *sæculum* refers to a long length of time, an age. The phrase meant, "for all ages of ages," or "age upon age." Its frequent repetition colored everything with eternity, even for me who did not understand its literal meaning.

Even when the monks were not together in church, I could see one or two of them cleaning the floor with dry mops or coming in to pray in silence. They would bow deeply toward the altar each time they crossed the middle of the church. It was clear that they had deep reverence for something connected with the altar, so I asked Bill about it. He explained a few facts about Christ in the Eucharist, the Tabernacle where the Body of Christ is kept and the red vigil light as a sign of his presence. He also explained that the solemn ceremony, the Mass, which they had celebrated one morning while I was there, had been in commemoration of the recent death of the very same Trappist monk who had visited our family in Shanghai a year or two before, Benoît Morvan.

I took it all in without comment, as part of the new world in which my brother lived. Another impressive element it had was its continuity, day in and day out, night and day, and these men seemed to be happy praying and working in silence, in a context which I could see was intensely Christ-centered. The crucifixes in every room told me the same thing. Bill also explained how the long chant in church at the end of the day in total darkness was a traditional song to Mary, the Mother of Christ.

My first visit to the monastery had been impressive, but I was somewhat saturated by then with a string of intense experiences: leaving Shanghai and my parents; the rolling trip across the Pacific; the cross-continental plane trip, which in those days was in slow, propeller-driven planes; above all, seeing my sisters and brothers again. The monastery was just one more part of all that, and I was only 16. I wanted to settle down again, even though it was in an unknown school.

My following visits to Bill, during some of my Easter or summer vacations, would deepen my first impressions of the monastery. On one of them, Bill told me, probably thinking that I already knew, that Mother had decided to enter the Catholic Church. I was caught by surprise, said nothing, just wept silently. Bill must have realized what he had done and we soon finished our conversation. I went instinctively to the guest tribune in the church. You could probably call what I did a type of prayer, but it was more a question of placing my whole situation—and that of our now divided family—in God's hands. I did not ask for anything in particular, though perhaps I was implicitly looking for God's will in this somewhat tragic situation. In any case, I rose from those minutes in the guest tribune with a clear, twofold conviction that guided me for the next months and years.

On the one hand, I saw that I was really led to the Catholic Church in a way that I had never been to any of the Reformed Churches. I was sincerely impressed by the Christian quality of these monks who had given themselves to the Person of Jesus with a depth of intensity which I had never met or heard of before, even among persons like Albert Schweitzer, whose life I was reading, or the lovely Anglican missionary nuns, dressed in their full blue habits and serving God in China. There was, I saw even then, this mystical quality to Catholic life which I was touching here in the monastery and had never touched before, even though I had been immersed in the best of Protestant Christianity. This impression was reinforced by the fact that none of these Catholic religious people were trying to talk me into becoming a Catholic, nor did they criticize the Protestant world. They accepted and respected me as the person I am, whereas among Protestants I had often heard deep criticisms of the Catholic Church. I sensed that maybe the Catholics were actually more evangelical than the Protestants.

At the same time, however, I understood that I was too young to make any decision now about my future. The time had not arrived, but would. My task was to live each present moment. Things would be given to me at their proper time. I should wait, see and let my life unfold. Underlying this watchful attitude, though I was not fully conscious of it at the time, was a deep trust that God knew what was best for me, would take care of me and show me what he wanted, as perhaps he was doing at that very time.

Mount Hermon

After a night in Helen's small apartment on Beacon Hill in Boston, I made the three-hour train trip into western Massachusetts and the Berkshire Mountains, arriving at the little Mount Hermon train station in the middle of a snowy winter day. In some way my whole trip from China during the previous five or six weeks had been an apprenticeship in solitude, so I was not really disturbed by being in totally unknown surroundings. I had also grown up in Massachusetts and was used to the snow. Fortunately there was a taxi at the little station and the driver knew just where to take me: the administration building of the school, where I was welcomed very kindly. They knew I was coming and where I had come from, and were used to children of missionaries. I roomed with David Burdge, from Milford, Connecticut, and began classes the next day in the middle of the junior year.

It was only after settling in at Mount Hermon that a deep wave of homesickness came over me. I compared everything to Shanghai, to S.A.S., to being at home. Actually, it was a necessary part of growing up. Perhaps the real problem was that I did not speak to anyone about what was going on inside me, nor did I want to. I had never done so in my life and I have every reason to think that no other member of my family had either. Our somewhat Victorian, success-oriented upbringing, in which individual consciences were sincerely respected with an emphasis put on personal good behavior, saw no real reason for sharing what was intimate in the human heart, although my mother's innate maternal sense often attempted to draw things out of me. So I did not become really close to anyone at Mount Hermon, though there were many fine people there among both students and faculty.

I was much more open in my weekly letters to my parents in Shanghai. From their experience with my older siblings, they knew what I was living through and wrote back frequently, especially my mother. Their letters kept my boarding school experience in perspective and I commented to them how things were going in general and how good my teachers were, especially my two successive English teachers, Judson Stent and Jack Baldwin.

In Mr. Stent's junior English class, we had organized debates, which involved studying on the assigned theme, preparing arguments and possible rebuttals with their counter-arguments, then the actual 40-minute debate with another classmate in front of the class. I was assigned the position of arguing in favor of a "United States of Europe," this being in 1949, when a European union or common market was still only hypothetical. It was a new subject for me—as it probably was for the rest of the class—but I championed it so well that Mr. Stent gave me a good mark and soon asked me to be, during my senior year, the "Floor Officer of Cottage One," that is, the senior student living in one of the three or four smaller residences for freshman newcomers, in which Mr. Stent was the residing "Floor Prof."

The principle behind this system of smaller groups for incoming students was to provide as homey an environment as possible to them, since they were almost all entering directly from their own homes at the age of 13 or 14. I was pleased at Mr. Stent's trust and accepted, even though it meant living apart from the main body of my classmates, especially since I chose as my roommate Bill Bishop, a friend who, like me, had just come from S.A.S. His father had worked in Shanghai for the Y.M.C.A., the Young Men's Christian Association, and I had visited his home on one or two occasions.

Life as a Floor Officer for 20 young adolescents was both challenging and rewarding. It involved being an older brother, friend, companion, advisor and, in case of need, keeper of discipline. During the day, I would study and play sports like any other senior, choosing soccer, basketball and track without making the varsity team in any of them, but in the evenings, between supper and going to bed, I would make the rounds of the rooms to see that all was well, make some observation if necessary and answer any questions they might have about their studies. At least once a week I would have a talk with Mr. Stent, a shrewd, kind, middle-aged bachelor, who had lived in Cottage One for many years taking care of his mother. Like all teachers at Mount Hermon—in those days they were all men—he had an appreciation for religion and was especially interested in me as the son of a missionary bishop, since he himself had once studied to be a minister. After I graduated, we kept in contact by mail through the years, even after he retired, and were able to renew our conversations when he visited me at the monastery, not long before his death.

Despite my almost inevitable loneliness, Mount Hermon was a healthy experience, a good environment for growing up as a teenager, though not always easy. I never really integrated with the majority of my classmates, not only because of living in Cottage One, but even more from not trying to be "one of the boys." In practice that meant not smoking or "shooting the breeze," relaxing with them in the Recreation Room, dubbed the "Blue Cloud" because of its cigarette smoke. Though I liked sports, classmates and teachers, my basic interests were in more extended reading, deeper study of the assigned subjects and daily piano practice in the chapel basement for my weekly piano lessons.

I soon discovered the classical music room in the basement of the library and would often go there when I had a spare hour, to study while listening to a whole range of symphonies, concertos and sonatas. I was seldom interrupted, which gave the impression that others really did not share this attraction for classical music. The pieces that caught my fancy tended to be Slavic, especially Rimsky-Korsakov's *Scheherazade*. Its dramatic impetuosity, combined with the soaring lyricism and rich orchestration of Russian composers in general, still appeals to me, perhaps because it brings to the surface certain elements otherwise clouded over by a more sober upbringing and life environment.

I also found the room in the library where the daily newspaper was available, so I looked at it often to see how things were in China. On May, 24, 1949, only a few months after my arrival at the school, there was a first-page report on what I was looking for: the entrance of the Communist army into Shanghai. The article even contained an interview with one of my father's British friends, Charles Thomas. There had been almost no armed resistance, simply a withdrawal of the weakened nationalist troops and the cautious entrance of the Communist troops. It seemed that, for the time being at least, life there continued more peacefully than before and my mother wrote that the Communists had put some order into the usual chaos of Shanghai traffic. I did not know it at the time, but it was a week later, on May 30, that my mother officially entered the Catholic Church.

It was only many years later, after my father's death, that she told me some details about her change of Church allegiance. As it became clearer to her that the Roman Catholic Church was the real continuation of the apostolic Church founded by Christ, she saw that, to be faithful to her conscience, she had to enter it. She had to become a Catholic. Father Gatz warned her that it would not be easy, neither for her nor for her husband, the Bishop, but she was undaunted, so she told Daddy about her decision. He was, of course, deeply hurt and tried his best to dissuade her. There was never a question of divorce or separation, but both of them understood that a Protestant Episcopal Bishop could only with great difficulty function with a Roman Catholic wife.

I myself learned from experience that my father, generally the incarnation of evangelical meekness, even in family affairs, could become a tiger when it came to discussing the validity of the Episcopal Church, in which he had grown up and to which he had given his life. On the other hand, my mother had become equally convinced of her realigned faith and had just gone through, in her own mind and heart, the dialectical arguments presented by her husband, demolishing them one by one. The heat of their arguments increased exponentially, since my mother, though less versed in theology, had a keener intelligence than my father, who was more conditioned by his classical background and education.

It soon became clear to both of them that they could not go on arguing like this. It was destroying them and their marriage, so they agreed not to talk about their respective beliefs any more. There was no real meeting of minds on the issue of Church allegiance, but at least there was an exteriorly peaceful coexistence, especially for the sake of my father's ministry, where no one was yet aware of what Mother was planning. So it happened that, a few days after the Communist army marched into Shanghai, my mother wrote a note to Daddy:

> *Dear Billy, I just want to tell you that tomorrow I shall be officially received into the Roman Catholic Church. I know you will pray for me.*
>
> *With all my love, Dotty.*

Within a few hours my father replied with a similar note:

> *Dear Dotty, Let no man stand between you and your God!*
>
> *Affectionately, Billy.*

My mother was delighted, even 25 years later when she told me what had happened. It was truly a magnanimous gesture on my father's part, she felt, an expression of the true gentleman he was, in keeping with his respect for personal freedom of conscience. But when Mother told me what he had written her, I was aghast with dismay, then astounded at my father's astuteness. I saw what he had done, based on my own readings in Reformation history and on knowing my father's subtle keenness in playing with words. He had found a way to respect his wife's own religious decision and simultaneously to proclaim his own deepest convictions: "Let no man stand between you and your God!"

In the history of the Anglican Church, that phrase is attributed to Thomas Cranmer, theological advisor to King Henry VIII, named by the latter as the first Anglican Archbishop of Canterbury. Cranmer was the chief author, first of the Anglican *Book of Common Prayer*, then of the *Forty-two Articles* which define the dogmatic positions of the Church of England on the religious controversies of the Reformation. Almost immediately after finishing these landmark works of Protestant literature, he was tortured and burnt at the stake as a heretic under the new Catholic queen, "Bloody" Mary I. Thus Thomas Cranmer, besides being one of the original guiding lights of the Church of England, became one of its first martyrs and is venerated in the Anglican Communion as a saint.

By using Cranmer's principle, which might have been addressed originally to King Henry VIII himself, my father succeeded in having my mother think that he, her husband, was the man who should not stand between her and her God, which was indeed the lesser part of what my father wanted to convey. But he affirmed at the same time, and in the strongest of terms, his own deepest conviction that no *pope* should stand between anyone and their God: let no man tell you what to believe! This is the original and authentic meaning of Cranmer's directive, of which my father was certainly aware, since it rings as a trumpet call for the entire Protestant Reformation. I never even tried to explain all this to Mother, who was well into her 80s when she told me about this exchange of written notes. In God's mercy I am confident that she and my father are peacefully together again in heaven, where supreme truth and supreme love are happily united.

A Highway in the Heart

On my side of the story, a year after my mother's official entrance into the Catholic Church, close to the end of my second and last year at Mount Hermon, several different episodes occurred that were interrelated, though I was not aware of it at the time. They show how, underneath my daily school life, something else was happening, something even more intense and important. The result was that the half-century year, 1950, became the turning point of my whole life.

It started with a strange combination of a minor operation and a disastrous fire. During spring vacation I skipped going to the monastery to see Bill and went directly to John's Quonset hut in New Haven, because I was scheduled to have my tonsils removed at the hospital where he had some connections through his medical studies. The purpose of this minor operation was to put an end to my proclivity for catching one cold after another. I spent the night after the tonsillectomy in a ward of the hospital, where one of the nurses kindly gave me the morning newspaper, which I would not have received if I had been at John's. There on the first page was a picture of Bill's monastery in flames, almost totally consumed by a midnight fire that had destroyed the entire church and gutted most of the other buildings. I could hardly believe it, but was relieved to read that none of the monks had been killed. They had all been able to escape in time. That was in late March.

Back at Mount Hermon in mid-April, a second event occurred, a short dream which I have always remembered. I was at the end of a long arched corridor, like the nave of a church, and at the far end there was a figure, either alive or a statue. It was the Virgin Mary. That was the dream. When I woke up, my feeling was one of deep peace, a type of spiritual well-being. At the time, I connected it with my experience at Bill's monastery, looking from the tribune at the rear of the now-destroyed church and listening to the monks' solemn evening song, the *Salve Regina:* "Hail, Holy Queen!" I realized that I felt at home there and, although I would not have said so at the time even to myself, my heart was becoming Catholic.

A third event happened soon afterwards in the obligatory Bible class, which for senior-year students was a survey of the history of Renaissance and Modern philosophy as a background for differing interpretations of Sacred Scripture. The teacher was presenting the thought behind subjective idealism, the theory that nature has no objective existence independent of the minds that perceive it. It was the first time I had heard of such an unscientific theory, so I raised my hand and asked, "You mean these people think that things don't exist unless we think about them?"

"Yes, that's it," the teacher replied.

"But that's stupid!" I retorted, at which he shrugged his shoulders and my classmates looked at me somewhat dumbfounded, as if to say, "What's eating you?" or, "Who do you think you are, to question someone else's opinion?"

Many years later I discovered that, in the mid-thirteenth century, Saint Thomas Aquinas had dealt with a somewhat similar theory that denied our ability to know objective reality. He replied more elegantly than I had, "If that power is denied, then the one affirming such an opinion doesn't understand anything and therefore should not be listened to."[1]

1. Thomas Aquinas, *Commentary on the De Anima* (of Aristotle), III, 7. Quoted in B. Lonergan, *Verbum: Word and Idea in Aquinas* (Notre Dame, IN: University of Notre Dame Press, 1967), 78.

My classroom incident shows, of course, that without my really being aware of it, I was concerned—deeply concerned—about where truth lies. Looking at subsequent events, it is clear that the subconscious reason for my concern was not only the question of truth as the universal object of human intelligence, but more specifically where is the true Christian Church and how can we be sure? The first part of that question was soon answered for me, but the second part—which requires explaining how we come to know the truth—took me six more years to really understand.

The whole question of where to find the true Christian Church is why a fourth event in that spring of 1950 was so important for me. It was a totally interior experience. One afternoon I was alone in our room of Cottage One, looking out the window toward the big school chapel, not thinking of anything in particular. Suddenly a syllogism formed in my mind, that is, a couple of premises and their logical conclusions. It went like this: "If God loves mankind (perhaps today I would have thought, 'humankind'), which he does, he wants to teach us the truth about himself and about the most important things in our lives, that is, he does not want his children to be in error about the most important principles of their life on this earth and after death. But the Roman Catholic Church is the only Christian Church that claims to teach such important truths without error, that is, infallibly. The others leave it up to private interpretations which are admittedly open to error, sometimes serious error. Therefore, the Roman Catholic Church is the true Church of God, founded by Christ, the universal Teacher, and the Pope is God's instrument for carrying this out."

From that day on, although I had to learn the strict conditions under which the Pope and the Church are infallible, I understood that, if the teaching authority of the Christian Church is not at least minimally infallible, all other truths of Christianity fall to the ground and become objects of doubt rather than causes of joyful, grateful certitude. It was my less erudite version of what happened to John Henry Newman when, in search of the true Church, he read Saint Augustine's manifesto against excessive Christian regionalism, *Securus judicat orbis terrarum:* "Certain is the judgment of the whole planet." Perhaps more precisely, mine was a simpler version of Edith Stein's conclusion after devouring the autobiography of Saint Teresa of Avila, "This is the truth!" I did not fully realize it then, but on that spring afternoon in Cottage One, I had become, not only at heart but also in mind, a Catholic. My body had to follow, as Saint Paul understood after his encounter with the Risen Christ: "What am I to do, Lord?"[2]

It has been said that such a search for transcendental certitude is what causes religious fundamentalism and is really an immature flight from the obscurity of human existence. There is no doubt that, at the age of 17, I was still very immature, yet I instinctively saw that to search sincerely for the truth is an inner thrust of what is deepest in the human spirit towards all I was made for, namely permanent joy, the peaceful possession of lasting truth, the symphonic embrace of what is eternally real, and thus of true love.

I later came to see that both fundamentalism and its opposite, relativism, come from *not* making an adequate search for the truth. Fundamentalism takes a part of reality as the foundation of all else and so becomes blind, narrow and sometimes cruel. In reaction to it, relativism says that everything depends on each person's individual judgment. The proper search for, and possession of truth, on the other hand is characterized by "love, joy, peace, patience, kindness, generosity, faithfulness, gentleness, and self-control,"[3] that is, the fruits of the Spirit, which are opposed to both intolerance and unbridled permissiveness, because the deepest truth—human and divine—is love, the gift of self, and particularly that special form of self-gift which belongs so properly to the Church of Christ, namely forgiveness, mercy and reconciliation.

That afternoon in 1950, however, I would not have articulated my experience in any way. It was too intimate. I saw nothing wrong or selfish in wanting to know the truth about God's plan for the human family, about Christ and his Church. In the following days I saw that there was an immediate consequence of my

2. Acts 22:10.
3. Gal 5:22.

initial intuition, namely that an exclusively individual or private interpretation of the Bible, of God's self-revelation in Christ, was a self-contradiction, since Jesus is a public, social and universal Person. So it was totally logical, even necessary, that he continue his public presence through a social institution vested with his spiritual authority. At the same time, something inside me still said that I should wait, that I was not yet ready to take a concrete step toward the Catholic Church. As it turned out, it would not be a long wait.

A fifth, more superficial event was a result of the preceding ones. I had been appointed as one of a group of "student deacons," whose nominal responsibility was to help take care of the school chapel, but whose most important task was determining how and where to give away the modest contributions collected from the students' voluntary offerings during the year. There was a fixed annual contribution to a Protestant prep school in France and something for the missions in Africa. Without any premeditation, I suggested that we send a contribution to South America, which was surprising, since I had no contact with, and little knowledge of, anything in that part of the world. The other deacons replied at once, "That's in the hands of the Roman Catholics," to which I responded, "That's no reason for not giving them anything." The conclusion was that nothing was sent to South America.

There was a final event during my last weeks at Mount Hermon, different from the previous ones and mysterious for me until much later. The combined Drama Clubs and Glee Clubs of the two schools—Mount Hermon and Northfield—had put on a great performance of Gilbert and Sullivan's *The Mikado* and I was waiting outside the Northfield Auditorium for one of the singers to appear, Sally Johnson, with whom I had gone to two dances, including the Senior Prom. She was the type of young woman who appealed to me for her goodheartedness, normal attractiveness and generally wholesome qualities. Moreover, we enjoyed each other's company and this would be the last opportunity to see her before our respective graduations. But as I spotted her emerging from a side door, something strange took hold of me from the inside and I practically ran away without turning back. I couldn't stay. It was stronger than me and happened so suddenly that I could not resist this interior force. But the next day I had my second thoughts and wondered how and why I had acted in such an impulsive, irrational and unfriendly way. I was frustrated, embarrassed, and wrote apologetically to Sally, saying that I had had to get back immediately to Mount Hermon. She replied that she understood and gave me the telephone number of where she would be studying the next year in Boston.

For some time I tended to interpret my strange escape from Sally as an unresolved, unconscious fear of getting too involved with girls, but this would have been one of the few times in my life when such a fear had shown itself. My personality runs in the opposite direction. In light of where I was to go, I now see it as my first experience of Holy Fear, "the fear of the Lord" prophesied by Isaiah[4] for the Messianic age, which the Christian spiritual tradition enshrines as one of the seven special Gifts of the Holy Spirit. This gift of the Spirit had kept me from what might have radically thwarted God's Will in my life, but without telling me why, at least at that time, which I have learned to be a common feature of how God acts in the life of his children: "Be still, and know that I am God!"[5] In other words, "Trust me and be quiet!" He wanted to build his own highway in my heart and my job was to accept this without asking too many questions.

An important part of the final months at any prep school is deciding to what college or colleges one should apply. Personally, I did not have any particular attraction in this regard, but it seemed logical to go to Yale, where my father and both my brothers had gone. With those antecedents, it was more than likely that I would be accepted, and there was an additional incentive: the Yale-Mount Hermon Scholarship, awarded each year to a Mount Hermon graduate applying to Yale. It was never clear to me what the principal criterion for this award was, whether academic achievement, financial need, or simply a more general suitability.

4. Is 11:2-3.
5. Ps 46(45):10.

More than likely, it was a combination of all three factors. In any case, I applied for the scholarship and received it, for which I will always be grateful to Mount Hermon. Although it was not a full scholarship, it made things easier, especially for my father.

Since my parents were still in China, my siblings, Helen and John, were good enough to come for my graduation, John leaving his family for the weekend. At the graduation ceremony, besides the Yale scholarship and to my total surprise, I was given two other awards: one for being a good senior "deacon" in helping the needs of others; the other for poetry, based on a somewhat moralizing poem I had written on the danger that the modern world might become like one of the dead babies—probably baby girls—wrapped up in newspapers and waiting for the trash collector, that I had seen on the Shanghai sidewalks while bicycling to school.

New Haven

A few weeks after my graduation from Mount Hermon, my parents left Shanghai permanently on a Norwegian freighter bound for New York. The uprooting that this implied, especially for my father after 35 years of intensive ministry, was eased somewhat by the fact that the decision to leave China was made with all the other non-Chinese Episcopalian and Anglican missionaries when they saw that their continued presence as foreigners under the Communists was a hindrance, rather than a help, to the Chinese clergy and faithful. Since then, especially in the last decades of the 20th century, the Episcopal Church in China has joined other mainline Protestant Churches to form a single autonomous body under the surveillance of the government.

Mother and Daddy, from their freighter somewhere in the Pacific, sent word for me to meet them in August at the old summer home of Daddy's family on Nantucket Island, in the seashore village of Siasconset. We were together there for three weeks before I made the move to New Haven, to start my freshman year at Yale. Not once did they or I bring up the subject of our respective Church affiliations.

In retrospect I now see that the weeks at Siasconset that summer and during the following three years were significant in my life for a different reason, which at first appears to be ridiculous. Unknown to me, however, I was being trained in a general attitude toward adversity, and the instrument for it was the improvised sport of surfing, which could be described as the poor man's equivalent of surfboarding.

My version of surfing consisted in diving through a breaking wave—the bigger the better—as it arches its crest ten or twenty yards away from the sandy shore before crashing down and disintegrating on the beach a few seconds later. The best time for this was during and after a tropical storm in the Atlantic Ocean, that would produce swells up to fifteen feet high. In those days there were no lifeguards on the beaches, so young boys were free to be brave and my family did not seem to object, though they probably kept a watchful eye on me. The sport was to walk into the water and face these big waves head on, wait for the right moment, then dive straight into and through the advancing wall of foaming salt water, underneath the breaking crest, and come up in glory on the other side as the wave crashed down at the place I would have been if I had not dived through it. The ideal was to do this in time to ride in on the very top of the crest and, when it broke on the beach, to land standing up and walk away like a Roman gladiator after vanquishing his victim in the sandy arena.

Sometimes, it is true, I would miscalculate or hesitate and get "boiled," as we used to say, thrashed in every direction by the angry ocean wave like a piece of seaweed and thrown onto the beach like flotsam from a shipwreck, but then I could get up and redeem myself by conquering the next giant that came in from the sea. Surfing obviously appealed to my adolescent bravado, but the attitude of soul and body that it cultivates—an intensely alert, optimistic fortitude combined with a patient calmness in adversity—would prove invaluable in the years to come.

My parents spent the next nine months resting on Nantucket, then living in a rented apartment in New York City while Daddy looked for some Episcopal diocese which would accept him as an Assistant Bishop despite his Catholic wife. It was not easy to find such a place. At one point, my parents thought seriously of living separately, but the Episcopal Diocese of Philadelphia, where my father had served for a time six years before, came to the rescue and offered him work as rector of a small parish in East Germantown, combined with other duties. My mother told me that the Episcopal parishioners at the "House of Prayer," as this small parish was called, were grateful that she was a Catholic, since it meant that their parish minister was a bishop. My parents were both happy there and stayed until my father retired eight years later, in 1959, when he reached the age of 71.

Those eight years would be decisive for me in more ways than one. Like most college freshmen, the adjustment to a large institution, to new roommates, teachers, and a greater anonymity was not easy, despite the fact that the authorities at both Mount Hermon and Yale made a sincere effort to ease the transition. Since I was on scholarship, I worked several hours a day at the huge freshman dining hall, usually handing out silverware in the cafeteria line.

Academically, it seemed as if my shift to Yale had accentuated my ease in the exact sciences, with a corresponding reduction of ability in the required English courses. For some reason, it was hard for me to grasp the messages of English literature, which Mr. Baldwin at Mount Hermon had explained so well, and I flunked my freshman exam on Shakespeare. Fortunately, I was allowed to repeat it and just passed. As a result, I decided to specialize in what I seemed to be good at, so I geared my sophomore classes toward the exact sciences required for medical school.

Underlying my difficulties with English literature was another problem: the Catholic faith. Where was I going? I saw that some kind of religious orientation was part of my being, despite my interest in almost everything else, except partying, for which I didn't have the money even if I had wanted to. My first months in New Haven were all spent in getting adjusted socially and intellectually, but the religious dimension came to a head during Christmas vacation, which I spent with my parents in the house of one of Mother's relatives in Jamaica Plains, just outside downtown Boston. They had decided that my mother would go to Midnight Mass at the nearby Catholic parish, then she and my father would both go to the Christmas Day service at the Episcopal Trinity Church on Copley Square, in downtown Boston. I saw that my best course would be to go first with one, then with the other, so I accompanied my mother to Midnight Mass, then went with both her and Daddy to his daytime service downtown.

It turned out to be a more important decision than I foresaw. When Mother and I entered the moderately large Catholic church of Our Lady of Lourdes parish, a few minutes before midnight, it was packed full. There were only two places left in one of the pews on the central aisle way down in front, three or four rows back from the Communion rail. It was the last place I would have chosen but, to be with Mother, I accompanied her down the aisle during one of the longest 20 seconds in my life. I knew that Catholics genuflect toward the Tabernacle before entering their seats, and that this was both an act of faith in the Real Presence of Christ in the Eucharist and a public sign of Catholic identity. So what was I going to do? Was I going to genuflect or not? And this in the presence of all these people! I recall making an instantaneous silent prayer, something I was not in the habit of doing: "Lord help me to do the right thing!" We reached the pew, my mother entered first. I knew I had to genuflect, and I did.

I have no recollection of the rest of the Midnight Mass, except that I was intellectually and emotionally overwhelmed by the implications of what I had just done, although I said nothing to either my mother or my father at that time. It is hardly necessary to say that the Christmas Day service at Trinity Church, Copley Square, was an anticlimax for me. It was dignified, of course, but subdued and seemed empty ritual in comparison with last night, even though the large church was relatively full. Again, however, I made no comments to my mother and father, nor did I make any immediate plans for my future, since there was enough to think about with my freshman studies at Yale.

Nevertheless, there were two immediate consequences of my Midnight Mass experience, both of them on the more affective level. One was a final inner break with Sally Johnson, whom I mentioned above. She was studying nursing in the Boston area and had given me her telephone number so that I could contact her over the holidays, but after my Christmas experience I consciously let it pass. It would have to wait. It was not for me, at least then. My life had become too full. I never saw her again.

The other result was even more significant, but harder to put into words, since it was a purification of the heart. A short time after my Christmas vacation, with its Midnight Mass experience, I gradually realized that I was freer from the pull of emotional satisfaction of all kinds. It was sort of an emotional sobriety or inner restraint that had been given me, not acquired through my own efforts or simply by bodily mortification. It included a gift of chastity and a conversion of my affective life that I did not analyze at the time—I was not that intellectually trained—but it revealed a new type of friendship coming up to the surface of my life. It was also an inner confirmation of the path that God's mercy was opening up for me. I had not lost a thing and had found a true liberation, a greater inner harmony.

During that same Christmas vacation, I happened to see a small book on the living room table, *The Glory of Thy People*, by Raphael Simon. Something on the cover made me understand that it was about a monk, so I picked it up, started reading and finished it before returning to New Haven, not talking to anyone about it. The book was an autobiographical account of the conversion of a Jewish psychiatrist to the Catholic Church through his study of Saint Thomas Aquinas, then of his entry into the same Trappist monastery where my brother was. It was the first real book I had ever read about Catholics or the Catholic Church and served as an introduction to what conversion can mean. It is only now, as I remember this incident, that I realize how strange it was that this type of book appeared in the living room of my staunchly Protestant relatives. More than likely it was my mother who "planted" it there for me to read, just in case, exactly two years after she had first handed me Father Peyton's little Rosary book in Shanghai onboard the *General Breckinridge*. My father must have seen the book there on the table but did not say anything.

For the rest of my freshman year at Yale, my real interest was not in the studies but in the question of how to proceed in order to be consistent with what God was doing to me. One of the hardest aspects was that of not causing unnecessary suffering for my father, who had always been so good to me and was such a good person in his own right. It would be a terrible blow for him to have another son become Catholic. What should I do? I wasn't sure. So I waited, but I was becoming increasingly convinced that I had to make a final leap. But how?

A breakthrough came one day at a surprising moment, occasioned in part by our class in English literature. We were studying the works of the Irish playwright, George Bernard Shaw, especially his two plays, *Man and Superman* and *Saint Joan*. Shaw's key message in both these works is the importance of rising above one's milieu in order to achieve the best of one's humanity. I must have been thinking about this as I walked from one building to another on the central Yale quadrangle, called the "Yale Green," for suddenly I had a double insight into my own condition at the time. The first one was that I still had a lurking mistrust of exterior religious commitments, probably a mixture of human respect and a certain reaction against overly pious religious behavior. I saw that this mistrust is actually very common and is a form of pride desperately trying to avoid anything that might control, or even condition, my life. Even worse, this anti-religious pride, at least in me, was wearing the mask of humility, softly whispering, "Who are you to say or think that you know the truth more than others do?" I had to tear off this mask of human respect.

Almost at once came the second part of the insight, namely that this false humility is closely linked to an even deeper mistake, which is even more common than mistrust in organized religion. It is to think that personal freedom consists in doing what I want. I grasped, more by intuition than by logic, that my real freedom—my truest self, destiny and happiness—is, and will always be, to know and give myself to *what I was made for*. I must have consented interiorly to this important insight—of being made for God himself—because its immediate result was an experience of inner joy of soul, the first time I was aware of such a thing, at least explicitly. I was beginning to be set free . . . from myself!

A second result was that I started to go to Sunday Mass at one of the nearby Catholic churches: either Saint Thomas More Chapel for Yale students, on Park Street, or Saint Mary's Parish, run by the Dominican Friars on Hillhouse Avenue. One Sunday morning as I was walking to Mass, a car came up to the sidewalk beside me, stopped and the driver leaned out the window. It was my brother, John, with his wife, Kate, who had driven in from their village of Quonset huts to go to the Sunday service at a downtown Episcopal church. My heart dropped, although later reflection showed me that this was God's way of pushing me along the path he wanted me to follow. "Where are you going?" I heard.

I had to answer and did, though embarrassed, "I'm going to the Catholic chapel on Park Street."

"Oh, we're going in the other direction," they smiled and drove off. Now my family knew, or at least they would be watching.

The next step was to contact the priest in charge of Saint Thomas More Chapel, which I did before the Easter break. The first time I rang the doorbell of the small rectory, no one answered, so I came back another day. This time I found him, Father Edwin O'Brien, a Yale graduate himself, a middle-aged priest of the Diocese of Hartford and chaplain to the several hundred Catholic students at Yale. I explained my situation, he was interested and told me to think things over, study for my midyear exams and come back after they were all over in three or four weeks, which I did.

Father O'Brien was organizing a small class for converts, in which I was the youngest member of a group of five or six, one of whom was the Japanese Buddhist wife of a Yale graduate student. The group had a class together each week for two months before the end of the school year, using a short catechism for adults. Each week we would cover 15 to 20 pages, so the brunt of responsibility lay on each member's personal reading. The only four elements of these classes that remain in my mind are, in the first place, a picture in the book we used, showing Saint Thomas Aquinas with a white dove over his head and the caption, "Saint Thomas Aquinas preserved by God from error." Fortunately, I did not give it too much attention, but it shows how a good thing can be piously exaggerated.

The second item was a question I asked Father O'Brien, "In the history of the Catholic Church, when was the doctrine of Purgatory introduced?" Without much hesitation, he correctly replied, "Well, there was really never a need to introduce it, since the teaching on Purgatory was present even before the time of Jesus. The Jews used to pray for the dead, that God would free them from the sins they had committed during their life on earth. The primitive Church did the same thing and we still do. Purgatory is the state after death when the souls of good people are purified from any sins they had committed, so that they can enter Heaven as soon as possible."

The reply was a good one and corrected the idea I had brought with me from my Protestant upbringing, which was that Purgatory was one of those "Catholic doctrines" added to the Gospel in order to explain what happens after death. Father O'Brien could have referred to Saint Paul's explanation, in his First Letter to the Corinthians, of a final purification as a consequence of Judgment Day:

> The work of each builder will become visible, for the Day will disclose it, because it will be revealed with fire, and the fire will test what sort of work each has done. If what has been built on the foundation survives, the builder will receive a reward. If the work is burned up, the builder will suffer loss; the builder will be saved, but only as through fire.[6]

I also remember the comment of the young Japanese, "For a Buddhist, the hardest thing to understand and accept in Christianity is the doctrine of the Trinity: first that God is a Person, and then that there are *three* Persons! It is very difficult." Her words made me newly grateful for my Christian upbringing, even though it had the effect of tending to make me take the Blessed Trinity somewhat for granted.

A final episode in the instruction class was a vehement discussion that took place between two of its members in one of our

6. 1 Cor 3:13-15.

meetings concerning an item touching the Episcopal Church and its approach to the Eucharist. My first impulse was to intervene, solve the problem and show how much I knew, but something inside me told me that it was better to keep quiet, since there was so much emotion involved in the discussion and I was younger than everyone else. After things had subsided, Father O'Brien turned to me and said, "Bruce, your father is an Episcopal Bishop. Do you know what the Episcopal Church says about this?" I answered by stressing the plurality within the Episcopal Church itself, so that someone asked me, "Why didn't you speak up earlier?"

I replied sincerely, "I thought that peace was better than winning an argument." It was an ecumenical principle which can be abused, but in this case I think it came from my growing appreciation of the Catholic Church as something really holy, a sacred communion in the hands and heart of Christ himself, which should not be the scene of violent, emotionally charged arguments. In later years I learned that this was naive on my part. The Church is very human.

Once I had started the classes of formal instruction, I wrote the difficult letter to my parents. It was hard to give explanations for my decision to become a Catholic, not only in order not to hurt my father, but above all because it was difficult for me to pinpoint the reasons. The underlying one was that I had to be interiorly true to myself, to my conscience, to my deepest convictions about where truth, Christian truth, lies. More objectively, it was that the Catholic Church as I experienced it in its life, mysticism and teaching seemed increasingly more real, alive, Christian and credible than the very fine life and spirit of the Protestant Churches I was familiar with. When my father read the letter, he came immediately to New Haven to see me.

I met him in his simple room at the Y.M.C.A. in downtown New Haven close to the Yale campus and we talked there for two hours. It was one of the most difficult moments in his life: out of a job, few prospects for finding one because of his wife's conversion to Catholicism, and now this added humiliation of another theologically wayward son. Fortunately, there was no grave economic problem, since he continued to receive his salary from the Episcopal Board of Foreign Missions: nothing extraordinary, but enough for him and his wife to live on. Daddy was never arrogant, even the few times I saw him angry or vexed, and now he was humble and humiliated, yet always dignified and respectful. I myself had not prepared any particular speech or argument, nor did I feel the need to do so. It was enough to be sincere with this sincere father that God had given me. I instinctively thought of Christ's words "not to prepare your defense in advance; for I will give you words and a wisdom that none of your opponents will be able to withstand or contradict."[7]

It was good that I was not aware at that time of the heated discussions that had taken place between Mother and Daddy in Shanghai two years previously. As it turned out, I found myself putting the emphasis on what I had observed in Catholic spirituality, how Catholics seemed to cultivate humility and devotion to the Passion of Christ in a way that I had not experienced before and which meant a lot to me. Daddy could hardly argue with this and I got the distinct impression that he was basically concerned for my own sincerity, that I was not making my decision simply to imitate my older brother or just to follow the example of my mother. There was certainly an element of fatherly responsibility involved in his visit and our conversation was always peaceful, without any particular paternal message directed at my behavior or my future. Perhaps he basically wanted to tell me that he was, and would always be, my loving and caring father.

I found him so approachable, in fact, that at one point I asked him if he had ever thought of becoming a Catholic himself. His reply is significant for revealing his underlying attitude: "No. I believe that God's will is revealed in the situation in which he puts us. We should stay in the Church in which we were born and brought up."

He had answered my question, given me his message, which he himself sincerely observed, and I made no reply or commentary.

7. Lk 21:14-15.

Only later, reflecting on our conversation, I saw the contradiction between such an attitude of institutional stability and his life as a dedicated Christian missionary, or perhaps he applied this stability to himself and his family, but not necessarily to others. In any case, a critical examination of one's own presuppositions was more typical of my mother than of my father.

Final exams were approaching and our little catechism class finished its preparation without any fanfare. There was no public reception of candidates in those days, so the members of the group were received into the Church each in his or her own way, perhaps in their respective hometowns. I explained to Father O'Brien that I did not have any hometown, so he was more than happy to receive me himself, which he agreed to do in early June, right after my last final exam, in the nearest parish, which was Saint Mary's. It was in the sacristy of Saint Mary's, on Saturday, June 9, 1951, that I abjured all heresy, expressed my faith in Christ, in the Roman Catholic Church with its Sacraments and its Pope, and received conditional Baptism from Father O'Brien. My baptismal "sponsor" was the sacristan, a Dominican laybrother whom I had never met before, Brother Giles. There was no one else present.

The Baptism was conditional—with the words, "If you are not baptized, I baptize you . . ."—because I had almost certainly been validly baptized in the Episcopal Church as an infant in Nanjing over 18 years before. In fact my conditional Baptism could have been omitted, as it was for my mother, but I realized later that Father O'Brien had decided to do it this way because he intuited the possibility of my entering a seminary and becoming a priest, in which case at least conditional Baptism is required, to assure the validity of the many Sacraments which the priest will be administering.

After my official admission into the Church and my conditional Baptism, Father and I went back into the empty church and I proceeded to make my first sacramental Confession. At first I thought of presenting to God's mercy a general rundown of my past life, but Father O'Brien encouraged me to be simple. After all, Baptism washes away all sincerely regretted past sins. Since I really did regret any and all of my offenses against him who was the love of my soul, I only mentioned the two that I thought were the most flagrant: my frequent impatience and my general self-centeredness, that is, pride and sensuality. After a few gentle words from Father O'Brien, who was probably just as emotionally drained as I was, I received absolution for the first time in my life. It was a relief, a spiritual shower. There was no sensible experience of Christ, but I knew that it was he who had forgiven me, received me, cleansed me, embraced me. The next morning, at Sunday Mass in Saint Thomas More Chapel, I received my First Communion, totally unnoticed in the long line of communicants. It was done and I was in peace, somewhat dazed by it all.

That very afternoon I had a simple lunch in a cheap restaurant, took the short train ride to Stamford and reported the next morning for my summer job with the Bartlett Tree Company. After a few days' training I was told to go to their office in Boston, to receive work there. So my second Holy Communion was the following Sunday at the Paulist Center on Park Street, off the Boston Common. My third one would be in a country chapel outside Goffstown, New Hampshire, where I would spend the next six or seven weeks working with three older men spraying herbicide on the trees and brush underneath long miles of high-tension power lines. It was an education in itself, not an easy one, but it brought me down to earth, helped pay some of my living expenses and gave me an invaluable experience of the life of an itinerant hired worker.

In the middle of August I went to be with my parents on Nantucket Island, before returning to Yale. Meanwhile, my father had finally found his new work in the Episcopal Diocese of Philadelphia. For the first time since the Midnight Mass in Jamaica Plains the previous Christmas, I went to Mass with Mother. This time we both received the Lord in his Blessed Sacrament. It was in a small Protestant chapel in the village of Siasconset, kindly lent to the Catholic priest from Nantucket town for an early Mass on Sunday mornings. Later in the day, Mother went to the same chapel again with my father for the Protestant service, but I stayed home and prepared their lunch.

Eddie, thank you for your patience in following me this far. I'll tell you something about my next step in another letter.

Letter 3

BUT WHERE?

1952–1953

Dear Eddie,

Probably one of the reasons you recommended that I write these letters was to know a little more about how I came to discover the Catholic Church despite the opposite direction of my family background. Now you know. But there still remains the whole process of how we came to meet up at Spencer, so here are a few more details about that.

Yale sophomores are generally assigned to one of a dozen or so dwelling complexes called "Colleges," in keeping with the classical tradition of English universities. There they would live and eat for the next three years. Jonathan Edward's College was not my first choice, but it was a simple quadrangle of three-storey stone buildings without elevators and, of course, without TV or the Internet in those days.

The sophomores had suites for four students each: two small bedrooms, each with a double-decker bunk, and a central parlor with its door into the corridor. I took an upper bunk, with my desk in one corner of the central parlor. I and my three roommates had chosen each other at the end of our freshman year: Joshua Dranoff, later a distinguished Professor of Chemical Engineering at Northwestern University; Harry Alter, who was born in the Middle East and worked for many years in the petroleum industry with Saudi Armaco; and John Britten, doctor and professor at the University of Maryland Medical School. All four of us have since written articles in our respective fields. Our life style was simple and functional. None of us were party revelers or athletes, although I indulged in an occasional golf game with other classmates, especially on Sunday mornings. We had come to study and learn.

Two Concerns

For each of us the sophomore year was one of consolidation, a bridge between the newness of the first year at college and the more intense specialization that takes place during the last two years. Little by little during this sophomore year it became clearer what each one would major in, what type of specialized classes and research he would engage in as a preparation for a professional career or, as often happened, for further study in some graduate school, such as law, medicine, the sciences, business or the arts. I had pretty much decided, even before entering Yale, to do pre-medical studies, basically the sciences, especially chemistry and zoology. Perhaps today I would have included psychology and anthropology. The problem, however, was with me. What did I really want to do?

As I started my second year, I was not sure what I wanted to give the rest of my life to. The past 18 months had been too intense. I was still living on two planes, on the academic level with moderate intensity, but with maximum concern for what at that time I probably would have called "living my faith," integrating this new world of Catholic realities into my mental frame and daily life. Chief among these realities was the Eucharist. On my first visit to Bill after my entrance into the Church—I was hitchhiking back to New Haven from Nantucket Island a year after the disastrous burning of his monastery—while he was living and working with a few other monks in the one wing of the monastery that remained livable, he encouraged me to receive Holy Communion every day, which I began to do. It meant studying when I could in the afternoon and evening, then getting up for the 6:30 Mass, walking back to the college for a quick breakfast and bicycling to my first classes at 8 AM: an intense schedule, but well worth it. I carried with me every morning, like most Catholics at that time, the *Saint Andrew's Daily Missal*, with the Mass texts and readings in English—since the Masses were all in Latin—plus short commentaries on the different feasts of the year. It was my best introduction to Catholic life and prayer.

One afternoon, crossing the "Yale Green" on the way to my job at the Freshman Office, I crossed paths with Dick Unsworth, one of my Bible teachers at Mount Hermon who later became Headmaster of the combined Northfield Mount Hermon School. He asked me how I was doing and I told him simply that I had entered the Catholic Church. He politely asked if I noticed any difference with my previous Church allegiance. I said, "Yes, especially Mass and the Eucharist, the Real Presence of Christ." "But we have the Eucharist, too," he replied, to which I simply said, "But it's not the same thing," and we went our own ways. I have not seen him since.

What did I mean by, "It's not the same thing"? I had not had any special sensible experience of Christ's Real Presence in the Eucharist. Extremely few Catholics have, and I am not among them. Jesus' emphatic words to his disciples in the upper room, where he ate and drank with his immediate disciples, apply especially to Mass and Holy Communion, "Blessed are those who have not seen and yet have come to believe."[1] It is really better not to see, taste or "feel" the Lord, because the spiritual gift of believing in the words of God's only Son at the Eucharistic consecration, "This is my Body," is immensely more intimate, unifying and transformative than any sensible experience could be. So it is this double gift, the Body and the faith, that is different. This double reality, inner faith embracing the resurrected and transforming Body of Christ, has always been the dynamic core of Christianity, starting with the faith of Mary, the Mother of Christ, at his conception: "Let it be with me according to your word."[2] Living faith goes directly from the human heart to the divine heart, from the human mind to the center of God's loving wisdom, embracing it—Him!—without seeing or understanding the details.

Some years after leaving Yale, I became aware that a better appreciation of the religious culture which Jesus shared clarifies

1. Jn 20:29.
2. Lk 1:38.

what he meant to do at the Last Supper and confirms his Real Presence in the Eucharist. It is a question of his words, "Do this in remembrance of me."[3] Our Western understanding is that this means recalling what he has done for us as we celebrate the Eucharist, but Jesus' biblical mentality goes in the other direction and it is he who is creating a living memorial of his death and resurrection. The Jewish Paschal meal was a renewal of God's powerful blessing of salvation for his people, achieved in the past but made present by God himself for each celebrating family. Jesus is telling his disciples, "From now on it is I who will bless you with my saving presence, the new Covenant sealed in my Body and Blood. And you should renew it just like this." The remembrance, the memorial, is Jesus himself, remembering and saving his people proactively in his full Humanity, because that is what he did and does for his people then and now.

During that entire sophomore year my mind was continually involved on these two levels: the truths of Christian faith that had suddenly become so real, so overwhelming, and my studies, which were demanding in themselves. In two of my less important classes I was able to integrate the two levels. One of these classes was on 17th-century English literature, where I wrote a term paper comparing the Anglican King James Bible with the Catholic Douay translation of the Latin Vulgate, both of them from the 16th–17th centuries. In the other class, an introduction to musical composition where we studied the underlying harmony in the chorales of Johann Sebastian Bach, I wrote one or two chorales myself, using the Latin texts of the Mass. In light of my later work with liturgical music, this course in musical harmony was one of the three most useful subjects I ever studied, the others being English composition in my senior year at Mount Hermon and learning to touch-type in a special course for freshmen at Yale.

That year coincided with the moment when a well-known Catholic theologian, Father John Courtney Murray, S.J., was a

3. Lk 22:19; 1 Cor 11:23-25.

visiting professor at Yale. His specialty was the social doctrine of the Church, especially the relationship between Church and state, and his writings on the subject had a deep influence on the *Decree on Religious Liberty* promulgated ten years later by the Second Vatican Council, at which Father Murray was a theological advisor to the American bishops. Although I had never heard of him before and did not attend his lectures, which were mainly for graduate students, I often served his weekday Mass at the Thomas More Chapel. His tall, solemn, taciturn demeanor immediately instilled respect, yet without giving any impression of haughtiness. It was simply that life was a serious affair. He would thank me after each Mass, but not engage in any kind of conversation.

One Sunday, Father Murray was the celebrant at the main Sunday Mass at the Chapel. Since it was not a parish church, there was seldom a sermon or homily, but the gospel that Sunday ended with Jesus' words, "Many are called, but few are chosen,"[4] not the easiest phrase to explain. Since the Chapel was full of people, Father Murray, after reading the Gospel in Latin, which most of us were reading in English in our Sunday Missals, simply looked up and said, "This Gospel brings home the fact that God loves everyone, but he has his favorites." Nothing more, but among the innumerable homilies I have listened to, it is one of the very few that I will never forget: "God loves everyone, but he has his favorites."

On weekdays as I bicycled back and forth between classes, I would find myself meditating on such things as the Mass ceremonies, the Last Supper, purification of the heart, life after death, the meaning of sin. It was a mixture of being dazzled and being in love: two ways of saying the same thing. Gradually the conviction grew in me that I had to decide, or rather discover, my vocational orientation. It coincided with the need to choose one's major field of study. What should I do? I was beginning to admit to myself that maybe God was calling me to be with him and serve him more directly within the Catholic Church. But how, and when, and where?

4. Mt 22:14.

The first and, I think, only person who intuited my situation was, to my surprise, my sister-in-law, Kate, wife of my brother John, and herself a dedicated member of the Episcopal Church. After becoming a Catholic, I never overtly discussed the faith with either her or John, but on the occasion of a one-hour visit I paid them at that time, in their Quonset hut residence in West New Haven, she quietly observed, "Bruce, you are really enthralled with the Catholic Church, aren't you?"

I was taken off guard. "Yes, I guess I am," I admitted, somewhat embarrassed. "Did you notice?"

"It's easy to see," she said, perhaps hoping for a few more details, which I did not give her.

The normal course to follow at this point would have been to talk to someone who could help, probably a priest, but my inbred independence, my training in self-reliance and simply my pride kept me from even considering such a possibility. It was my problem; God and I can handle it, thank you. More specifically, I felt that I would not be helped by sharing my options with someone else. A few years later my brother John, by then a skilled ophthalmologist, wrote me something very similar about himself, "I have found that it is better to do things by myself, because I really know how to do them better than the people I could ask." There are different names for such an attitude.

So I continued with my unskilled personal discernment of what road to follow. Although I liked most women and got along well with them, they did not now attract me sexually or affectively. Something or someone else had taken hold of my heart. Medicine was a noble calling and I liked the exact sciences, but it was clear that they did not speak to or fill my heart, my inner desires which were coming more strongly to the surface. What *were* these desires? They could probably be described as a desire to do what the Lord Jesus wanted me to do, whatever that was; dedicate my life to something or someone worth my while and worth loving, to something where I could really be of service to others, where I could really help them become . . . not exactly "better," but more eternally satisfied, fulfilled, touched by divine joy, truth and life. At that time, "divine love" was, for some reason, not part of my vocabulary. Perhaps it sounded too pious. Divine life, truth, fidelity, joy, reality was what I was looking for, what I wanted to dedicate myself to. But how?

Fruits of Prayer

Christmas vacation came and went. Then Lent arrived and I wondered how I should choose a good book for Lenten reading and what I should give up as a type of Lenten sacrifice. For a book, I happened to find a small edition of *The Imitation of Christ*, which I could carry around in my pocket and read in short intervals during the day.

As for something to offer up for Lent, I knew that Jesus would like me to give him something precious, something I really like, even need, as a sign that God is the Lord of my life. Since I saw at once that what I most wanted and needed, humanly speaking, was more time for my studies, I resolved to get a part-time job, thus having less time for study. It seemed foolhardy and I knew it, but it was a real sacrifice and that was where I was at. So I went to Saint Raphael's Hospital, at that time a relatively small Catholic hospital, 10 minutes by bicycle ride from the Yale campus. It was run by some nursing Sisters and I asked them if they had an opening for an evening orderly, that is, an assistant for the sick or for the doctors. The Sister I spoke with looked me up and down, took my name and statistics, and told me that if there was an opening they would phone me, which they did within a week.

From then on until the end of the school year I worked four hours almost every evening at Saint Raphael's, doing a little of everything: giving bed baths, enemas and sheet changes to male patients; moving and installing oxygen tanks; helping doctors make spinal taps; wheeling patients to and from the operating room; going on ambulance calls. In the few free minutes between calls, I would either read a little of *The Imitation of Christ* or make a short visit to the hospital chapel.

By the end of Lent, I had narrowed my vocational field down to two general choices: the life of a Trappist monk or that of a missionary priest, preferably with the Marist Fathers because of their missions in the South Pacific and their devotion to Our Lady. The wonderful vocation of a diocesan priest in a neighborhood parish just did not appeal to me, not at all because of any bad example I had received, quite the contrary, but somehow I saw and felt that it was not for me. It was one example among several of how God speaks sometimes through one's "guts," one's deepest feelings, intuitions or attractions. It would happen to me again on several key occasions, as I hope to describe in some future letter.

Although I increasingly felt that God's providence and my deeper attractions were hard at work drawing me toward the monastery, it was not at all clear as to whether I should enter there as a brown-robed laybrother, like Bill, who spent most of the day at work to finance and maintain the monastery and its charities, or as a white-robed choir monk, like the ones I had seen in the two long lines in choir chanting in Latin day and night. I had talked with both kinds of monks in the Valley Falls guest house and they had all been most kind, spiritually transparent and peacefully happy in their special vocation, but I could not see myself, nor *wanted* to see myself, chanting in Latin for four or five hours a day the rest of my life. The lay brothers seemed more evangelical, simple and more intellectually humble, so that was where I decided to go.

Soon after Easter I was able to take a weekend off from my Saturday classes and my two jobs, and hitchhiked the 200 miles from New Haven up to the new monastery in the hill country near Spencer, outside of Worcester in central Massachusetts. On the last leg of the trip I was picked up by a group of monks returning to the monastery from somewhere, all in their black and white habits. They told me that Bill was working in the guest house. He was surprised to see me and I explained that I wanted to speak with whomever I should about my vocation. He asked no questions, as is our family way, and arranged an interview for the next morning with the abbey's vocational director, who Bill told me was a former student at Yale.

He was Father Thomas Aquinas Keating, a young, tall, thin, serious choir monk, who was to become much later the abbot at Spencer and a well-known author of books on the spiritual life.

At that time he was recovering from the consequences of a serious lung abscess and living in a small farmer's cottage on the monastery property. I explained my entire situation to him, the first time I had ever done so to another human person. It was an excellent experience for me and a good conversation. He listened quietly, did not object to anything, but pointed out that it might be better for me, with my relatively good intellectual formation, to think of becoming a choir monk and priest, to which I replied that I really had no attraction in that line and wanted to be a lay brother. He said nothing, acquiesced and handed me some application papers to fill out, telling me to come back in the summer. I returned to New Haven the next day, driven all the way by the father of one of the young lay brothers, Brother Paul Heide, who was returning to New York with his wife and daughter after visiting their son.

Now that I had made the first step at the monastery, I approached Father O'Brien at the Thomas More Chapel and told him what I had done and why, but when I said that I was going to become a lay brother instead of a priest, he exclaimed, "No, Bruce, you can't do that!" I replied softly and firmly, "But that's what I'm going to do," and the conversation ended there. I left his office to take up my daily round of Mass, classes, work and study. This time, however, there was a new element. My final vocational decision was approaching, much more important for me than any final exam. Although I was not disturbed by the recommendation of both priests with whom I had spoken, their words of caution brought home my need of a clear vocational discernment and choice. Besides, these men represented the Church with its centuries of experience, both were searching with me for God's will and both, independently of one another, happened to be former Yale students, something not too common. It made me more cautious. I needed and wanted divine light.

So I decided to make something like what is called a "Holy Hour," a time of prayer and adoration in the presence of the Eucharistic Christ. The key element of these 30 or 40 minutes in the Thomas More Chapel every afternoon was the Rosary, that is the five daily "decades" or series of an Our Father, ten Hail Marys and one doxology to the Father, Son and Holy Spirit, each decade dedicated to an event in the life of Christ. It is a prayerful meditation on the mysteries of Christ's life, death and resurrection, made in the presence of his mother, Mary, who herself had lived through most of them, "treasured all these things, and pondered them in her heart."[5] It was the first time in my life that I had prayed the Rosary and I felt that I should do so, especially now in my need of God's guidance as to how best to follow Christ.

This time with the Rosary every afternoon, usually before supper and my work at the hospital, was difficult. I was full of distracting thoughts and my imagination traveled all around the world. Most of my time was spent in trying to bring this "lunatic in the house," as Saint Teresa of Avila called it, back in line so as to think about the mystery at hand instead of about everything else. It was the typical battle of the beginner in prayer, and it was both difficult and humiliating, especially since I had plenty of other things I could be doing. So why did I keep it up? Something in me made me. The other possible activities were not half as important as this one, especially at this junction in my life. Occasionally, between Hail Marys and distractions, I would look at the Tabernacle, where the Living Body of Christ is kept in the Eucharist, and directly ask Jesus to help me. Once, when I was sure no one else was in the chapel and to conquer my religious backwardness, I went up awkwardly to the statue of Our Lady, lit a small vigil light, knelt in front of her and said something like, "Mary, now that I am a Catholic, I should have a devotion to you as the Mother of Jesus, but I really don't. Give it to me, if you want to. Help me be a good Catholic and give me light about what I should do in my life." There was no immediate answer.

One day at the end of May or beginning of June, after a typical 30- or 40-minute battle with distractions as I tried to pray in the chapel, I got up from my kneeling position, genuflected to the Tabernacle and walked out onto the sidewalk with a feeling of deep inner dejection. I was getting nowhere in prayer, my future

5. Lk 2:19.

was anything but clear and my final exams were approaching. A beggar was there on the sidewalk and asked for a handout. I decided to give him what I had in my pocket but was dismayed to discover that I had nothing except a ten-dollar bill. For a scholarship student in the early 1950s, this was a significant amount of money and giving it away would mean not buying anything for at least a week, but without much hesitation I handed it over wordlessly. Why? More than just self-denial or detachment, it was like a desperate act to live the Gospel in the middle of my personal misery and to "give the money to the poor,"[6] without any desire to think about it: God is God. Who am I to argue? What value is money?

Only a day or two later, after a similar struggle with the Rosary, I got up once again, genuflected, and walked out onto the same sidewalk. As I opened the outside door to the chapel, everything became suddenly and totally clear. Perhaps the beggar had prayed for me and the Lord had heard his prayer. There were no words, no sensible consolation, but simply an intellectual enlightenment, an inner certainty about what I should do in regards to my future. It was the Gift of Counsel and it was unexpected, like the coming of the Holy Spirit on the first Pentecost. The apostles had prepared themselves through prayer, but it was not clear to them what they were going to get. Their job had been to persevere in prayer. The Risen Christ would do the rest, and he did.

I understood what God wanted of me and what he himself would do in my immediate future. I was to enter the monastery as a choir novice, not a lay brother, and if God wanted me to change or go elsewhere, he would tell me through my superiors. That was it. It was settled and I was at peace. I had discovered at last my vocation, or rather had been discovered by it, and had no regrets about not entering the lay brothers. In fact I had very few questions at that time. The Lord of my life had shown me the course to follow. My heart was tired but grateful, and looking forward to the future.

6. Mk 10:21.

I told Father O'Brien as soon as I could and he correctly said, "But Bruce, before anything else you need to be confirmed," that is, receive Confirmation, the Sacrament of spiritual anointing by the Holy Spirit for bearing witness to Christ in one's personal vocation. Of course I agreed. I had overlooked Confirmation because of all I was more concerned with. So without any special preparation it was arranged that I would join a group of younger adolescents in a nearby parish when the Archbishop of Hartford came the following week to administer Confirmation. But Father O'Brien was shocked when I appeared that day at the Thomas More Chapel in my usual student's clothes: pants, open shirt and sweater. "But Bruce, go back and put on a coat and tie!"

I appeared again within 15 minutes, more elegantly clad, and we drove together to the parish. There I met my "sponsor," a member of the parish whose name I have totally forgotten, got gently slapped on the cheek by the Archbishop, anointed and sacramentally strengthened by the grace of spiritual Confirmation. It was all over in a few hours and I returned in time for my work in the hospital.

The Plunge

Since it was clear what I should do about entering the monastery, I wrote to Father Thomas about my change of plans and went to see him after my last exam. Almost incredibly, under my three-month regime of minimum study but maximum spiritual vigilance, my final marks at Yale went up an average of two points, from 87 to 89.

Father Thomas, however, gave me some disconcerting news, a first frustration in my vocation plans. I would have to go to school for another year before entering the monastery as a choir monk. It meant studying at a special kind of pre-seminary, The School of Saint Philip Neri, on Newbury Street, downtown Boston, run by the New England Jesuits for the considerable number of veterans who felt called to the priesthood, but lacked sufficient Latin. The course jammed four years of Latin in one, quite an achievement, and it worked well, although it died a natural death 15 years later, after the Second Vatican Council, when Latin was no longer required to begin seminary studies.

At the same time, it was clear that an extra year before entering the monastery would be helpful to me as a recent convert from a Protestant Church. Nine months living and studying with the other 30 young men from different parts of the country, sharing their life stories in a boarding house run by a delightful Irish widow, "Ma Campbell," on Beacon Street was an irreplaceable introduction into normal Catholic life. Under her homey direction, we would do our studies, go to one of the morning Masses at Saint Cecilia's, the nearest parish, kneel around the living room statue of Our Lady after supper every evening, say the Rosary together and end with the sung *Salve Regina* ("Hail Holy Queen"). It was easy, too, to go for evening adoration to the Eucharistic Shrine on Boylston Street.

To help pay for my expenses, I took a part-time job as driver of a small school bus for some French Dominican Sisters who were running a primary school for French-speaking children in Brookline: Saint Dominic's Institute. It gave me my first—but certainly not my last—insight into the details of religious and convent life. One of my three roommates, Dick Hannigan, and I have been close friends ever since, all through his life as seminarian, parish priest, army chaplain wounded in action in Vietnam, then back to his home parish in Fitchburg, Massachusetts, and his retirement from active priestly duty. He passed to the Lord from a heart attack shortly after the turn of the century, but I kept in touch with his only sister, Catherine, superior general of the Sisters of the Presentation.

The experience of healthy young religious men and women was certainly the key element of those months at Saint Philip Neri's. The Latin classes themselves were well conducted by the Jesuit faculty and Father Mortimer Murphy was an especially good teacher, one of the best I've known, with his lively sense of humor used with exquisite pedagogical skill. Between classes, three or four of us would go into the closed stairwell and sing in three-part harmony, the echo magnifying our voices. One of our trio was Paul Smith, a young African-American from Detroit, who became a parish priest of that diocese and the dynamic principal of an inner city parochial school. We kept in touch over the years until 30 years later, in the 1980s, he was shot dead on the street.

One particular event turned out to be especially important for me. It took place in the small school library, a converted classroom, where I had gone to study. There on a side table I happened to see a thin booklet with large letters, *The Mystical Body of Christ*, and the subtitle, *Mystici Corporis*. It caught my eye immediately and I took it up. It was the encyclical letter of Pope Pius XII on the nature of the Christian and Catholic Church, written ten years previously, in 1943, but which I had never heard of. My catechism class with Father O'Brien had not even mentioned this phrase, but I vaguely remembered having heard the expression, "mystical body," without really understanding its meaning, in conversations between my parents or with visitors to our Shanghai home. In any case, I dropped everything and spent the lunch hour in the library, devouring the booklet.

It was fascinating, the first time I had ever read anything like it. The Church is a human institution founded by Christ, but much more than that. It is the living body of the Risen Christ. The risen Head of this body is in heaven, its divine soul is the Holy Spirit and its members are on earth, in heaven and in Purgatory, ready to enter God's fullness. The Pope, as successor of Saint Peter, represents Christ on earth as visible pastor of the universal Church in unity with the other bishops throughout the world. As the Body of Christ, the Church unites heaven and earth, eternity and time, divine grace and human nature in a sublime communion of mortal persons that mirrors the divine communion of the three divine Persons. I left the library intellectually and emotionally enraptured, captivated with this vision of universal unity in the Living Christ. Future readings and reflection, would only explain more deeply what I had sensed in this encyclical, especially the fact that the Church as the living Body of Christ was one of the great insights of both Saint Paul and Saint Augustine, especially in the latter's commentaries on the Psalms: "Christ as God, himself unchanged, took to himself our created nature in order to change it, and he made us one man with himself, Head and Body. . . . God could give no greater gift to us than to make his Word, through whom he created all things, our Head and to join us to him as his members."[7] Over the years this has become the air I breathe.

Toward the end of that school year, in the spring of 1953, I made a final visit to the monastery before entering. Father Thomas asked me to speak with Father Raphael Simon, whose autobiography I had read two years previously in Jamaica Plains. It was a sobering conversation, partly because of his psychiatrist's tone of voice, as he told me, "It would probably be better for you to wait before entering in order to finish college, preferably in a Catholic university like Fordham, in New York."

I replied as calmly as I could that I thought I had enough intellectual formation, that I didn't think more college education was what I needed.

"Your education," he answered, "has not been in a Catholic context."

"I'll do whatever you decide," I said, subdued.

It was a blow, although it did not alter in the least my vocational orientation. I returned to Boston feeling somewhat like a criminal waiting for his prison sentence and watched in dread for a letter from Father Thomas, who would have the final word. The letter arrived two or three weeks later and it was a surprise: they had decided that I should enter that summer. No reason was ever given to me for this final decision, but time would show that God's providence was behind it, because a two-year delay would have significantly altered the future events in my life.

June and July passed peacefully enough, a final good-bye to my classmates at St. Philip Neri's, then going to stay with my parents in North Philadelphia, where I got a three-week job cleaning industrial kitchens. After July Fourth, Mother, Daddy and I drove up to Siasconset on Nantucket, where we relaxed through the month of July. I used the spare moments to wallpaper or paint

7. Augustine, *Sermon on Psalm 85*, 1.

almost every room of the old family summer house. On August 1 we took the ferry back to the mainland and Daddy drove us up to Spencer, where we arrived in mid-afternoon. The next morning we said good-bye. Mother told me later that they thought I would not make it through the first year, probably because I was too "normal." She felt that I might be entering the monastery to escape having to work for a living, since I was only 19 at the time.

Father Thomas told me to spend a few days at the guest house helping the brothers there, then to speak with the Novice Master, Father Hilarion, and arrange with him a time to enter the community as a postulant. The brothers put me to work helping them to clean the many guest house rooms and make the beds. I did so with Brother Matthew, a gentle, kind man in his thirties, whose older brother had entered the community before him. While we were making a bed together, he on one side and I on the other, I asked him how long he had been in the monastery. "Seven years," he replied.

I was aghast. Seven years seemed like an infinite time of separation from family and friends, never to leave this single place, never to see the ocean again, never to play tennis or golf, never to travel or go on vacation! My face must have shown what was racing through my disturbed imagination, because Brother continued at once, "And I have no regrets, I've never been happier." I was relieved, but it shows that I had never given much thought to what I was about to do or to its human consequences. It had been too much the work of God himself. I must have been blinded, or seduced. But since leaving Yale, I had never doubted what God's vocational will for me was, nor have I doubted it since then.

Father Hilarion said to enter the next day. And so began my ongoing experience as a monk, a pure gift from the Lord. But more about that in another letter.

Letter 4

FIRST FORMATION

1953–1958

Dear Eddie,

My first three letters were really kind of a preparation for this one, since the discoveries I was being led into were almost all inside myself. You entered the monastery three years before I did, so you know that in the 1950s the passage from the status of guest to that of Trappist postulant was something like a leap in the dark. Entering a monastery meant trusting in God's personal call and in this institution, which had a decent reputation as a center of lived spirituality. There was no trial period as there is now, no "observership" or temporary experience of monastic life for possible candidates. It was sink or swim, and the newcomers tried to swim as best they could, thanks to the help of everyone else in the novitiate, especially the novice master and the submaster. At Spencer, these latter were Father Hilarion Summers and Brother Theophane Boyd, later known in monastic circles as the author of a short book, *The Magic Monastery*.

Postulancy

There were around 20 young men in the choir novitiate when I entered, and another 20 or so in the separate novitiate for lay brothers, both groups using the same building, a converted horse barn 100 yards downhill from the main monastery. There we slept, prayed privately, studied, showered and changed clothes for work, which was either outside—on the farm, in the garden or at the construction site of the new buildings—or indoors, mainly cleaning up the new monastery. I remember that one of my jobs as a novice was to help you cut up big pieces of meat and put them in the deepfreeze for future use in the guest house. We would all pray early morning Vigils and the seven other daily Offices in the choir of the big church with the professed choir monks, all in Latin, which I discovered to be surprisingly understandable.

Everyone treated me most kindly. Because of the strict rule of silence—which is not a vow, but a norm to help maintain an adequate context of prayer—I only spoke with the superiors and the brother in charge of my work for the day. In such an atmosphere of silence, looks, smiles and gestures are enough to communicate recognition and friendliness or their opposites. By their look or smile I could sense that the members of the community were pleased to see Brother Luke's younger brother. At that time, it was expected that someone would take a new name when entering any form of religious life, which shows the relatively little importance given then, at least in practice, to the sacrament of Baptism. When I saw that none of the choir monks had the name John, I leapt at the chance to be named after Christ's beloved disciple, so from my first days in the novitiate I was "Frater John."

My honeymoon lasted about ten days. It took that time for me to really become aware on a gut level that this was for keeps, that I was expected to stay here for the rest of my life. It had dawned on me in the guest house before entering, but now I began to touch it existentially, with almost an obsession: no more travel, no more ocean surf, tennis, golf, planning my own day, living with people I knew, the family or my chosen roommates, in other words, doing what I wanted. From now on my life would be just this set of buildings, persons and routine activities, period! Nothing was going wrong in the monastery; on the contrary, everyone was most kind and considerate, but it was just that I wanted to get out of there. My whole inner system was clamoring for it. Nerves, memory, desires, thoughts: all wanted OUT. This was too much.

I tried not to show all this, of course, and the fact that we did not speak to each other made this easier to accomplish, but several days and nights passed without much of an oasis in the desert. I would go upstairs to the little novitiate chapel, kneel before the Tabernacle and tell Jesus, "Lord, if you can spend your eternity shut up in a Tabernacle like this, forgotten by most people, I guess I can do the same in this place."

I was playing the hero, but not really asking for the strength to stay. That would have been too much, because I wanted out. Yet somehow I kept staying. My pride and self-esteem were involved, but there was also something deeper, more central to my being than mere memories, desires or thoughts.

One morning while the novices were changing from their white robes into their work clothes, I sat down in the main hallway of the novitiate to wait for them, since as a postulant I wore my shirt and pants throughout the day. Although it was only eight o'clock in the morning, I was interiorly exhausted by what was going on inside me, and I must have shown it on my face. Without being aware of it, I had sat down on the stool outside the novice master's door, the sign that I wanted to speak with the novice master, which was in fact the last thing I wanted to do! Some novice must have seen me there, interpreted what was happening, and gone at once to tell Father Hilarion, who came almost running from where he had been changing his clothes.

I was caught off guard. Father Hilarion took me by the sleeve of my shirt, opened the door to his office and said, "Come on in." There was no way out. It was a new situation for me, since during the week that I had been in the monastery I had seen no need to talk with the novice master. I and the Lord could handle things very well, at least so far. In those days, Trappist monks and nuns all over the world knelt to speak with their superiors. So I knelt on the floor at the side of Father Hilarion's desk as he asked, "So how are you doing?"

Fortunately I was sincere enough to say the truth, "I want to leave."

Father Hilarion probably expected such a reply and he was undoubtedly used to talking with homesick candidates, so he simply asked, "Well, how long do you think you can stay?"

It was at that point that I unexpectedly expressed, for the first time and without any hesitation, in fact with a sincere conviction, the inner certainty I had received over a year before in New

Haven, when it became clear what Jesus was calling me to do, so I said, "I'll stay until you tell me to leave."

Father Hilarion was clearly relieved and, in a way, I was too. We conversed a little more about my work and my reading. He encouraged me to live each moment as a gift from God and to come back to see him sometime in the next week. I left his office in something of a daze, but in peace. At least I had been true to the grace I had received, although the need to fight against feelings, memories and thoughts was a new form of warfare, which I was not used to.

It had been a sobering experience, but I soon understood how, once again, God's spirit had strengthened my abysmal inner weakness at a critical juncture of my life. And I had learned—or was beginning to learn—two fundamental lessons: first, the sharp duality that exists inside me, the "spirit" and the "flesh,"[1] which Jesus referred to in his own agony, or more precisely, "the law of the Spirit of life in Christ Jesus" and "the law of sin and of death";[2] and secondly, the practical importance of being open with the novice master, and with superiors in general, as instruments of freedom and truth in this otherwise dangerous duality of flesh and spirit.

After that, my life as a postulant continued peacefully enough. My longings to leave had been pushed into the background by recalling, to myself and to Father Hilarion, my commitment to staying until told otherwise, which has never happened. In fact that initial conversation with the novice master marked the beginning of a period of successive inner clarifications. There was nothing really spectacular about them, but they have marked me interiorly from then on and hopefully into eternity. I'll try to explain them here as best I can, because they were the real substance of my novitiate.

About a week after my first unscheduled talk with Father Hilarion, I was working with Brother Anthony, a professed lay brother, pouring the asphalt pathway linking the new monastery

1. Mt 26:41.
2. Rom 8:2.

with the old farm buildings, outside the community refectory. While I was walking from one end of the pathway to the other, intent on what I was doing, a captivating inner presence filled my heart in a way I had never experienced before. It was the presence of an eternal Love, an interior Lover who could only be divine. It was totally unpremeditated on my part and without any motive or stimulus outside me. There was no voice or image, just the inner presence of a Person who loved me like a spouse. That is to say that I was the spouse. It was not that I was thinking of God, or of Jesus as my Spouse, but rather that I was being embraced from the inside by a nuptial Lover. More than just "joy," it was the cause, the Author, of joy and I melted in gratitude.

Although the experience itself only lasted a few seconds, its impact has never left me. Exteriorly, I kept walking and working, but interiorly my first reaction was, "Thank you, Lord," then the realization that this is what spiritual marriage must mean, something I had read about in the life of Saint Teresa of Avila. And my conclusion at that moment was how beautiful life in the monastery could be, no matter what happened exteriorly! In my next talk with Father Hilarion I mentioned this spousal experience and his comment was simply, "That's nice."

It was only years later, while preparing a conference on initial monastic formation, that I became aware of the important connection between this spousal experience and what had happened the previous week. God wanted me to commit myself intentionally and verbally in the presence of his visible representative in my life to staying in the place he had chosen for me, before giving himself to me in a new, much more intimate way. Good Friday had to come before Easter Sunday, no new life without a previous death. At the time of my postulancy, though, the last thing I thought of was to theologize on the experience. I just enjoyed a new inner certainty that I was loved by God, belonged to him and was on the right course. I asked Father Hilarion how long I would have to wait before receiving the novice's habit. He smiled laconically as was his custom, "So you want to stay?"

In those days, the postulancy for choir novices was only a month long, which seems a short time, but mine had been especially intense. They told me that the date for finally changing my shirt and pants for a novice's white robe and scapular was set for the first week of September, so I began a week's retreat beforehand, which consisted of working in the morning and having the afternoons free for reading and prayer. Father Hilarion told me to read what was called the *Spiritual Directory,* a book of several hundred pages translated from the French, giving rather detailed ascetical and spiritual advice for newcomers to Trappist life. It reflects the spirituality of 19th-century French monasteries with their emphasis on fervent prayer, personal mortification and growth in faith and humility, not a bad combination in itself, though approached in a tone that would strike us today as overly moralistic, even military, not to say self-sufficient. I took it all in stride, perhaps naively so, and when Father Hilarion asked me how I liked it, I said it was helpful.

Much more helpful, though, were the one or two afternoon hours alone in the little novitiate library, which has since been changed into the secretary's office. I wasn't aware of it at the time, but I received several important lessons about my life, which later years proved to be both meaningful and prophetic. They came one after another in the course of my reading, starting with a little book I happened to see on the shelf: *Novices of the Lord*. The title caught my eye, so I looked through it and saw that it studied the interaction between Jesus and the 12 apostles as the model of what occurs during one's formation in religious life. I had never really thought of monastic life in those terms and the image appealed to me. I had become not only a disciple of the Lord, but also a follower of Jesus' own way of life as described in the gospel. That vision brought everything into focus and has held up through the years.

A second lesson, more in the form of an intuitive prophecy, was that Jesus did not plan to give me any active ministry in behalf of the average Catholic or Christian person. My life would rather be particularly dedicated to those persons whom he had loved and chosen more especially for himself. This was not surprising in itself, considering that I was to be a Trappist monk, but I sensed that it was a special inner message for me. Once again, I did not ask any questions about this, nor did I think it necessary to present it for discernment to Father Hilarion. In fact I forgot about it for many years, until I saw that it was really happening in my life.

A third intuition came on the heels of the other two. It was that my life in the monastery was not just local, but universal, worldwide, since I was entering not just a local house, but also a far-flung religious Order, with communities all over the world. It was not that I would necessarily do a lot of traveling—though that turned out actually to be the case—but simply that my cloistered life, if lived as it should be, would touch other people all over the world. Here also, I did not dwell on this premonition, but it was not difficult to accept, since I had already experienced life in other countries and had even thought of the possibility of becoming a Catholic missionary since, after all, "catholic" means universal.

A final intuition came during morning work. I was cleaning the windows of the abbot's future living quarters, diligently spraying them on both sides with some type of window cleaner and wiping them as clear as possible. The inner message came, "That's what I want you to be like, transparent. Let me shine through you."

"Oh, O.K., Lord," and I kept working. This incident occurred very near the time when I had the honor of being the first person to break one of the glass windows in the new monastic cloister, crashing the dry mop's wooden head into one of the lower windowpanes.

This combination of six lessons learned or reinforced inwardly during my short postulancy—openness to my superiors, flesh and spirit at war in me, Christ's spousal love, living as one of his disciples, with a non-active role in his Church on a worldwide basis and letting him polish me from within—all these fundamental orientations made my official entrance into the novitiate relatively easy and painless. One weekday morning, in the presence of the 40 or so professed choir monks and 15 or 20 choir novices, I prostrated on the floor of the chapter room in front of Dom Edmund, the abbot, and asked for the mercy of God and of the Order, so that I could become a novice. It was the first such ceremony in the new monastery's big chapter room. The abbot asked me to stand up and, after a few words—which I have no recollection of—he put the novice's habit of a white tunic, hooded scapular and cloth belt over my shirt and pants. I was a novice and happy to be one. There was one lay brother present in the back, as an exceptional favor: my brother, with whom I had not exchanged a single word since entering the community over a month before, although we had exchanged occasional smiles. I'm sure his prayers had helped me.

Novitiate

With each change of situation in the monastery—postulant, novice, professed monk—there comes a greater sense of belonging, which normally produces a deeper, peaceful joy in God's service. This does not necessarily mean that life becomes easier, but it does mean a life of greater commitment and spiritual understanding. At the same time, each person's monastic journey and each monk's novitiate experience is uniquely personal. For some, it can be more like a honeymoon, but later their professed years might be marked by trials and problems. For others it can be the opposite: the two years of novitiate can seem like a continual purification, a time of many contradictions and frustrations, but if they live through it, their profession commitment can be all the deeper and their years as a monk richer and more peaceful. It is impossible to know ahead of time what is going to happen, although it will almost certainly not be what we expect, which means that the best attitude is one of total abandonment and trust in God's loving wisdom.

Probably my attitude, as I began my two years as a novice, was something like this state of trusting abandonment. I had no plans or preconceived ideas. In fact my ignorance of monastic life was very great, but I was eager to learn, so my novitiate was basically a happy one. The major difficulties came later. Contrary to what the outsider usually thinks, there is little time to spare in the monastery. There is always something to do and part of the practical wisdom of life according to the Rule of Saint Benedict is the balanced alternation of different activities from before dawn until early evening, when the monk goes to sleep in his cubicle or bedroom with a real desire to get some rest. One soon learns the discipline of changing from sleep to sung night prayer, then to silent reading, breakfast, personal prayer and reading, liturgical prayer, manual work, more sung prayer, lunch, rest, work, prayer, supper, final prayer together and sleep again, all of this according to a timetable established by centuries of human experience not one's own. It is meant for the average, normal human being and you accept it or you leave.

Personally, I have found this Benedictine rhythm to be not only wise and flexible, but also liberating. It has repeatedly freed me from my self-will, from my "flesh" in the sense Saint Paul gives to that word, that is, the self-centered, self-serving tendency of fallen human nature. Often it is a relief to change gears from what one is doing at the moment, but just as often it has seemed like a built-in frustration of the work at hand, or a sudden break in the reading I was getting so much profit from, or the prayer that I was just beginning to relish. What is really happening is that the monk is learning to die to self, even in the best of activities, and to be more dependent on God's *when* and *how*, without asking too many *why's*. Fairly early in my novitiate I saw that monastic life was not meant to be a straightjacket, but a school for learning, even exteriorly, to be children of God, "led by the Spirit of God."[3]

Nothing had prepared me, however, for an abrupt change in our novitiate life, which constituted perhaps my biggest trial of these two years. One afternoon, during one of his conferences to us, Father Hilarion explained that the abbot had asked him to go as novice master to Spencer's recently founded daughter house near Berryville in northern Virginia. Our new novice master would be Father Thomas, whom I had dealt with as the monastery's vocational director. I was undone, because I had opened myself entirely to Father Hilarion, even though he was far from perfect, and he had patiently accepted me as I am, answering my questions with simple, affectionate common sense. I had never

3. Rom 8:14.

experienced such a relationship before, nor had I ever made such a conscious effort to be open with another person as I had with him. Many in the novitiate, though not all, had had a similar experience and we were somewhat scared of Father Thomas, a totally different person, whom we felt would be considerably more difficult to relate to and probably more severe in his teachings and advice. After saying goodbye to Father Hilarion, I wept for the first and only time in my novitiate years.

Father Thomas

The change of novice masters was not easy, probably especially for Father Thomas himself. In several ways, his personality and background were more like mine, since he had gone to Yale, with a more reserved demeanor and a better intellectual education, but that was not what I was looking for, or needed. The contrast between the two men was epitomized in their favorite spiritual authors. Hilarion's special favorite, at least at that time, was Caryll Houselander, an English lay mystic, pastoral counselor and writer of spiritual books during and after the Second World War, whereas for Thomas it was Saint John of the Cross with his keen, seemingly pitiless analyses of the trials and pitfalls that characterize the spiritual journey.

It was Father Hilarion who had cracked open my Victorian reserve and put me on the track to becoming a simpler, less sophisticated child of God, but I saw what God wanted me to do and I tried my best to be open to Father Thomas as a person and as God's representative in my life for the final 18 months of my novitiate, which I began to hope would pass as rapidly as possible. When I managed to tell him about my experience of God's spousal love, he cautioned me not to go too fast; that was for later on.

About a month after the change to Father Thomas, I decided that I should be frank with him about our relationship: "Father, I am having a difficulty which I think I should explain. It is hard for me to be open with you," I said to him.

"I know," he replied, "I'm a difficult person. I'm sorry."

I had never in my life heard such an expression of humility from anyone, much less from a minister of God, and I was deeply impressed by this humble sincerity on the part of my new novice master. Moreover, he did not ask anything from me, nor did he even try to give me any advice. Our relationship improved from then on and I began to accept him as he was, even with a certain tenderness and compassion different from my somewhat sentimental dependence on Father Hilarion.

Time would prove that this change of novice masters was one of the most important events in my early monastic life. What Thomas lacked of Hilarion's simplicity, he more than made up for by the spiritual quality of his conferences and the deep respect he showed for each person's intrinsic worth. At the end of my novitiate years, I told him that I thought he had been overly nondirective in my regard, but that I was immensely grateful for all he had given me.

Two long series of talks given to us by Father Thomas—what Trappist jargon calls "repetitions" because of their repeated emphasis on the same basic truths—have stayed in my memory through the years. One was based on a commentary on the Rule of Saint Benedict by the well-known abbot of the Belgian monastery of Scourmont, Dom Anselme Le Bail. Instead of a verse-by-verse analysis, Dom Anselme developed the twelve fundamental spiritual principles on which the entire Rule is based, which is what Saint Benedict is trying to teach. Unfortunately, I no longer have my notes to these conferences, but the twelve principles are embodied in the following five points:

- The first one is that Jesus Christ is Lord and God, "our King," as the Rule says. We are in the monastery to serve him in the school of his service by giving ourselves entirely to his will, which is one of redeeming love.

- The second principle is that God is everywhere and we should reverence him at all times and in all we do, exteriorly and interiorly. This inner attitude of reverence and respect is a continual prayer, the soul of all prayer.

- Thirdly, the way to God is the same way he took when he came to us as man, namely, humility: "Take my yoke upon you, and learn from me; for I am gentle and humble in heart, and you will find rest for your souls."[4]
- The fourth principle is more external and is the basis of the phrase often attributed to Saint Benedict: *Ora et Labora*, pray and work. What the Rule prescribes and what we need is a healthy balance among the three basic activities of prayer, work and meditative reading. In a more general way, the Rule presents a remarkably creative balance between such contrasting elements as community and solitude, docility and creativity, asceticism and discreet charity.
- Finally, almost as a synthesis of the other principles, is the inner relationship of monastic life to the life of the Church, the Body of Christ. The monastic community is the Church in miniature, with its structured leadership, its mystical union with Christ, its Sacraments and communion in all things good. It continues the life of the first Christians in Jerusalem, who "devoted themselves to the apostles' teaching and fellowship, to the breaking of bread and the prayers . . . [They stayed] together and had all things in common; they would sell their possessions and goods and distribute the proceeds to all, as any had need."[5]

The second series of talks was Father Thomas' own commentary on the Gospel of Saint John, based to a great extent, as he repeatedly said, on Saint Augustine's similar commentary. The spiritual interpretation of the different "signs" or miracles performed by the Lord opened my eyes to what the Scriptures contained and could teach, also establishing the bridge between the gospels and the Sacraments. In other words, our life should be based on God's self-revelation in his beloved Son, over and above all other spiritual authors or passing spiritual fads.

4. Mt 11:29.
5. Acts 2:42-45.

Inner Formation

Running parallel to these ongoing "repetitions" or conferences, which took place once or twice a week, there were several lessons given me more interiorly during these two years. One afternoon while I was standing in choir waiting for Vespers to begin, not thinking of anything in particular but probably looking at the Tabernacle, I was unexpectedly given a personal word from God spoken like a peaceful thunderclap to my intellect. It was this: *I do not love you because of what you do, but because of what I do in you*. I was startled, since it was the first time any kind of verbal sentence was given to me in this way. In fact I looked around in choir to see if anyone had spoken to me, but everyone was minding his own business, hopefully praying silently in preparation for sung Vespers.

There was not much I could do about this clear message from the Lord except to welcome it as a divine correction of an inner attitude that I was slowly becoming aware of. It had the effect of making me much more self-critical and sensitive to my "do-good" attitude, which I began to see was a self-justifying anxiety to control my own spiritual situation, even my relationship with Jesus, saying to myself, "He will love me if I do this or that." This new type of spiritual warfare—for which the inner message, *I do not love you because of what you do, but because of what I do in you*, was something like a battle cry—was going to last through my novitiate and only come to a head a few years later. I began to ask myself where this Pharisaical attitude in me came from. How did it appear? Despite all that God had done and was doing in my life, I was instinctively putting the emphasis on my own good deeds, my good monastic observance, my faithfulness to prayer, singing well, working hard, smiling at everyone, doing what I was told.

Little by little I came to the conclusion that this continual self-justification was due in part to an ethic of generous service to others flowing from my family heritage. I will be judged by what I do, how I behave, because that is what occurred in my family and in all my schooling. In fact the Bible itself often says something very similar: "Let your light shine before others, so that they may see your good works."[6] The principal cause, however, seemed to be original sin, *my* original sin. Sin, I began to see, is not just bad behavior, but means putting another person in God's place as a norm for one's being and acting. It is idolatry, for which the Bible often uses the human image of adultery, betrayal of a spousal relationship. The idol, this other thing or person put in the place of God, is usually ourselves: in other words, ME, my self-fulfillment, my talents, my health, my behavior, my personal growth.

I began to see how this was one of the dramas of the entire New Testament: the Pharisees in the gospels,[7] the "old self" in Saint Paul[8] and the "beast" in Revelation.[9] Paul's groan became my own, "I see in my members another law at war with the law of my mind, making me captive to the law of sin that dwells in my members. Wretched man that I am! Who will rescue me from this body of death?"[10]

It is a good question, and I became more and more desperate for an answer, "How can I get out from under this continually self-justifying betrayal of my Lord?" Without becoming a real source of anguish or worry—because I implicitly trusted that God would do something about it—this inner Pharisaism increasingly haunted me and became the shadowy background for the more positive experiences of my novitiate years.

One of these experiences occurred shortly after the "message" I had received in choir. Coming into church one day a few minutes before one of the sung Offices, I stayed in the back, knelt down and prayed silently, instead of going directly into choir. As usual, it was more a prayer of self-donation than a petition for any particular grace or intention. This time I received not a

6. Mt 5:16.
7. As in Mt 23:2-33.
8. Eph 4:22.
9. Rev 13:5.
10. Rom 7:23-24.

message in words, but a conviction, a felt image of a much deeper reality inside me. I was inhabited by a majestically flowing river, that was unruffled by the occupations of the moment, superbly beautiful, peaceful and powerful. This river linked me with other people through whom this same river flows, to form a transcendent, divine communion of unconquerable joy. "So this is what sanctifying grace is!" I exclaimed to myself. The *Catechism of the Catholic Church* describes this interior river as

> an habitual gift, a stable and supernatural disposition that perfects the soul itself to enable it to live with God, to act by his love. . . . Sanctifying grace is the gratuitous gift of his life that God makes to us; it is infused by the Holy Spirit into the soul to heal it of sin and to sanctify it.[11]

It is very true that "grace, since it belongs to the supernatural order, escapes our experience and cannot be known except by faith. We cannot therefore rely on our feelings or our works to conclude that we are justified and saved,"[12] so it would seem that God gave me at that moment a certain intensity of faith, perhaps the Spirit's Gift of Understanding, intense enough to produce in me the image of a river in full flood. It is an inspired image that has stayed with me for the rest of my life: "The waters of a river give joy to God's city, the holy place where the Most High dwells."[13] Many years later, traveling by car to Gethsemani Abbey in Kentucky, I was able to stop on the banks of the Ohio River, on its majestic way through West Virginia into the Mississippi, and I saw firsthand this visible image of divine grace. Maybe people who live there permanently have the same experience when they visit a monastery!

Some months later, during my second year in the novitiate, two other significant experiences occurred, both events related to the Liturgy but taking place as I was reading the texts beforehand,

11. *Catechism of the Catholic Church*, nn. 2000 and 2023.
12. *Catechism*, n. 2005.
13. Ps 45 (46):5. See also Ez 47:1-12.

seated on one of the wooden novitiate benches. The first one was during Advent. I was reading the texts from the prophet Isaiah, the Messianic Song in chapter 26, which begins:

> We have a strong city; he sets up victory like walls and bulwarks.
> Open the gates, so that the righteous nation that keeps faith may enter in.
> Those of steadfast mind you keep in peace: in peace because they trust in you.[14]

God wanted me to open my gates, so that true faith could enter in, along with a deeper love and an unconquerable trust in the Lord of my life, who gives peace to the humble ones who don't even try to justify themselves. What made these verses especially poignant for me was the Latin Vulgate rendering of the third verse, which reflects the Greek Septuagint rather than the original Hebrew: "The old error has passed away; you will keep peace, peace because we have hoped in you." The old error—my old error—was not to trust God with all my heart and mind, but to try to justify myself rather than peacefully humble myself before the Lord. I had to pass through from the moral virtues into the theological ones, and this passage put the Spirit's finger into the wound of my inner situation. Christmas would be a new birth and my ancient error would fade away slowly but surely.

The following summer I was preparing for the Feast of the Sacred Heart by reading the texts of its Liturgy, when I suddenly realized that there was something about this feast that struck a deep chord in me. This caught me by surprise, since pictures of the Sacred Heart never appealed to me, but I soon was confirmed in my new awareness. Soon after my simple profession I came across a picture of Saint Faustina's vision of Christ with rays of divine mercy pouring out from his hands and heart, and her simple act of theological hope, "Jesus, I trust in you!" In the stormy years ahead I was to learn in different ways never to mistrust the loving mercy of the Heart of Christ. The Sacred Heart

14. Is 26:1-3.

is not the most important feast of the year, but it expresses the very human and totally divine love of Christ, which is the living soul of Christmas, Easter and Pentecost.

It was some years later, on another Feast of the Sacred Heart, that I realized the intimate connection between the blood and water that came out of the pierced side of Christ on the Cross[15] and the river of sanctifying grace that I had experienced as a novice. The source of our interior flood stream is the very Heart of Christ, opened on the Cross to become the new river that "flows out of Eden to water the garden, and from there it divides and becomes four branches,"[16] which flow through the different parts of the world. The prophets saw this as "a river that could not be crossed,"[17] flowing from the side of the new Temple of God's people, and "everything will live where the river goes."[18] Ultimately, the river is the Holy Spirit himself, pouring out the inner wealth of divine life through the whole Christ, Head and members, the complete Church, into the hearts of men and women to renew the face of the earth through them.

Just before being ordained to the priesthood, after my solemn profession, I dedicated my priestly life to the Heart of Jesus, since "from his fullness we have all received."[19] In a similar way, at the end of my novitiate and just before simple vows, I gave my entire life to Mary, for her to use in the ways that she, as spiritual mother of all the world, knows will be most sure to guarantee that God's "will be done, on earth as it is in heaven."[20]

There were also less subtle, but equally important lessons to learn about growing up as man and monk. As a corollary of learning to depend on God rather than on my own abilities, I began to accept not achieving things, not looking for the self-satisfaction of success, and to be satisfied in simply doing as well

15. See Jn 19:34.
16. Gen 2:10.
17. Ez 47:5.
18. Ez 47:1-2,9.
19. Jn 1:16.
20. Mt 5:10.

and as peacefully as possible, with as much love as possible, the task at hand, which in monastic life can be almost anything. It meant, in other words, not looking for the next oasis in the desert, but accepting to live on a continuous journey of attention to the Beloved, rather than in a series of successes, even spiritual successes. It was at this point that I began to see how success-driven my whole education had been, even from my earliest years, but success in God's eyes is totally different.

In this same line, but with an even greater abruptness, came an incisive word from the abbot, Dom Edmund. He was disappointed that I and the other novices were not singing more vigorously in choir. He spoke to me about his concern in one of my private talks with him, which took place once every two or three months. He probably brought it up because he knew from my brother that I had some musical training, but there was an underlying reason that I was also aware of: the abbot had an ongoing disagreement with Father Thomas on this subject. My novice master, with his deep appreciation of the interior life of prayer and of Carmelite spirituality, thought it better for the novices to concentrate on the more spiritual side of the rich monastic liturgy: the biblical and patristic readings, the Psalms as Christian prayer, the sacramental symbolism of almost everything we say and do. This required a spiritual attention which seemed somewhat incompatible with the details of singing Gregorian chant under the direction of the choir master.

Haltingly, with fear and trembling, I tried to express this in one of my private talks with the abbot: "Reverend Father, giving more voice in choir can be very distracting."

The reply came at once, "But the gift of yourself is the heart and soul of the Liturgy!" It was like a flash of lightning revealing not only the heart of the Liturgy, but also the heart and soul of the abbot and, above all, the inner dynamic of the vocation God had called me to. I had not studied any theology then, but I saw in a flash—and for the first time in my life—how heaven and earth are ruled by the law, the principle, of self-gift. That is what love is and that is what true reality is, divine trinitarian reality and human reality, which is really human only when it is in God's image and likeness.

I have no recollection of the rest of that conversation, the abbot in his chair and I on my knees at his side, but the next day in choir I forced myself to sing more loudly, what seemed to me, and probably to others, to be too loudly, especially for a novice. As we were processing out of the church, Dom Edmund was waiting at the sacristy door and made a sign for me to speak with him there. He beamed, grasped my hands and exclaimed, "*Fili mi* (Latin for 'My son'), that was the way you should sing, that is how we should all sing!" I never told him everything else his few words to me in his office had meant for me, and would mean for the rest of my life, namely that the gift of self is the heart of God and of the Body of Christ, the Church, which means all redeemed humanity.

Closely related with that episode was a more simple and private one, this time at work. The novices were picking up hay bales from the fields, loading them onto a truck, then riding on top of the bales—which was the best part—to the barn, where we unloaded them and piled them up inside, all of this, of course, in silence. As we leaped up onto the truck for the ride to the barn, force of habit made me look for a place apart from the rest, where I could be more alone. It was not a totally deliberate habit, but probably reflected my years at Mount Hermon and Yale, where my different interests had made me feel and be "different." This time, however, something opened up inside me and I experienced a sudden conviction that it was much better to be with the others, not only for this ride to the barn, but also as a principle: it is generally better to be with the others, with the community. I saw it as applying to daily life, the reality of the Mystical Body of Christ: we are members of each other and our vocation is not an individual, private affair. I must learn to live this and show it more freely in all its aspects.

A beautiful, unexpected confirmation of this conviction occurred one day very shortly afterwards while all the white-robed monks walked peacefully from the noon prayer Hour to the refectory for lunch. It was a sunny summer day and the novices, as usual, were the last in line. I glanced up toward the front of the line and saw the whole community clothed in the brilliant light of midday. It lasted two seconds, but the impression was of an eternal communion of transformed saints journeying together in the light of the resurrected Christ. With lessons like that, life in a monastery becomes much more bearable! In fact it becomes incredibly rich, even though the disciples at Christ's Transfiguration still had to pass through his Passion and Death.

The last two of my three years in the novitiate also meant the beginning of priestly studies, coinciding with the two required years of scholastic philosophy. Every morning, Monday through Friday, a group of eight or nine of us would have a class with Father Hugh, laboring through a Latin textbook written by an austere-looking German Benedictine monk, Joseph Gredt. The best I can say about it is that it was a strange new world, into which Father Hugh, later first abbot of Berryville, did his best to introduce us. I understood very little about such things as matter and form, substance and accidents, major and minor syllogisms, act and potency, or the degrees of abstraction, especially as expressed in Latin. It was only three years later, while studying Theology, that I would begin really to see what they were dealing with and to appreciate their underlying importance.

Profession and Prayer

The autumn of 1955 approached and the superiors decided that I should pronounce my simple temporary vows for a period of three years, on the Feast of the Holy Rosary, October 7, with Frater Stephen, who had entered a few weeks after me. It was a simple ceremony, once again in the chapter room and once again with Brother Luke sitting alone in the back corner as the only lay brother present. I stayed another year in the novitiate before moving to the "Upper House," that is, the newly built monastery uphill from the converted farm buildings which housed the novitiate. It was especially during this third year in the monastery that I became more at ease, more at home, in the prayer dimension of my life.

Prayer is not an easy subject to talk or write about and I am no expert in it. None of the books I have read on it have helped me much either. It is not that they are wrong, quite the contrary, but my personal experience coincides remarkably with the homey advice Father Hilarion gave me when I asked him how best to pray. He simply said, "The most important thing in prayer is to be sincere." The classical monastic writers would agree. The key to prayer, as to all Christian life, is purity of heart. It is the heart that prays, more than the mind, the imagination or the mouth, but I had to find this out for myself by trial and error. It was not easy for me to spend a long time in silent prayer. Since nothing particular happens during it, the common temptation is to think that it is a waste of time and to apply, in a gross misinterpretation, the words of Christ at the Last Supper, "Rise, let us be on our way!"[21] He said it as a prelude to his Passion and Death, but we usually think it in order to *escape* from a mysterious passion and death which we do not fully understand.

Nevertheless, I instinctively saw that I should be faithful to the prescribed times of silent communal prayer in the early morning after Vigils and in the afternoon after Vespers. I found it good, too, to add a half hour just before Vespers. So during most of my first five or six years in the monastery I had a total of over three hours of Liturgical prayer every day and over an hour of silent prayer, also made in church, alone or with others. Prayerful reading, in the form of both *lectio divina* and prayerful theological or biblical study, occupied another period of at least two hours a day and sometimes three. Finally, there was a fourth form of prayer which is often overlooked but of great importance, namely continual prayer, at work and at such times as walking indoors or outdoors, during meals, or during classes and conferences. At that time, I was not formally aware of these four types of monastic prayer—in the liturgy, in silence, at reading and throughout the day or night—but that did not prevent them from being the heart and soul of my life and that of all my brothers, since prayer in these different forms is one of the most normal expressions of sincere love of Christ. We want to be, in mind and if possible in body, with the person we love.

21. Jn 14:31.

Slowly I became used to persevering in what is called "dry prayer." This is a term which describes a strange mixture of desire for God, for Jesus, and a difficulty in concentrating on things of faith during times of silent prayer, whether with the mind, with one's feelings, or with the imagination. These three elements of one's interiority—thoughts, desires and images—seem to go off on continuous side-trips, distractions, useless wanderings into the past, the future or the impossible, and one is left with a stripped-down desire for God and for his kingdom. Dry prayer is one of frustration and a more or less peaceful struggle to continually come back to the Lord. It will differ from one person to another and depends a great deal on each one's temperament, affectivity, capacity for concentration, intellectual development and, of course, God's totally gratuitous graces given as his wisdom and mercy see best.

The underlying temptation in such dry prayer is to give up, with a feeling that, "Prayer is not for me." The cure to such a temptation is to see a normal rhythm of daily prayer as a primary expression of true love: love of God, love for self as a servant of the Lord, and love for one's neighbor, since the spiritual process of prayer, especially when it is difficult, benefits and will benefit everyone. It is most important to encourage ourselves and others to persevere in it.

My experience is that God also encourages us—though in a hidden, gentle way—to persevere. Often after a dry and distracted prayer session I have left the church humiliated: "Lord, have mercy on me, a sinner!"[22] But as I walk away an inner peace appears to reassure me that all is well. My reaction is often a complaint, "Lord, why don't you give me this type of peace while I'm praying?" But there is no immediate answer. Probably he would say something like what he said to Saint Anthony in the Egyptian desert and to Saint Catherine of Siena when they were in a much worse situation than I have ever been in: "I waited to see you in action. And now, because you held out and did not surrender, I will ever be your helper."[23]

22. Lk 18:13.
23. St. Athanasius, *The Life of Saint Antony*, 10.

A paradoxical part of this dryness is that while walking in the cloister toward the church for another prayer session, sometimes with a certain sense of dread, there can suddenly be a heartfelt conviction that this is for the best, that prayer is really worthwhile, one of man's supreme activities, the lifeblood of the Mystical Body of Christ, but as I kneel or sit down, look at the Tabernacle, close my eyes, the good thoughts disappear. What thoughts take their place? Only God knows, and perhaps it would be better if he didn't. But am I praying? Are you praying? The answer is Yes, not perfectly, perhaps not purely, but truly and sincerely. At least your body is at prayer and probably an important part of your heart is, too.

When I tried to explain my combination of prayer and lack of prayer to Father Thomas, he encouraged me to keep going. Later, in one of his afternoon talks, he outlined the teaching of Saint John of the Cross on the question of dry prayer.[24] He pointed out a few characteristic signs which, taken together, show that God is active in lifting the human heart to himself. There is an inability to concentrate one's thoughts in prayer, but at the same time a lack of desire for any particular sensual satisfaction and an increasing need to be alone with God without thinking of anything in particular. In one place John of the Cross describes remarkably well what my prayer was during most of my formation years, and my own experience mirrors his advice:

> I go to my prayer fully intending to adore God and to unite myself to Him. Without any warning, my imagination goes off at a tangent, and is occupied with a thousand different things. If I do not want these distractions, and they distress me; if, as soon as I am aware of them, I recall my thoughts gently to the subject of my meditation or, better still, remain quietly in the presence of God, then they are not voluntary, because my intention to adore God and be united to Him has never changed. Even if the whole time of my prayer passes in this way, my

24. See St. John of the Cross, *The Ascent of Mount Carmel*, II, 13, and *The Dark Night of the Soul*, I, 8-10.

> prayer is none the less pleasing in God's sight. . . . Beware, then, of losing patience or hope when the imagination thus runs wild. Do not suppose that your prayer is worse or less pleasing to God. Do not listen to yourself or to the devil, who would like to induce you to give it up as a waste of time. Do not take up a book for the purpose of occupying your mind. . . . Neither should you strain yourself or weary your mind or body in order to drive away these distractions. Such efforts are useless. Far from calming the imagination, they only irritate and excite it all the more.[25]

There are several common instruments or proven techniques that have helped me persevere in dry prayer. It is not that they change it for something else, which would not be good for anyone, but they make it more bearable and peaceful. The first is to have a book at hand and, if there is enough light to read by, to take it up—but only for a few minutes—to bring one's thoughts and imaginations back into focus. It is not so much "for the purpose of occupying your mind," as John of the Cross says, but more as a bodily and mental proof to yourself that you really do want to give your thoughts to God, even though you can't. To prolong such reading, however, would turn it into one more distraction. In terms of traditional monastic *lectio divina*, this principle means not getting stuck in *lectio* and *meditatio*—spiritual reading and reflection on it—so that one seldom enters into *oratio* and *contemplatio*, personal prayer and inner contemplation, which is the whole purpose of *lectio divina*.

Another common instrument of prayer, which I have found most helpful, is the use of short phrases or even single words, often called ejaculatory prayer. Hindu spirituality refers to *mantras*, sacred verbal formulas repeated in prayer, meditation, or incantation. The word comes from the same Sanskrit root as our words "mind" and "mental." The Christian prayer tradition, quite independently of other religions, developed these short repetitive

25. *Spiritual Maxims*, 15, in: *Collected Works of St. John of the Cross*, trans. K. Kavanaugh and O. Rodríguez (Washington: ICS Publications, 1964).

prayers from the very beginning. John Cassian, in his 5th-century *Conferences*, which are inspired by the even earlier tradition of the Egyptian desert monks and perhaps even of the Hebrew prophets, encourages the use of the Psalm verse, "O God, come to my assistance. O Lord, make haste to help me,"[26] to be repeated at all times and all places. Saint Benedict, in his 6th-century Rule, does not go into so much detail, but recommends that the monk "always say to himself in his heart what the publican in the Gospel said," namely, "God, be merciful to me, a sinner!"[27] From at least the Middle Ages until our day, probably the most common ejaculatory prayer is simply the Holy Name, "Jesus." The Eastern Christian prayer tradition has developed this into the "Jesus Prayer": *Lord Jesus Christ, Son of the living God, have mercy on me, a sinner*, made popular in our day by the short Russian book, *Way of the Pilgrim*. The use of simply the Holy Name of "Jesus" is a very legitimate abbreviation of this, which seems to have sprung up spontaneously in the hearts and minds of millions of believing Christians. It is the name of the Beloved, God's and ours.

From my novitiate days until the present, I have found myself repeating the name of Jesus in prayer, often replaced by, "My Lord." I find that it comes to my lips in two very different circumstances: at prayer in church and also outside the church, walking, working or waiting. If it is a long walk or wait, or when I am driving a car, I often replace it with a decade of the Rosary, bringing Mary into the scene. In church, I use it both as a means to keep my heart and mind more focused in silent prayer and as a type of silent baptism of the Psalm we are singing, while the other side of choir is singing its verse, or in the brief pause after one of the readings. The result is that all the activities of the day are united in a love-song to and of the Lord. I can't say that my prayer is continual, but the name of Jesus has been my way in that direction ever since my novitiate.

It was during my third year of novitiate, that is, after my simple profession, that three somewhat different events happened. There

26. Psalms 39(40):13 and 69(70):1.
27. Lk 18:13 in RB 7, 65.

was a change of superiors at the foundation in Berryville and Father Hugh, my philosophy teacher, was sent to replace Father John, who returned to Spencer. Such a change was not unusual, but for me it meant a change of name, since it would be confusing to have two Johns among the choir monks, so they asked me to choose some name not shared by anyone else. I narrowed the choice down to Daniel or Augustine and chose the latter, mainly for his commentaries on the Gospel of John, whereas Daniel, though a prophet, came from the Old Testament.

The second event was more pleasant, though purely personal. During my final Lent in the novitiate I asked for and was given to read the work of abbot—now Blessed—Columba Marmion, *Christ in His Mysteries.* Marmion was an Irish diocesan priest who had voluntarily exiled himself to Belgium and had entered the Benedictine monastery of Maredsous, where he was eventually elected abbot. *Christ in His Mysteries* is not Marmion's major work, which is *Christ, the Life of the Soul*, a more complete presentation of the life of faith; but I wanted to share in Marmion's penetration into the mysteries of Christ's human life, which we celebrate in the great liturgical feasts. I had only gone a few pages when I read the following:

> The mysteries of Jesus are states of His sacred humanity; all the graces He had, He received from His divinity in order that they might be communicated to His Humanity and, through His humanity, to each of the members of His mystical body "according to the measure of Christ's bestowal."[28] The Word, by taking on a human nature from our race, has, so to speak, married to Himself the whole of humanity, and each soul . . . partakes of the grace that inundates the sacred soul of Christ.[29]

I was dazzled, intoxicated by the realization that through and in the human nature of Jesus *humanity has become a wedding feast*, even now, embodying in its own way, in what we call "the Mystical Body of Christ," the eternal divine wedding feast between

28. See Eph 4:7.

29. C. Marmion, *Christ in His Mysteries*, trans. Alan Bancroft (Bethesda: Zaccheus Press, 2008) 29.

the Father and the Son in their Holy Spirit. It is the privilege—or rather the grace and responsibility—of baptized Christians, especially Catholics, and even more especially of monks, to live this reality, which is only possible through the humanity of Christ.

This dazzling vision of what human existence not only can be, but *is*, combined four different strands in my life that had not really come together, either mentally or emotionally, until then: the uniqueness of Christ, Lord and Spouse of my soul; the spousal love God has, which I should also have, for each of my brothers precisely in the all too apparent weaknesses of their human personalities; the beauty, therefore, of a monastic community, where this unity in diversity is expressed as a permanent way of life; and the meaning of the prophetic vision from an airplane flying over Beijing eight years previously. What I had seen from that slow-moving plane was a transcendent golden city—something like a brilliant treasure trove—shining in the wasteland. Now I began to understand that the true city was not so much Beijing's "forbidden" one but rather "the city of God, the holy habitation of the Most High. God is in the midst of the city; it shall not be moved!"[30] That was what had enchanted me as a youngster without my knowing why, and here it was in reality, "the holy city Jerusalem coming down out of heaven from God. It has the glory of God and a radiance like a very rare jewel."[31] That radiance is what Marmion was trying to describe.[32]

The third event at this time was more obscure and difficult to understand, even to myself. I began to experience something

30. Ps 45(46):4-5.

31. Rev 21:10-11.

32. Elsewhere, he applies the reality of spousal love to the Church's liturgical prayer: "See her there, this spouse, proud of her position and station, assured of rights which are eternal and have been sovereignly won by her Divine Spouse – see her boldly enter into the sanctuary of the Divinity, where Christ her Head and Spouse, ever living, prays for us. Between the two of them there is the distance from earth to heaven, but the Church crosses that distance through faith, and she blends her voice with that of Christ in the heart's embrace of the Father . . . . How could such a prayer *not* be pleasing to God, seeing that He receives it from Christ?" *Christ in His Mysteries*, 401.

like a peaceful cloud that would come over me for a few minutes during silent prayer. It implied three different effects. During that brief time all distractions ceased; it was like an infused recollection, but not centered on any particular thought or truth of faith. Dryness also disappeared and was replaced by a new presence, but of something of which I had no idea. It was mysterious and at first I was somewhat disturbed by not being able to explain this strange newness. Its third quality was its total unpredictability. It really corresponded to the Lord's words to Nicodemus, "The wind blows where it chooses, and you hear the sound of it, but you do not know where it comes from or where it goes. So it is with everyone who is born of the Spirit." And like Nicodemus I thought, "How can these things be?"[33] When I mentioned this to Father Thomas, he asked, "How often does this happen?" to which I replied, "Perhaps once or twice a week." He showed surprise that it happened so often but did not give any concrete advice, and I wondered if perhaps I had not explained it adequately.

It was in this combination of circumstances that I left the novitiate and joined the larger, older group in the new buildings. From then on, my daily life would be within a different subcommunity, that of the 50 professed choir monks, within the total community of over 150, which included the choir monks and novices, and an even larger contingent of lay brothers.

Life with the Professed

Monastic life is a fascinating combination of the two dimensions of human existence, the exterior and what goes on inside. There are the anecdotal events of daily life including one's physical health and vital systems, and then there is what goes on inside, one's loves, convictions, motivations, deepest emotions and life with God. Even atheists have this hidden life with a God whom they neither know nor admit. Jesus himself, God become man, lived these two dimensions. In fact, he lived them to the full, as did his Holy Family of Nazareth and his immediate disciples.

33. Jn 3:8-9.

Every believer is called to this experience, so that "through the Church the wisdom of God in its rich variety might now be made known," as Saint Paul wrote.[34] Even in the monastery—perhaps *especially* in the monastery—each person has a rich variety of grace, an unforeseeable mixture of exteriority and interiority, work and prayer. My first years among the professed monks were characterized by such a variety. It took place in two separate contexts, both of which implied spiritual turbulence and strife.

The first, more important one, was connected with my passage out of the novitiate. As the weeks went by, I felt increasingly alone, almost abandoned. The closely knit novitiate setup gave way to the more anonymous, sober and mature spirit of a large group of older men, each with his own work to do, and fewer structures of interaction such as shared work or meetings with a novice master. The prior and subprior, Fathers Owen and John, were fine men, excellent monks, but their task was not so much that of formation or personal spiritual attention, but simply being healthy cogs or lubrication in the wheel of daily monastic life. They and all of us looked to the abbot, Dom Edmund, for spiritual inspiration, which he gave abundantly, but necessarily at a certain distance. I tried to see him once a month.

My sense of psychological and spiritual loneliness came to a head two or three months after coming to the Upper House, that is, during Advent and Christmas of 1956, while working as secretary for the mail order department of Trappist Preserves, processing the many Christmas orders that were coming in. The work was so intense that everyone in the small office had to work both morning and afternoon, then skip Vespers and return after Compline for another three hours, until the day's orders were finished, often close to midnight, which meant not getting up for Vigils the next morning. It was a total change from the regular, prayerful timetable of the novitiate and I became increasingly distressed by it all. I was missing Advent, my favorite Liturgical season, and Christmas was approaching without any adequate

34. Eph 3:10.

preparation on my part. The fact that I was working like this in the spirit of obedience and at the service of the community did not impress me very much, nor did the spiritual quality of the men I was working with. I tried to put up a good front, but that façade was decaying rapidly.

Finally Christmas Eve came and we stopped our work. Interiorly exhausted, I went back to the choir offices, but it was all different. What I wanted was interior harmony with my Lord and I lived everything else at a distance, the first time in my life such a thing had happened. I had no clear idea of what was happening and no clear person to whom to turn for help, so I signaled to Father Thomas that I wanted to go to confession to him after one of the abbot's morning chapter talks. I knelt down in front of him and said sincerely, "Bless me, Father, for I have sinned. I am having a hard time and feel that I'm falling straight into hell," and then broke out in tears. He treated me kindly and compassionately, quoting a text from the readings at one of the Christmas Masses, which has stayed with me ever since: "When the goodness and loving kindness of God our Savior appeared, he saved us, not because of any works of righteousness that we had done, but according to his mercy."[35] It was the same old lesson that God had been trying to convince me of since my first weeks as a novice.

A few days later I spoke with Dom Edmund to inform him that I had changed confessors from Father Xavier, who happened to be my work chief in the mail order department, to Father Thomas. He replied passionately and at once, "You did? You shouldn't have!"

I reacted like Eve in the Garden of Eden, "Maybe it was the devil."

"Yes, maybe it was," the abbot answered.

At that moment, kneeling before my abbot, I had my first and only ocular "vision" of the face of Christ, looking sadly at me from over the shoulder of the abbot. The sight lasted less than a

35. Titus 3:4-5.

second, but was enough and I got the Lord's message without need for words, "When will you learn to trust me?" I gasped, shocked, and hastily left the abbot's office.

From there, I went directly to the church, but stopped and knelt, as many of us used to do, before the large painting of Our Lady just outside the church door. I simply said to her, "Mary, you are the help of the helpless. Help me." I got up and was immediately flooded interiorly with an extraordinary experience of the Holy Spirit living in me and transforming me into a child of God. This lasted for some 48 hours. It was like experiencing all the mysteries of the Christian faith in a single Christmas package: Trinity, Incarnation, Redemption, Inhabitation, Divine Sonship, Personal Unification, Eternal Peace and Mary's spiritual motherhood. I will never forget this whole Christmas experience of despair, condemnation, confession, reprimand and inner redemption. It seems that my very immature heart needed something like this to finally make a real break with my novitiate, begin something new and feel more at home among these professed monks and brothers. And Mary gave it to me.

Seeing that the abbot and the Lord he represented for me both preferred that I return to Father Xavier for confession, despite his human limitations, I did so, explaining things to Father Thomas, who of course had no objection. Later Dom Edmund apologized for his bluntness, which I think was because he saw that he should not impede anyone from going to the confessor of his choice, although I already knew that there was a certain tension between him and Father Thomas.

Reflecting on this whole incident, I came to several conclusions. The first was that it had been another important part of a long lesson in how I should trust the Lord, even when I felt as if I was falling into hell. I should not worry even when my whole monastic and spiritual life is turned upside down. The psalm verse we know so well, "Even though I walk through the darkest valley, I fear no evil; for you are with me,"[36] is beautiful to read or

36. Ps 22(23):4.

sing, but it can mean traveling very close to hell. Yet God never abandons those whom he calls to himself. I know by experience.

A second conclusion is that my momentary vision of the Face of Christ was probably the simple overflow onto my imagination of a more substantial grace of theological hope which the Lord gave me at the moment my abbot spoke his harsh words to me, which were like a verbal slap in the face. What happened afterwards—the experience of all the Christian mysteries in a single package—points in that direction.

Thirdly, it all points to what is really central to monastic life, not regularity of observance but purification of the human heart from all false loves, especially love of self, and most especially any type of spiritual self-satisfaction or self-seeking in what appears to be a good life. In other words, to grow out of spiritual immaturity, a few dark tunnels of failure, contradiction and divine mercy are absolutely necessary. This old inner self that cries out for freedom, even more than for truth and love—what Saint Paul calls the "old man"[37]—is like a spoiled child. Somehow, it has to die in order to grow up and God will do his best to put this spoiled child to death, to the degree that we let him. That is what the monastery is for, so that those who live may live for the Lord. My years of simple profession were basically that. The dry prayer continued, but faith and hope were growing.

Another type of enlightenment occurred during those years. One winter over half the community came down with flu and had to stay in their cells for several days. This meant that the necessary work was cut to a minimum and I was asked to substitute for the ailing guest master, which I did despite my lack of experience in anything like large-scale hospitality.

The community's system was—and still is—to receive lay persons over the weekends and priests from Monday to Friday. So for my first Monday supper, there was a dining room of 10 or 11 priests, among whom was an elderly monsignor from a large city parish, all dressed in their clerical suits. Everything was going

37. Eph 4:22.

smoothly until time for dessert, when the monsignor started exchanging remarks in a loud voice with his neighbor, who looked increasingly uncomfortable as the elderly priest kept raising his voice. I decided that the best solution was to finish the meal faster than usual and most of the new guests got up from the table. Soon the monsignor also got up and walked toward the door, at which time I finally understood what was happening: he was drunk.

"Are you O.K., Father?" I asked, as he grasped the doorknob. He grunted and made for his bedroom.

I looked up at one of the other priests, who was smiling at the situation, "Looks like he had to have a drink," he said.

"Yeah," I replied and left for my own supper as the dishwashers arrived to take over.

But I was emotionally upset at my first experience of a drunken priest. It was not that I was scandalized, just saddened to realize that some priests are still bound to such things as alcohol and need help to face a retreat in a Trappist monastery. The intensity of my reaction showed my immaturity, but it also reflected the abysmal contrast between a priest's mission to continue Christ's life on earth and any notorious moral weakness he might have. I never sang Compline with such inner vehemence as that night: "O men, how long will your hearts be closed, will you love: what is futile and seek what is false? . . . Do not sin: ponder on your bed and be still. . . . Lift up the light of your face on us, O Lord!"[38]

Theology

Along with this type of interior roller coaster, something else was happening that was more intellectual than spiritual or emotional, yet was important for me: an intellectual conversion. Leaving the novitiate meant passing from philosophy to theology. Spencer was blessed with two successive teachers of theology from the Dominican Order, Fathers John Mulgrew and Dominic Hughes. My first year was Father Mulgrew's last at Spencer and we had

38. Ps 4:2-6.

a splendid course on St. Thomas's "Tracts on the Sacraments" in general and, more specifically, on the Sacraments of initiation, that is, Baptism, Confirmation and the Eucharist. This was pre-Vatican II scholastic theology, but using Saint Thomas's *Summa Theologiæ* as our textbook, which is both more difficult and more sublime that any ordinary textbook. It teaches the student to think, since Saint Thomas was, above all, a teacher of teachers.

In the long run, however, it was Father Hughes who really taught me theology. Well trained in Thomistic philosophy, he was at home in Part One of the *Summa* where Saint Thomas treats the nature of God as One, yet in Three Persons, something absolutely unthinkable if it were not for the words and gifts of Christ. Thomas begins with the possible names of God, in reply to the fundamental question "How we can think and talk about God?" The key to his answer is what is called "proportional analogy," meaning that terms derived from our knowledge of visible reality can truly, though imperfectly, be used of God, not just poetically—as in images, similes and metaphors—but as really applicable to God's inner being when it is a question of the most noble, "transcendental" characteristics of being. Thus God's "strong arm" is a metaphor, but his truth, love, beauty and power are much more than poetic; they are real and correspond—proportionately—to what we understand by those words. What is the proportion? That God's truth is to the divine Being in the same way that our human truth is to our human being.

It was in the middle of this section on naming God, however, that I began to have real personal difficulties, provoked by the combined clarity of both Saint Thomas and Father Hughes. My problem was this: these people were writing and talking as if things were really what we call them, as if the substance of a table or chair were "tableness" or "chairness," or as if the rainbow was really a rainbow, whereas I knew from modern science that chairs and tables are really just a conglomeration of atoms and molecules with a great deal of empty space between them, formed into wooden tree trunks which human lumberjacks and carpenters have made into something useful and convention has come to call "chairs" and "tables." And rainbows in the sky are, after all, just an interaction of light rays, water drops and optical reflections. So isn't our knowledge of almost everything dangerously mixed with a series of false perceptions? And if that is so, how can we dare start talking about knowing God?

When I tried—for the first time in my life—to present these difficulties in a private talk with Father Hughes, he looked at me with disbelief, possibly because he saw that I was presenting the classical arguments of modern scientific man, and also that he was well prepared to surpass them. He explained how the human mind is made to go beyond atoms and molecules, to capture, know and understand each object's particular meaning, not just what its material components are, something that modern science does not even try to do, nor can. This inner meaning is each object's nature, what makes it to be what it is—and not what something else is—for an intellect that *understands*, not one that simply measures weight, velocity, mass and distance. The measurable quantities and qualities of something are its material element, but there is also, underneath and supporting the measurable elements, the substantial reality of each entity in itself. This is what only a spiritual intellect—human, angelic or divine—can apprehend. Then, by an informed judgment, the intelligent person says, "This is true and good."

Going into more detail, Father Hughes gave me an impromptu course in epistemology, the study of knowledge, which I should have learned in our philosophy course, but of which I had understood very little because of the unfamiliar Latin vocabulary. Father Hughes explained that the human intellect—unlike the angels and God, since we receive our information through the senses—must abstract the nature of each object from its atoms, molecules and other components, such as its relations to time, place and other circumstances. This is precisely the function of the active light of human intelligence that sees that this object is unique: this *chair* rather than that table; or *you*, rather than he. The result is a concept, an idea in the mind, that prepares for the final act of human knowing, which is a judgment that this concept, this idea, is true, that it corresponds to what is: "This is really so." It is something like God's satisfaction at the end of each moment of creation: "God saw that it was good,"[39] which becomes, after the creation of man and woman, "Indeed it was *very* good."[40]

It took me several days to begin to absorb this new vision of what things and people are, which was on such a different plane from my whole previous mode of thinking, based as it was on the mathematical measurement of observable quantities accompanied by a certain neglect, even mistrust, of the mind's deeper spiritual capacities, rather than on trust of their innate veracity. Father Hughes recommended that I read a short book by Etienne Gilson, *The Unity of Philosophical Experience*,[41] which opened my eyes to the disasters wrought by two forms of intellectual skepticism: a certain illuminism that thinks that any real knowledge we have can only come directly from God, and what is called "nominalism," the theory that our general concepts of things and persons refer to their names, what we call them, more than to what they might be in themselves, which is a matter of useless speculation.

Nominalism constantly doubts the mind's ability to know objective truth and is as old as ancient Greek philosophy, but it was reborn in the late Middle Ages. This led to the Protestant reformers' doubts about the validity of Christian tradition, their emphasis on subjective inspiration, and a theory of extrinsic, nominal redemption ("justification") of the human being by faith alone, without any interior change of heart. It resulted not only in doubt, but also in a pessimistic attitude about the goodness of persons and things. In the philosophy of the 17th and 18th centuries, it led to the denial of all knowledge that cannot be validated empirically by human measurement. The meaning, the substance of things, was taken to be their measurable usefulness for humans, rather than their inner identity, and thus our knowledge of God became, not a cause for joy in adherence to the truth, but

39. Gen 1:10.18.21.25.

40. Gen 1:31.

41. New York, Scribner's, 1937, republished in 1999 by Ignatius Press. Another book in the same line is: Jacques Maritain, *Three Reformers: Luther, Descartes, Rousseau* (New York: Scribner's, 1955).

a matter of doubt, hardly worthy of the human person, because it could not be measured or calculated by us.

Father Hughes' private class to me on the foundations of human knowledge thus explained an important historical factor in the Protestant Reformation that I had sensed, but had not understood. Christian faith is a gift from God, but if it is all just a question of names that can change arbitrarily, what difference does faith make? On the contrary, "the Son of God, Jesus Christ, . . . was not 'Yes and No'; but in him it is always 'Yes,' for in him every one of God's promises is a 'Yes.'"[42]

So I saw that my questions about the faith, especially about theology, were all right, but doubting about the faith is different, since faith is a certitude based on God's spoken, written and Incarnate Word that produces deep peace and joy. For the first time in my life I understood that a significant part of this joy in believing is to realize that we, through the intellect God has given us, can know him, ourselves, others and the world. There is an infinite difference between human reasoning and divine truth, but they are not opposed. Correct human reason prepares us to believe and, when faith submits our whole being to God's Word in Christ, it leads our reasoning to its highest destiny, which is to know the supreme Truth and to be sure of what is most important for human existence.

Personally, during my five years of formal theological studies and ever since, I never found the intellectual effort involved in such study to be an obstacle to prayer. Theology is not prayer, nor prayer theology in the common meaning of the two words. One is the use of human reason enlightened by Christian faith; the other is more exclusively the work of living faith and love, occasionally helped by the use of reason. In practice, I found that prayer and study were mutually helpful, provided that one never substitutes for the other, since they purify each other from self-centered motivations.

It could be objected that Saint Bernard of Clairvaux repeatedly warns, like Saint Paul, against the "knowledge that puffs up,

42. 2 Cor 1:19.

but love builds up,"[43] but both Bernard and Paul are referring to knowledge for the sake of self-aggrandizement, not a serious search for a new fullness in the truth that can and should go hand in hand with "speaking the truth in love."[44] The common experience is that sincere study about the things of God, especially about God's Word, soon shows us how little we know. It is vital to accept that fact and to study in a spirit of peaceful gratitude, which then easily leads to prayer and, through prayer, to service and humble love.

It would be hard to pinpoint a particular part of theology that has been more helpful than other parts. Perhaps the most important elements for me were the two big advantages to be gained from using Saint Thomas' *Summa Theologiæ* as a basic text, namely that he teaches his readers to think logically and theologically, that is to say with reason and with faith, and at the same time shows the unity of Christian doctrine as coming to us from God and guiding us back to him. This unifying characteristic comes from Christ's words at the Last Supper, "I came from the Father and have come into the world; again, I am leaving the world and am going to the Father."[45]

Those two advantages of the *Summa*—showing me how to think as a believer and how all truth is unified in Christ—have outweighed the disadvantage of needing to engage in supplementary reading to keep abreast of more contemporary thinking, especially since the Second Vatican Council. In practice, I found that four sections of theology were especially helpful and meaningful: those on how we can name God, which I mentioned above; on the interpersonal relationships within the Blessed Trinity as divine models of what human thinking and loving is meant to be; on the nature of human acts and virtues; and on the sacramental world of sacred signs, especially the mystery of Christ's Eucharist.

43. 1 Cor 8:1.
44. Eph 4:15.
45. Jn 16:28.

Lost and Found

My first two years of theology at Spencer took place as I was living through the last two years of my simple profession. After my desperate attempt to change confessors and save myself from falling "into hell," which I described above, I was able to adjust exteriorly to life with the other professed monks, but interiorly something was happening that was not at all clear. Only many years later could I see that the Holy Spirit had taken this whole time to drag me slowly out of myself—out of continual self-reliance, self-sufficiency and self-protection—into a land of total trust which opens out to self-sacrificial love. Christian love, *agape*, is a continual gift from God. It is not made on earth, but "from above, coming down from the Father of lights."[46]

The goal of living "from above" rather than "from me" has probably been the basic lesson that God has tried to get through my thick, stubborn head through all these years, ever since my high school days at Mount Hermon. The shift from vice to virtue, then from the moral virtues to the theological ones, is full of lights and shadows, hidden and indescribable joys, but also many subtle pitfalls, tricks which crafty human nature and an even craftier enemy of God and man throw into the way of simple spiritual childhood. Learning what these tricks are and how to avoid them takes time, years, and demands a vigilance that seems to last well into old age.

My years of spiritual and theological formation were an introduction to this school of inner stripping of self. This deprivation, or spiritual poverty, did not come from outside. In fact, the brothers were most kind to me. It was a gradual, deeper and more permanent expression of my Christmas grace of destitution, losing what seems to be myself, in the name of an interior trust that what Jesus says is true: "Those who lose their life for my sake, and for the sake of the gospel, will save it."[47]

The technical name for this seemingly blind trust is "theological hope," the often forgotten steppingstone between faith and

46. Jas 1:17.
47. Mk 8:35.

love, which explains the simple ejaculatory prayer, "Jesus, I trust in you." Hidden pockets of self-reliance have to disappear, which is a work that no human teacher can accomplish. Only the Spirit of the Risen Christ, who is "meek and humble of heart," can do it. My task was to resist this inner process as little as possible and admit, like Job, that

> With him are strength and wisdom; the deceived and the deceiver are his. He leads counselors away stripped, and makes fools of judges. He looses the sash of kings, and binds a waistcloth on their loins. He leads priests away stripped, and overthrows the mighty. He deprives of speech those who are trusted, and takes away the discernment of the elders. He pours contempt on princes, and looses the belt of the strong. He uncovers the deeps out of darkness, and brings deep darkness to light. He makes nations great, then destroys them; he enlarges nations, then leads them away. He strips understanding from the leaders of the earth.[48]

Suddenly a breakthrough happened, and it was on Pentecost, 1958. I had been assigned to be one of the cantors to sing Psalm 94 at the beginning of Vigils at 3:30 in the morning, usually one of the drearier moments of the monastic day, since we are all trying to wake up. Perhaps as a challenge to sleepiness, Saint Benedict assigns this Psalm to be sung or recited at the start of every predawn prayer service: "Come, ring out our joy to the Lord; hail the rock who saves us!"

As I began singing the Psalm with two other monks, I was filled with such jubilation that I practically bellowed out the words of praise, "Let us come before him giving thanks, with songs let us hail the Lord, . . . for he is our God and we the people who belong to his pasture, the flock that is led by his hand."[49] Yes, we really are God's People and he has taken care of us as his beloved children, alleluia! A surge of energy swept through me that in some way has continued to this day, over 50

48. Job 12:13-24.
49. Ps 94(95):2-7.

years later. The battle's over! We've won! "Who will separate us from the love of Christ? . . . We are more than conquerors through him who loved us!"[50] I felt ready for anything, or nothing. What mattered was not me, but him, the Conqueror.

The abbot immediately noted the difference in my attitude toward everyone and every event. There was now an inner security that brought not only joy to the heart, but also forgetfulness of self and enthusiasm for the task at hand. Jesus' promise had been fulfilled, "that my joy may be in you, and that your joy may be complete,"[51] and I had been reborn in him, dead not only to sin, but also to its root, the curse of self-reliance, self-achievement and self-perfection. "I" had died—at least in a new way—because Christ, the Victor, had killed me, who am the enemy, as Isaiah had foreseen:

> In the Lord God you have an everlasting rock.
> For he has brought low the inhabitants of the height; the lofty city he lays low.
> He lays it low to the ground, casts it to the dust.
> The foot tramples it, the feet of the poor, the steps of the needy.[52]

Somehow I sensed that the Lord of my life had achieved—through a type of infused inner destitution—what is otherwise impossible, namely he had reconciled intellectual integrity with a life of love by uniting mind and heart in the transparent beauty of his own pulsating heart. The theologians can figure out what to call such a rebirth. It was not that I had been totally transformed into Christ or made sinless, but through his mercy, wisdom and patience with me I had emerged from darkness into the light of an enraptured faith in him who had died for me and had risen again to lead me to the Father. I felt ready for my final commitment to the Lord, my solemn profession. The abbot agreed and told me to get ready.

With that I'd better end this already long letter about my first five years at Spencer. More later.

50. Rom 8:35-37.
51. Jn 15:11.
52. Is 26:4-6.

Letter 5

EXPANSION

1958–1962

Dear Eddie,

Although you are a few years older than I am, we both can remember how the end of the 1950s coincided with an important moment in the history of the Catholic Church in the United States, a moment more important than most of us realized at that time. The many Catholic veterans of World War II who had benefited from the G.I. Bill were often the first members of their family to achieve a college education and were now advancing in their professional lives, forming a powerful minority within middle-class America. Priestly, religious and monastic vocations, like ours, had multiplied. Parishes, seminaries, monasteries and religious houses in general were full of these men and—to a lesser extent—women who combined their traditional Catholic faith with healthy degrees of human experience, personal discipline and intellectual sensitivity. Besides, the war experience had also produced a much greater integration of Catholics into the mainstream of North American culture. There was even talk of a Catholic president in the person of our own young senator from Massachusetts, John F. Kennedy.

Profession and Ordination

It was at that moment, toward the end of 1957, that Pope Pius XII issued his call to the Church in Western Europe and North America to send more missionaries to foreign countries. He made his appeal more specific: the bishops and religious communities of Europe should send their men and women to the young Churches in Africa, while those in the United States and Canada should do the same for the traditionally Catholic countries of Central and South America.

American monasteries were not exempt from this call, although the Benedictine Congregations responded more enthusiastically to it than the Trappists did. One reason for this may have been that the Cistercian monasteries in Spain were already thinking of making foundations in Spanish-speaking America, whereas the Spanish language was, at that time, much less familiar to North Americans than it is now, a half century later. European monasteries, on the other hand, almost always established their African foundations in their own country's colonies, which were soon to become independent, meaning that their own language would be used, often even in the liturgy.

Despite the inherent challenges involved in such an undertaking, our abbot, Dom Edmund, who had a deep appreciation of the Church as the universal Body of Christ, was able to read the two simultaneous signs of the times: the Pope's call to help in Latin America, and the large number of young monks present in his monastery. Under his leadership Spencer had already established foundations in Oregon, Virginia and Colorado, and the number of young monks was still growing, so he began to think of South America. But where? And how?

Father Gabriel Bertonière, a faithful friend and companion during our shared novitiate and time of simple vows, has written a detailed history of these years at Saint Joseph's Abbey,[1] so it is enough to say that during Lent of 1958 Dom Edmund and four other monks of the community disappeared without a word of explanation. Strict Trappist silence prevented asking too many questions and I was beginning to learn the difficult lesson of minding my own business and accepting the fact that I did not control matters in the monastery. After ten days or so of

1. See G. Bertonière, *Through Faith and Fire: The Monks of Spencer 1825–1958* (New York: Yorkville Press, 2005), especially 445-458.

this prolonged absence, I slyly asked the second superior if the abbot was visiting one of our daughter houses, but all I got in reply was a vague, "He probably is doing something for them."

Suddenly, after over two weeks away, the group of five returned, all tanned by the sun, so I concluded that the next foundation would be in Florida, Texas or perhaps Arizona, since there was already a Trappist house in California. Holy Week was on us, but one morning shortly after Easter there was a special meeting of all the solemnly professed monks, those who constitute the official "chapter" of the monastery for voting on the most important decisions to be made, of which I, in simple vows, was not a member. It was obvious that the decision had to do with the abbot's mysterious absence and in all likelihood meant a new foundation. That afternoon, judging by the faces of the monks, it was hard to guess what had been discussed, but the next morning as I sat down at one of the tables in the common scriptorium to prepare for the theology class, the monk opposite me, Father Eugene, was reading the *Encyclopedia Britannica* and in my curiosity I read the title on the top of his page, even though it was upside down: *Argentina*. It all became clear.

A foundation in Argentina would be great and somewhat exotic. "How far away can you go?" But there was no immediate attraction to it in my heart, even after its approval by the vote of the solemnly professed monks. So I continued with my normal life of prayer, morning study and afternoon work, which consisted in helping the farm manager, Father Richard, in his preparation for spring planting by testing the soil of our fields and pastures. It was toward the end of that spring that I had the Pentecost experience described in my last letter to you. Sometime after Pentecost, Dom Edmund announced the composition of the group of founders for the new house in Argentina, which would be on a donated parcel of 2000 acres cut out from a much larger farm over 200 miles south of the city of Buenos Aires, near the town of Azul. Several young professed from my age group were slated to go in the founding group, especially Fathers Gilbert and Stephen, and Brother Thomas, which made the Azul foundation more poignant for me.

The summer of that year was understandably filled with the community's growing sense of an historic event, the very first Trappist foundation south of the Rio Grande, in fact 5000 miles further south. The seven or eight first founders were studying Spanish with Father Amadeus, who had lived several years in Chile, and plans were in place for a second group and even a third, to go in the first months of 1959 to help in the construction of the new monastery.

My solemn profession was coming up, but because of the foundation it was delayed until mid-November after the departure of the first group. I would make it with Brother Francis, who had also gone to the School of Saint Philip Neri in Boston and was destined to be production head at Trappist Preserves for many years. It was natural that the importance of the foundation eclipsed that of our profession, not only for the community as a whole but also for me personally, since my commitment to the Lord had been repeatedly renewed and just as often confirmed both externally and interiorly.

The departure of the founders at the end of October, simple enough in itself, proved to be especially significant. About 50 of us waved goodbye to them in back of the laundry-wardrobe building as they drove off, but the event touched something inside me that was different from my reaction to Spencer's other foundations. I had no sense of identification with these other daughter houses, since my vocation was to Spencer, but now I was feeling something more than just an attraction. It was an interior pull toward South America. What should I do?

I went immediately to the church and laid it before Jesus: "Lord, what do you want me to do? Should I volunteer to go on the foundation? Show me what I should do." The reply was an interior peace, an almost sensible sweetness of spirit. At that time I had not read anything about the *Spiritual Exercises* of St. Ignatius of Loyola, but what I experienced was what he describes there as an important criterion for discerning interior movements of the human spirit: "I call consolation every increase of faith, hope, and love, and all interior joy that invites and attracts to what is heavenly and to the salvation of one's soul by filling it with peace and quiet in its Creator and Lord."[2] This sense of peace in thinking of offering myself for the foundation impressed me, but I was only two weeks away from my solemn profession, so I put South America aside for the time being. Time would tell. If God wanted me there, he would keep pulling. My job was to give myself to him.

Mother and Daddy drove up from Philadelphia for my profession day, which also gave me a chance to speak with Bill, my brother. He was now the abbot's private secretary due to the fact that, besides his gifts as pianist and carpenter, he had a facility for writing, perhaps more than for speaking. Moreover, he was admired by both the abbot and the community as an example of combining work, prayer and service to all. With Mother and Daddy present, we spoke about the Argentine foundation, since Bill was about to go there with Dom Edmund on one of his visits. In fact Bill was learning Spanish in preparation for the trip. As usual, I did not tell anyone of my growing attraction to go, but during my next talk with Dom Edmund I said something like, "You know, I have a real attraction for the foundation, so if you'd like me to go, I'd be willing to." He smiled, thanked me and said nothing more about it.

The abbot actually seemed more interested in my priestly ordination than in my offer to go on the foundation, especially since I was nearing the end of my four-year theology course. When he asked how I felt about becoming a priest, I told him sincerely, "No one can ever be really worthy or ready for ordination, but if you want it, I have no objection." I have no recollection of ever having made an official, written request to be ordained.

Perhaps this does not sound enthusiastic enough, but it reflects what has always been my vocational orientation, which is to follow Jesus, and for me that means as a monk. The rest is secondary, whether it be solemn profession, ordination to the priesthood or building a monastery at the North Pole. Besides, there was that experience outside the New Haven chapel with its message that

2. St. Ignatius, *Spiritual Exercises*, 316.

I should enter the monastery as a choir monk and God would let my superiors know if he wanted something else.

Once the abbot's decision about my ordination was made, the events followed one another without much turmoil: first the ordination to the subdiaconate and the diaconate, both administered by a visiting bishop from South Africa, then a few months later the solemn ordination to the priesthood, which was presided at by Cardinal Richard Cushing of Boston. Mother and Daddy were on hand for the occasion and greeted the Cardinal in the reception room after the Mass, Daddy's gentle reserve contrasting with the Cardinal's more pontifical extroversion. I didn't help matters by instinctively addressing His Eminence as, "Father." Actually Cushing seemed to be less at ease in the situation than anyone else. Perhaps he was expecting an Episcopalian bishop to be like the Archbishop of Canterbury. Father O'Brien from Yale came for the occasion, as did some other friends from New Haven and "Ma" Campbell from our Beacon Street boarding house in Boston. Daddy did not mention it, but there was an interesting coincidence in the time of my ordination, occurring as it did in the same month as his retirement from active ministry at the age of 70. He and Mother were moving to Princeton, New Jersey, where he and Uncle Donald, who had been together in China for so many years, had bought a duplex house for their retirement. They and their wives would share it for the next 12 years until Mother and Daddy were obliged to enter a retirement home.

For me, the key event in relation to my ordination to the priesthood was my first Mass at the high altar of the abbey church with Father Xavier as my assistant. The ceremonies were familiar enough, although it was the first time I had lived through them in public. When the consecration came, with my words pronounced in the Name of Christ, "This is my Body," a special type of inner peace welled up from inside me and, as I raised the consecrated Host for all to see, the peace expressed itself intellectually, almost in words: "It is much better to believe like this, without seeing." There was no great consolation or joy involved, but simply a lasting confirmation for me, at the beginning of my life as a priest, that the Eucharist is truly the Mystery of Faith at the center of my earthly existence. Within a few years the Second Vatican Council would proclaim it as "the source and summit of the Christian life, . . . for in the blessed Eucharist is contained the whole spiritual good of the Church, namely Christ himself."[3]

To Rome

Even before my ordination, Dom Edmund had thought of sending me to Rome, to complete my theology. It was an interesting possibility and coincided with the opening of a new, enlarged house of studies for Trappist monks in Rome called *Monte Cistello,* on land that had belonged to the Order's Roman abbey of *Tre Fontane,* in the western section of the modern city of Rome, called the "EUR" (*Esposizione Universale Romana*).[4] As usual, Dom Edmund was thinking on a large scale and eventually over a dozen young Spencer monks went for at least a year of advanced studies between 1958 and 1962. My turn would come in the school year of 1960-1961.

During the 15 months between ordination and departure for Rome, I was given the job of sub-master of choir novices, something like an older brother responsible for the novices' work assignments and any practical help they need, supplementing the more spiritual and intellectual work of the novice master. It was during those months that one novice master, Father Owen, left to be superior of the Argentine foundation and Father Regis took his place. In fact I think that your own departure for Azul, Eddie, coincided with that of Father Owen, which was why I had taken your place as sub-master. Providentially, my own difficulties when novice masters were changed during my novitiate helped me to support several of the young men during this similar

3. Vatican II, *Lumen Gentium,* 11, and *Presbyterorum Ordinis,* 5, quoted together in the *Catechism,* n. 1324.

4. When the House of Studies, the Abbot general's residence, and the central secretariat of the Order were all moved in the 1980s to more modest quarters a mile away on Viale Africa, Monte Cistello was sold to Hewlett-Packard computers and is now the national Italian headquarters for the Hewlett-Packard-Compaq corporation.

transition. They, too, had their difficulties. There were about 12 novices at the time, three of whom have persevered through all the following half century and are still sterling members of the community: Brother Robert, Father Aquinas and Father Kizito.

During these same months, while talking about the novitiate with the abbot, he looked at me and said, "I've thought about your offer to go to South America. How would you like to go to our future foundation in Chile after your year in Rome?"

"I'll go wherever you send me," I replied without hesitation.

He seemed pleased and simply said, "Then it would be good to start studying Spanish. Speak with Brother Marius." Marius, still a simply professed monk, had taught Spanish before entering the monastery.

I left the abbot's office with an almost excessive enthusiasm for learning Spanish, which I had never studied in my life. I was thrilled. The next few months were a combination of working with the novices, getting ready for Rome and learning the basics of Spanish grammar and vocabulary. A few months later, Dom Edmund changed my destination from Chile to Argentina, saying that they needed someone like me there. I think he had in mind my more international background and somewhat better theological training.

Storm clouds began to gather over the community, however, in the summer of 1960, when Dom Edmund announced one Sunday morning that Dom James Fox, the abbot of Gethsemani Abbey in Kentucky, would be coming for an unexpected visit. It was, in fact, the beginning of an Apostolic Visitation made in the name of the Vatican's Congregation for Religious. The point at issue was not clearly explained but seemed to be principally the way in which the Argentine foundation was being handled. One or two of the monks felt that there should be greater emphasis made on adaptation to the simple rural life on the pampas, rather than using Spencer, or the European culture of Buenos Aires, as a frame of reference. Soon, however, the Visitation developed into an overall examination of Dom Edmund's way of governance, especially his pushing a second South American foundation, to be made less than a year after that of Azul. The foundation in Chile had indeed been approved by the vote of the solemnly professed, but with much less of a majority than that of Azul the year before. The Visitation increased this latent opposition and it was clear that the abbot was not happy about it, nor was he used to being contradicted, especially by an Apostolic Visitation.

Official investigations are hardly ever pleasant, and Dom James's Visitation was to last almost a year, including trips by him to all of Spencer's daughter houses. I talked with him for about 20 minutes shortly before going to Rome and explained that I really did not have any complaints about how these projects were being handled, so I asked Dom James something concerning Thomas Merton, about whom we talked during the last part of our conversation. It was in the middle of this tense uncertainty about the future that the six or seven founders of what is now the monastery of Miraflores in Chile left Spencer at the beginning of September, and our group of seven students departed for Rome a few weeks later.

The seven of us went to Manhattan's West Side wharf in a rented limousine, leaving Spencer in mid-morning. All set to go, I had ten minutes to spare and, knowing that this was a turning point in my life, I instinctively went to the library, knelt down at a table and read chapter 17 of the Gospel of Saint John:

> Father, the hour has come; glorify your Son so that the Son may glorify you, since you have given him authority over all people, to give eternal life to all whom you have given him. And this is eternal life, that they may know you, the only true God, and Jesus Christ whom you have sent. I glorified you on earth by finishing the work that you gave me to do. So now, Father, glorify me in your own presence.[5]

Yes, Father, glorify your Son in all that was happening and would happen to me and to the community that had mothered me over the last seven years, so that we may all glorify you. Amen.

Mother and Daddy, who had driven up from Princeton that morning, were at the wharf to wave me off before spending the weekend in New York to celebrate their 42nd wedding

5. Jn 17:1-5.

anniversary. Our ship, the *S.S. Olympia* bound for Naples with one stop at Lisbon, backed out of its wharf in the late afternoon. As usually happens on my transoceanic boat trips, I got seasick the first two days, then recovered and enjoyed the unique experience of the ocean's unlimited horizon. I had traveled five times by ship across the Pacific before my 17th birthday, but this was my first time across the Atlantic, where the waters are noticeably more choppy and storms more frequent.

Our little group supported each other well on board ship, partly because it was our first real experience of talking freely among ourselves. Our superiors at Spencer were wise enough to have given us few, if any, explicit norms of behavior for our trip to Rome, so we used our common sense. From that time on, I have had a special bond with four of the group, all of whom are still at Spencer: Brother Roger, Father Matthew, Father Robert and Father Placid, who now rests in the cemetery in the peace of the Lord after a sudden death from cancer in his early 60s. The curiosity of our fellow passengers was naturally aroused by this contingent of young clerics, so we had several occasions to explain who we were, especially in private conversations. The crew, most of them Italian Catholics, were kind enough to celebrate with us the feast of Saint Placid with songs and ice cream.

On another occasion, a small group of young Jewish men and women cornered Father Robert and me, to ask what Christian monks were and did. Unaccustomed to such a type of dialogue, we did our best to present the God of Christians in a way that those of Jewish faith would understand and that would also explain our way of life. I spoke first and tried to summarize Saint Paul's teaching on Christ as the new Adam, the restorer of the fallen human race, while everyone listened politely but without much comment or enthusiasm. So Robert took the approach of the artist he is, which was much more successful. He started from the innate human desire for beauty, truth and goodness, then showed how we believe that these transcendent qualities come to their perfection in the man, Christ, and how the monk wants to give himself with all his heart to this beauty, truth and goodness. They were impressed, and so was I. There's no one like an artist!

We passed gloriously through the Straits of Gibraltar and the Pillars of Hercules on a sunny afternoon and docked at Naples the next day. The abbot general, Gabriel Sortais, had sent a van down to get us, so we drove up past Monte Cassino, where Saint Benedict had written his Rule for monks in the 6th century, and arrived at Monte Cistello, ready for our Roman adventure. Classes began the following week.

The theology lectures at the *Angelicum*, the Dominican college not far from the Coliseum, were nothing special, apart from the fact that they were all in Latin. On the other hand, being in Rome for the first time, seeing the places which one has heard so much about, is a privilege in itself. It was the year before the opening of the Second Vatican Council and the theological world was living in expectation of the event. Probably because Pope John XXIII, when he had been Apostolic Nuncio in Paris, had known the abbot general, he made a point of visiting our House of Studies and greeted each one of us personally. Not speaking Italian, I simply knelt in front of the Pope and received his blessing. My impression was one of great kindness on his part, although I had never been so close to anyone who was so corpulent, especially around his face and neck. I had the impression that he suffered from it, yet was always very much at ease and interiorly joyful. Hopefully the episode has helped me learn that appearances are deceiving or, as God taught his prophet Samuel, "The Lord does not see as mortals see; they look on the outward appearance, but the Lord looks on the heart."[6]

The year in Rome also provided a type of experience which is probably typical of monks away from their monastery, namely, a heightened æsthetic sensitivity. One day soon after classes started, I was walking in the central patio of the Angelicum and passed an open window. The friar inside must have just turned up the volume on Anton Dvořák's *New World Symphony*, because out poured the gorgeous harmonies of its final movement, which I had not heard since leaving college nine years before. It was the

6. 1 Sam 16:7.

Mississippi River in sound, carrying with it the toil of the entire new continent and lifting it up to heaven in the majestic lyricism of a full stringed orchestra! I longed to stay and listen, but had to get to class.

Toward the end of the year, something similar occurred with the physical beauty of a simple, non-seductive young woman. It was not an erotic experience in the usual sense of that word, but a momentary bedazzlement caused by the suddenly perceived beauty of one of God's creatures. In themselves, these are naturally contemplative experiences, but it goes without saying that fallen human nature is easily seduced by them, and monks and nuns especially need to be on their guard when traveling—even by Internet—since their lives deprive them of a considerable number of æsthetic pleasures precisely to enhance their perception of other beauties. Self-discipline in this regard, a sense of sobriety, becomes increasingly important because growth in union with Christ means growth in love, both human and divine which, when true, are inseparable. This means, however, that if someone sincerely given to the following of Christ is caught off guard, he or she can fall into a pit of still unpurified human affection or æsthetic contentment. When this happened to a well-known priest and theologian, a Trappistine abbess wryly commented, "He left the Council of Trent to follow the counsel of Constance," the name of his lady-friend. But in many cases it is not too late and the person can, in the mercy of God, climb out of the pit, hopefully having learned a lesson or two about the human heart.

Toward the end of that year in Rome, the letters we kept receiving from Spencer were increasingly gloomy. Dom Edmund's future was uncertain and he himself wrote me—probably the letter was drafted by my brother and just signed by the abbot—asking me if I would think of going directly to Azul after my studies, without returning to Spencer. I answered saying that I would do whatever he asked but would appreciate a clear request from him, so that my going to Azul would not be interpreted as any type of rejection of the Spencer community. He replied at once with the following letter that could not have been clearer:

Dear Father Augustine,

As your Superior, I am requesting you to go to South America upon the completion of your studies at Rome and to devote yourself to the Cistercian life in one or other of our houses there. In fulfilling this directive of your Abbot, you may be sure that you are not following your own will, but the Will of God, and therefore His fullest blessing will be with you.

Your devoted father in Christ,
fr. Edmund Futterer, O.C.S.O.
Abbot of Spencer

Change of Abbots

Dom Edmund's letter made me realize the precariousness of his situation, but that was secondary. I was much more concerned for my brother, Bill, with his close spiritual, emotional and even artistic bonds to Dom Edmund. The fact that he was now his private secretary did not help matters and he had already contacted me several times while I was in Rome, twice by phone, to tell me that things were not going well, that several key members of the community were inclined to favor Dom Edmund's resignation and, if that happened, he (Bill) would have a hard time living there. Given his Protestant background and personal history of resistance to institutions of any sort, I sensed that this meant leaving the Church entirely, though this was left unsaid. At the same time, I did my best to keep all this from the other Spencer men studying in Rome, though they also began to take for granted that there would soon be a change of abbots at home. Meanwhile, Bill mailed me an airplane ticket for my flight from New York to Santiago, Chile, from where the brothers would arrange my trip to Buenos Aires.

It was in this context that we at Rome went through our final exams, some doing better than others. Without receiving especially high grades, I was given a Licentiate in Theology, which permitted me to teach the subject, something which I have never officially done, although I have given many conferences and classes on related subjects, above all for those in their first years of monastic formation. After finishing our exams, Father Robert and I joined up for a short trip to Lourdes and to the Benedictine Abbey of Montserrat, near Barcelona, then to several Trappist monasteries in Spain before returning to the USA, he to Spencer and I for a few days with my parents in Princeton before making the long plane trip south to Chile.

It was through my parents that I learned what the situation really was at Spencer. Bill had told them the essential facts so that they could relay them to me, namely, that Dom Edmund had seen that he should resign, but did not want to do so until the Apostolic Visitation had come to an end, so he had gone to the new foundation in Chile with his assistant secretary, Brother Simon. The community at Spencer was increasingly demoralized, including Bill, who was there disposing of all the abbot's personal and nonessential files, but would soon leave, perhaps to be with Dom Edmund but, if not, to leave the monastery for good. Dom James, the Apostolic Visitor, had told Dom Edmund not to send any men from Spencer to either of the South American houses, which is why Dom Edmund had asked me not to return to Spencer.

What my parents knew, however, and did not want to tell me, was that, on one of Bill's trips with Dom Edmund, he had met a charming Portuguese young woman, separated from her husband, whom he was seriously thinking of marrying. Although I was not aware of these details, I could sense how the wind was blowing—which my parents probably wanted me to do—and could see that Bill's heart was no longer that of a monk, perhaps not even that of a Catholic. Exhausted from my trip and from the emotions caused by these converging circumstances, all I could do was weep silently, which I did in the presence of my parents. They understood that it was not despair, just deep sorrow, though Mother was careful and brave enough not to join me in my grief. And perhaps Daddy, though concerned for his eldest son, was inwardly not unhappy about it all. In any case, both of them were well acquainted with analogous ecclesiastical problems in the Episcopal Church.

I had slept very little for almost a week, so when I finally arrived after a long plane trip at the little Chilean monastery outside Santiago, I slept for 14 hours straight, waking up to my first South American morning on a new and beautiful day. It was a different world, thanks be to God, and I was most willing to be there at the beginning of a new adventure: Cistercian life on a new continent. Dom Edmund greeted me warmly, but it was clear that he was no longer the same, no longer the master of the situation. In fact he was now a broken man, though still in his early 60s. It was crystal clear that he should resign as abbot. When I mentioned this impression to one or two of the brothers there, they could only agree.

The week spent in Chile, at what was called *La Dehesa,* "the meadow valley," was my first experience of Trappist life on a small, domestic scale, something that has become increasingly common in our Order today, since almost a third of our communities around the world at the present time, 2010, have less than 15 members. The seven or eight founders in Chile, one of whom was Father Richard, my work boss on the Spencer farm, were a happy group and most kind. After several days spent on horseback, riding around the Andes foothills in search of lost cattle, the time arrived to proceed to Argentina with Dom Edmund and Brother Simon. The abbot had decided to go with me there, ostensibly to see how the construction of the new monastery was proceeding, but most of us sensed that it was to say goodbye. For me it would be the introduction to my new home.

The three of us flew not only over the Andes to Buenos Aires, but also from there to the Azul monastery, the latter trip in a Piper Cub rented for us by a wealthy Argentine friend of the abbot. From then on, and during the next 50 years, I would make the trip between Buenos Aires and Azul by bus or, less frequently, by train, a question of about four hours.

The 15 brothers at Azul—you were among them, Eddie—gave us a warm welcome and immediately put me to work at the construction site. We slept in something like a large shed near the entrance to the farm, with the chapel, kitchen, dining room and showers in another building ten yards away. Each morning, after praying together, celebrating Mass and having breakfast, we would walk the half mile uphill, Indian file, to the future monastery, work until noon, return downhill for lunch and a nap, then up again and back for Vespers at the end of the afternoon.

Brother Gerard, who was in charge of the whole construction project, asked me to help one of the professional bricklayers who was working with us. The job was simple enough, carrying pails of wet cement or plaster from one place to another or cleaning up the floor and walls after the brick work was finished. However, after a few days, I felt increasingly uncomfortable with my Argentine boss, whose name was Antonio. I could understand his Spanish all right and he treated me fairly, but his mannerisms, gruffness and, above all, his handlebar mustache made me uneasy. This unease even turned into a slight fear and dislike which, of course, I tried to keep to myself, but I began wondering what I should do. Was I going to have this feeling about all the Argentines I met? My concern began to bother me even during the night, but I was understandably hesitant to speak with anyone about it. I wanted to stay here, but not like this.

Suddenly, after about ten days of this mixture of unease, pride and prejudice, I saw the cause of my reaction and, seeing it, was interiorly released. During my early teens, growing up in Newton, Massachusetts, during the 1940s, the bunch of school kids I hung out with would take advantage of the cut-rate price for the Saturday matinee movie show at the neighborhood theater. It was especially for youngsters like us, probably to keep us off the streets and out of mischief. The show almost always included a Western. The heroes of these movies were, of course, the cowboys, whereas the villains were not so much the native American Indians, who came off fairly well, but rather the Mexicans: sly, cunning men, obviously untrustworthy, usually robbers or worse, with a thick Spanish accent, broad straw *sombreros* and almost always with some kind of a big, black mustache. No wonder I was having a problem with Antonio!

It was a classic case of the mechanism of projection and it was a liberation to see that the problem was not irreversibly myself, nor much less the Argentines, but those sly, mustachioed villains who were waiting all these years in my emotional memory for the first opportunity to be projected onto a likely victim. I might add that, over the course of the years, I have felt on several occasions that I have been the victimized object of a similar type of projection: that of the "ugly American," the insensitive, frivolous, haughty tourist. This happens not only in Latin American countries, but also—perhaps even more—in Europe.

In time I have come to love the Argentine people dearly in the sincerity of their remarkably intelligent goodness or, in the case of some, in the shadows of their lurking arrogance. For half a century now I have rejoiced and suffered with them and have never regretted coming to the country, even to the point of becoming a naturalized Argentine citizen. Few countries or people are as naturally gifted as they are, but their future will hopefully consist in using these gifts to work with—rather than against—one another, and in creatively striving for what is noble, good and useful to everyone, since they have much to give.

Only a few days after our arrival at Azul, Dom Edmund received a telegram from the monastery in Chile, saying that a large envelope had arrived for him from Dom James by registered mail. Surmising its importance, the abbot left immediately with Brother Simon for the return journey to Chile. It was, as he expected, the decision of the Holy See that he should present his resignation as abbot of Spencer and go to some other monastery of the Order, not a foundation made from Spencer. It was a hard blow, and his first reaction after handing in his resignation to Dom James at Gethsemani was a type of nervous collapse. My brother rushed from Spencer, took him by car to a hospital in the Midwest and, after a week or so of rest and recuperation, they parted company, never to see each other again. Bill went temporarily to Princeton to begin looking for work, and Dom Edmund went to the monastery of Calvaire in New Brunswick, Canada.

Word of all this gradually reached us at Azul. When a Trappist abbot resigns, it is the abbot of the founding house, called the "father immediate," who makes the important decisions in the community until a new abbot can be elected. In Spencer's case this meant that Dom Emmanuel, the young abbot of Bellefontaine in western France, would convoke all the solemnly professed choir monks of the community for an election within the next few months. He did so almost immediately, and asked all of them, even those on Spencer's three dependent foundations, to come together for the election at the end of August. So the six of us at Azul—Fathers Owen, Amadeus, Gilbert, Stephen, you, Eddie, and me—began preparing for the long trip, as did our brothers at La Dehesa in Chile and Snowmass, Colorado. It was a leap in faith, because what would happen afterwards would depend almost entirely on the abbot to be elected and on the counsel he would receive. But the spirit of our small group was good, for we were convinced that God was behind what we were doing. Besides, the construction of the permanent monastery had advanced so far that it would be ridiculous to close everything down. The new foundation in Chile, however, was in a much more questionable situation.

We were met at New York's Idlewilde International Airport—renamed two years later in honor of John F. Kennedy—by Spencer's acting treasurer, Brother Alan, who drove us directly to the monastery. Dom Emmanuel spoke with me almost immediately and seemed deeply relieved when he saw that I had no thought of following the course of either my brother or Dom Edmund. On the contrary, I expressed my conviction that it was time for Dom Edmund's resignation and my fear that Bill had already, to a greater or lesser degree, lost his Catholic faith. Dom Emmanuel, who had little personal knowledge of Protestantism—and perhaps just to comfort me—did not agree with my pessimistic opinion concerning my brother, but it soon proved to be true. On the other hand, he confirmed my impression of Dom Edmund's general health, saying that there were medical signs of his having had either a heart attack or several slight cerebral hemorrhages.

The abbatial election was held within less than a week, a strictly democratic process dating back to Saint Benedict's prescriptions in the 6th century. The new abbot-elect was Father Thomas, my former novice master, who at that time was acting superior of the foundation in Snowmass. Of all the possibilities, he seemed the best equipped to face the difficult, highly complex situation of Spencer and its foundations. It was a task that he immediately set himself to, and he speedily confirmed all three foundation projects, at least until he could visit the two houses in South America personally. Before our small group could return to Azul, however, he decided to organize a year of pastoral studies at Spencer for all the younger priests, which meant that most of us would stay at Spencer for another seven or eight months. Fathers Owen and Amadeus returned at once to Azul, but Edward and Stephen went to Colorado the following summer, at which time Gilbert and I returned to Azul along with our first two Argentine candidates, Leandro and Manuel, who had finished their two-year novitiate at Spencer.

The Pastoral Year was a wise decision on Father Thomas' part. It gave nine months of reflection and peace to many of those who had most suffered through the Apostolic Visitation at Spencer or had worried about it at Rome or on the foundations. The classes were on pastoral practice, homiletics, canon law, psychology and sociology. Father Gilbert and I worked in the afternoons with our Argentine men to prepare a Spanish prayer book of psalms and hymns for our lay brothers at Azul. I also had the opportunity to take part in the meetings of the new abbot's private council, since I was temporarily assigned to be one of the subordinate superiors, whom we called "president," for lack of a better word. Someone kidded me for having been given this service as a consolation prize for having been born outside of the United States, which keeps me from becoming president of the country.

End and New Beginning

Some weeks after Father Thomas' election, Bill visited the monastery to finalize his official request for dispensation from his monastic vows. The new abbot and several of the brothers with whom he had worked did their best to try to dissuade him, but his mind and heart were convinced that he should leave. He and I talked for about an hour, during which he described his situation, as I did mine. I knew better than to try to argue with him, but simply asked questions, to which he replied with a certain controlled tension. He was not at ease, and it was distressingly clear that the events of the last year, especially the criticisms directed at Dom Edmund and indirectly at him, had alienated Bill from both the monastery and the Church. In other words, he was in "protest mode" and would continue to be so for a few more years.

He told me that, thanks to a family friend, he had found a job with an insurance company, but he omitted mentioning what I soon learned from my parents, that he had married in the civil courts the Portuguese woman he loved, Maria, and was living with her in a small rented apartment in Back Bay Boston. As it turned out, his job with the insurance company was the beginning of a successful career as computer programmer and eventually one of the vice-presidents of a major international accounting firm.

Needless to say, Bill's departure was a deep emotional purification for me, yet I never even considered following his example, which would have contradicted everything I lived by and was created for. Two years later, when Bill wrote me urging me to leave the monastery as he had done, a rage of anger welled up inside me at his attempt to undermine my God-given vocation. How strange God's ways are! It is as if he had wanted Bill to enter the monastery just for the sake of Mother and me. In fact, soon after becoming a Catholic and while still in China, Mother had written in a type of diary: "I must be sure that it was not because of Bill—Br. Luke—that I was entering the Church, that even if he should renounce it, I would keep on,"[7] which she did until she passed peacefully to her reward 35 years later.

Among other lessons to be learned from Bill's history is the prudence of having recent converts from other churches or religions pass two or three years in a normal Catholic setting—if such can be found—before entering a monastery. A more general principle overlooked in Bill's case is that, to the degree that someone is intelligent or cultured—the two qualities are not the

7. See the text of her account in Appendix 1.

same—the person needs, not *less* intellectual formation in the faith, but *more*.

Such people may behave well exteriorly, even on a religious level, but unless they have really assimilated the faith, they can, as St. Augustine says, "run well, but in the wrong direction," that is, they can live and work well but for reasons that prove to be inadequate. This is because every human person necessarily has his or her theological vision, even if it be primitive. Sooner or later each person has to explain, perhaps only to themselves, why and in what way they believe in God or why and to what extent they deny his existence, at least in practice. The more intelligent a person is, the easier it is for them to construct a theological justification for their preconceived ideas or prejudices, which is one of the dangers of a personal interpretation of the Bible. That is where a healthy catechesis is vital and cannot be taken for granted. For more intellectual persons it should be all the more thorough, preferably including moments of defending the faith or teaching it.

At the end of our pastoral year, in July of 1962, Father Gilbert and I, accompanied by our first two Argentines, made the long trip to Buenos Aires and then to Azul, leaving Spencer in mid-summer and arriving at our destination in mid-winter. This time it was for keeps. There, as we got off the bus in Azul, happened to be Father Leandro's youngest sister, Alicia, and it was a joy to witness their delight in seeing each other again. My first letter was to Father Robert at Spencer, and I remember writing him, "At last I've been able to give everything to the Lord!" Perhaps I remember this because—as so often happens—I soon discovered that there was more to give.

The three years spent in building the permanent brick monastery—all of it finished except for the church—had been a challenge for everyone, but one crowned with a certain degree of visible success, a *fait accompli*, a classical monastic gem rising up out of the Argentine pampa. But the building project had also been something of a honeymoon, uniting the brothers in a functional team spirit. Now that it was over, however, and we were living in it, what were we to do? Traditional Trappist spirituality provided a twofold answer: give yourself to prayer and follow the observances, that is, the flow of community life as prescribed in Saint Benedict's Rule and in the Trappist Book of Regulations. It was not a bad recipe, especially because of the primacy given to prayer, but the life's lack of normal interpersonal communication, combined with an emphasis on external good behavior, tended to foster a type of well-intentioned social immaturity.

It was in this context of classical Trappist life on a new continent, in a different cultural framework and, above all, in a much more reduced, intimate, domestic setup, that our group of 20 men started living together as monks, and I was soon given the task of directing the formation of our Argentine novices. It all would have been different and more difficult had it not been for the Second Vatican Council, which began its first session that October. But it will be better to talk about that in another letter.

Letter 6

LIFE AT AZUL
1962–1982

Dear Eddie,

The first group of founding monks had arrived at Azul on October 28, 1958, the day Cardinal Giuseppe Roncalli was elected as Pope John XXIII. Four years later, shortly before the beginning of the Second Vatican Council, our new monastery's novitiate was opened. The presence of young Argentines was both a blessing from God's mercy and a psychological stimulus for all of us, but for the time being I was just trying to survive a combination of difficulties.

New Circumstances

First there were the unheated buildings, which represented a challenge during the winter months and early spring, that is, from mid-May to mid-October. The system of centrally heated air blown into the different rooms proved to be a failure, besides being relatively expensive. Even more difficult, however, was the disappointing contrast of leadership styles between what we had known at Spencer under Dom Edmund's energetic insistence on faith, prayer and fraternal charity, and the instinctive emphasis on regular observance which characterized Father Owen, despite his personal kindness and humility.

There were also certain tensions, especially for me, in my relationships with one or two of the other founders. In some way it was a milder version of what had occurred in my dealings with Antonio, the Argentine bricklayer with whom I had worked the previous year during my first days at Azul. The fact is that there is a big difference between the inner dynamics of a big community of 100 men, as Spencer was, and those of a much smaller group of 15 or 20. Each person becomes more important and the psychological tension is considerably more intense.

Perhaps these and other difficulties many of us at Azul were having during the first months of living in the permanent monastery were preparing the way for a different kind of event that October, when a 19-year-old candidate arrived unannounced at the monastery. Father Owen was in Rome at the Order's general chapter, so the brother who received him told him to go around the building to the back garden, where most of us were weeding potatoes, and to speak with me, the second superior. He was a thin, gaunt young man, seemingly of few words but with an inner intensity that at first made me wonder if he was emotionally balanced. His name was Luis José Olivera, from one of the suburbs of Buenos Aires, who would become, some 20 years later, the monastery's first abbot and then the first non-European abbot general in the 900-year history of the Cistercian Order. I told him to stay a few days, then return home and, if he still wanted to be a monk, to come back for a longer trial period before entering the novitiate, all of which he did. He became an excellent novice. Father Owen gave him the name Bernardo.

Something totally personal happened to me shortly afterwards, and this will be the first time I have ever told anyone about it. Since we were using the chapter room as a provisional chapel, the brothers responsible for maintaining the new buildings decided to block off the entrance into the large unfinished church. This meant boarding up the big door at the far end of the main cloister. To make it more presentable, they put a small wooden shelf in the middle of the doorway and placed on it an elegant 30-inch statue of the Virgin Mary at prayer, which Brother Paul had brought with him from Spencer. It was especially striking when seen from the other end of the cloister's Roman arches and it caught me totally by surprise, since no one had mentioned it in public ahead of time.

As soon as I saw Our Lady there at the end of the arched cloister, I remembered the dream I had had at Mount Hermon over twelve years before, soon after the monastery in Rhode Island had burned down. I had seen a long arched corridor and, at the far end, the figure of the Virgin Mary as a channel of God's peace in my life. The coincidence was far too exact to be by chance, and was a powerful sign for me that this faraway monastery was what God had in mind for me all this time, despite the many human weaknesses and frustrations involved. The simple statue of Our Lady was also a sign of something even more important, namely, the reality in my life of this person, Mary, the Mother of Jesus. She has played a very discreet role in my life, almost always in the background, but at key moments—my becoming a Catholic, my vocational discernment and now my commitment to a totally new monastery—she has come to the forefront, gently showing me, like a true Mother, the way to follow her Son.

There was a further connection between my new monastery and Our Lady in the fact that Argentina is the only country that I know of whose national colors—blue and white, expressed especially in its flag—were chosen because of their association with Mary, in particular with Our Lady of Luján, the country's official Patroness. Moreover, our monastery is in the township of *Azul*, the Spanish word for *blue*. The name was not originally related to Mary, since it derives from the native Indian description of the "blue hills" lying between the monastery and the present town, like the Blue Hills of Greater Boston, the Blue Ridge Mountains of the eastern United States and Australia's Blue Mountains. For me, however, the Marian quality of our city's name embodies the best of the Argentine spirit and the mission of our monastery to be a spiritual center of gravity, like a blue jewel, a Marian sapphire, shining in the middle of the pampas and, like her, "a wholly unique member of the church, . . . its exemplar and outstanding model in faith and charity."[1]

December came and brought its usual hot weather. This meant that Advent and Christmas, instead of being celebrated more intimately indoors, often under the gentle mantle of the first

1. Vatican II, *Lumen Gentium*, 53.

winter snow, was precisely the time of hard work outside, in the garden or at the wheat harvest. For Argentine city dwellers, it marks the beginning of summer vacation time and, instead of coming home for Christmas, they tend to travel elsewhere. For such an intensely agricultural country, the wheat harvest is of prime importance and the many migrant farm workers, traveling south with the harvest, are away from home at Christmas time.

For those who are liturgically sensitive, living in the southern hemisphere means that Christmas coincides with the summer solstice, the sun setting well after Compline, which has several consequences. The symbolism of *sol invictus*, the sun that declines and is continually born again as a sign of Christ's new birth, suddenly disappears. No more white Christmases, icicles or sleigh bells in the snow. And after December 25 the days start getting shorter, not longer. So there goes Christmas!

Or does it? Little by little, over the course of the years, those of us from Spencer were forced by circumstances to live the Christmas mystery in a new way, for what it really is, namely our heavenly Father's Beloved Son taking on himself our human nature and becoming a man "who in every respect has been tested as we are, yet without sin."[2] One of the very earliest Christian hymns, a type of first-century Christmas carol, said it clearly:

> Christ Jesus, . . . though he was in the form of God,
> did not regard equality with God as something to be exploited,
> but emptied himself, taking the form of a slave, being born in human likeness.
> And, found in human form, he humbled himself."[3]

So the Christmas crib at the Azul monastery shows no snow, evergreens or holly, but in their place the Holy Family is usually surrounded by the first sheaves of our own ripe wheat, since Bethlehem means "House of Bread" and the Babe has become, in his human flesh and blood, the holy Temple where we eat the

2. Heb 4:15.
3. Phil 2:5-8.

Bread of Life. Perhaps the people of the southern hemisphere have the special mission, particularly in a century of globalized technology, to show to the world the simple charm of the humble humanity of Christ, the first and greatest of all Christmas symbols.

The Novitiate and Vatican II

It was soon after Brother Bernardo's entrance that Father Thomas asked me to be responsible for the formation of the monastery's novitiate. There were four or five postulants and novices at that time, a number which soon increased to seven or eight. They were from different backgrounds and were temperamentally diverse, but a solid core of them were interiorly convinced of God's call to this particular Trappist monastery, so that they have persevered through all these years: Bernardo, Juan, Gaspar, Omar, with Eduardo arriving later. Helping the Holy Spirit form such men was a challenge, for which no one is ever really adequate. My talks to them, which were two or three times a week, centered on three subjects: feasts and seasons of the Church's liturgy, the Rule of Saint Benedict, and the history and spirituality of Western Monasticism with special emphasis on the Cistercian tradition. As often happens, the novice master learned more than the novices.

Because I had to give my talks in Spanish, they needed more preparation on my part than if I were speaking in English; but I found that the time I had available for such preparation was disappearing, due to the desire of the young men to speak with me privately. At first I set up a certain timetable for these private conversations, but it became clear that our candidates wanted and needed more of my time, to such an extent that they began eating into my personal schedule of prayer, reading and study. After a few months, this situation became a real crisis in my life. Here I am, talking about prayer to the novices and I don't have enough time for my own prayer, precisely when I need it most! I was in a double bind, and a spirit of shyness, uncertainty and proud self-sufficiency kept me from discussing it with my superior, which would have been the logical and correct course of action.

However, God is merciful to sinners, especially to this one, so one afternoon when I had a few minutes available before talking to the novices, I went into the chapel, knelt down and prayed silently for whatever they and I needed. To my surprise, I got an answer, something like the word I received one afternoon during my own novitiate: *I do not love you because of what you do, but because of what I do in you.* This time it was even simpler: *If you take care of them, I'll take care of you.* My surprise was stronger than my gratitude at that moment, I think for two reasons. First, I took these words as a directive, pointing at the attitude God wanted to see in me, more than as any type of consolation or encouragement; and secondly, the message was not what I myself would have given if I had been in God's shoes. I would have said: "If you take care of them, so will I." That is, "I will help you in the formation you are giving them." I thought that God should back up my efforts. But he was telling me something else in answer to my concern for not having enough time for prayer or study, namely, that he was just as interested in me as in them and that I should trust more in him than in organizing my own timetable: *If you take care of them, I'll take care of you.*

One never forgets these inner locutions, especially when they are few and far between. This one had come almost ten years after the first one, and a third one, probably the last, would be given a quarter of a century later, all of them unexpectedly, in church and in three different countries. For the first one I was standing; for the second, kneeling in prayer; and for the third, sitting during Mass. The basic message has been the same, which shows how hard it has been for me to accept it: "Trust in me, because your life is in my hands!" In the middle of my pride and my hesitations, how can I thank God enough—how can I thank the Spirit of the Risen Christ!—for not only giving me a sign of his love, but especially for his extreme patience in trying to teach me how to respond? And the first response to love, especially divine love, is to trust the Lover, "for his love endures forever!"[4]

4. Ps 135(136):1-26.

I think I have learned to trust him in the big decisions, events and crises, because they clearly surpass me, but in the smaller ones I still tend to fall into the trap of thinking that I can handle the situations myself.

The Second Vatican Council had opened and, like the whole Christian world, we watched it closely, above all through the weekly *L'Osservatore Romano* in Spanish. Throughout the following three years, until December 1965, I read the résumé of almost all the conciliar interventions, plus any major article or commentary on the issues involved. The result was a prolonged, in-depth updating of my theology courses and a quality exposure to the problems and the splendor of the Church in the world of our times. At the time of the Council itself, at least for me and generally for the Church in Argentina, the focus of interest was on the central Dogmatic Constitution on the Church, *Lumen Gentium*. With the passage of time, however, I have come to appreciate the even longer Pastoral Constitution on the Church in the Modern World, *Gaudium et Spes*.

The conciliar interventions of two European archbishops particularly impressed me. The first one was that of Cardinal Montini of Milan at the end of the first session. He was already singled out as the most likely successor to Pope John XXIII and his programmatic intervention showed that his reputation was well deserved. He first pointed out how the work of the Council in its future sessions needed a guiding principle to unify and coordinate the different commissions as they drew up their respective documents. He then proceeded to present such a principle and how it could be applied. The central focus of the Council should be the Church itself in its life of union with Christ and service to the human family. Around this central hub there would be an inner circle of documents concerning the life of the Church: Divine Revelation, the Liturgy, and the missions of Bishops, Priests, Laity and Religious. Then there would be a second circle around the first one, made up of those documents concerning the Church in relation to other churches and religions, that is, ecumenism and interreligious dialogue. Finally, there would be an outer concentric circle representing the Church in the contemporary world, its missionary activity and its use of the mass media.

Time proved that this vision of the future Pope Paul VI was, indeed, the most adequate one for fostering the work of the Council and producing its remarkably harmonious body of teaching. Seven years later, at the beginning of our general chapter in 1969, I was inspired by Montini's intervention and his image of the three concentric circles to suggest something similar for the work of our Order's renewal. First should come a statement on Cistercian life in itself, as lived in each local community, then a clarification of the relationships among our various monasteries, and finally an adequate presentation of our life to those outside the Order, especially to the Holy See. Once again, the image proved to be successful.

The other noteworthy intervention occurred in the Council's third session. It was a remarkably acute analysis of atheistic communism and what the Church's approach to it should be, given in a brief speech by the young Polish archbishop of Kraków, Karol Wojtyła, who was created cardinal soon after the Council and became Pope John Paul II. It was an eye-opener for me, since my image of Poland and its Church was that of a downtrodden group of coalminers; yet here was a young, clear-thinking Polish bishop speaking with total competence about one of the most important pastoral problems in the Church and approaching it from a deeply theological perspective, yet without falling into clichés or stereotypes. In fact, it was that intervention which caused Wojtyła to be named to the commission working on the Church in the Modern World, in which he played an important part.

The Heart

Perhaps what most needed updating in me was a tendency to a more speculative, abstract moral theology. This approach was not due just to the texts I had studied for the theology classes at Spencer and in Rome, but also to the general emphasis on correct Christian living in which I had grown up. The Council's call to review such an approach forced me to rethink what I had learned, not so much from Saint Thomas Aquinas,[5] who goes immediately to the roots and principles of what we do, as from a so-called "pastoral" judgment on human behavior based, above all, on the Ten Commandments, Church law or manuals of pastoral ministry. The Council was asking us to start from the teachings of Christ—especially from the Sermon on the Mount and the supreme commandment of loving as he has loved us—instead of from a preestablished list of commandments, virtues or vices. I was finally beginning to understand that mathematics, logic and the scientific method were not enough, not really adequate, to deal with Gospel living, which means listening and responding to God's Word as to a love letter written by the Holy Spirit in the flesh and blood of Christ and in the life of his Body, the Church.

Two or three simple interior experiences at that time expressed this inner renewal in my life, which I now see as part of the new Pentecost that Pope John XXIII talked about. One afternoon I was kneeling in our little winter chapel with my eyes wide open, not thinking of anything in particular, when a type of inner prayer, a deep desire for God and love for his kingdom, came up from inside me, but from neither my thoughts nor my lips. "This must be what they mean by the *heart*," I thought. It seems strange that I was only discovering this now, after 15 years in the monastery and many more of reading the Bible, but it shows how "heady" my intellectual education had been with its stress on knowledge, rather than on being or serving. Even my broader human formation had been mainly self-functional, that is, geared to succeeding in whatever is undertaken, with an emphasis on exterior, measurable results.

But what is the measure of interior, personal quality? Even after 15 years of relatively intense monastic life, with two years of philosophy, five of theology and another four or five teaching lived spirituality, I still was not at all sure what characterizes the personal interior quality of a human being. At the same time, however, one can sense that a certain, indefinable interior quality is there, or not there, present or lacking in a person, which

5. In his *Summa Theologiæ*, St.Thomas starts his consideration of human acts with the universal search for happiness (ST I-II, 1-5).

is why the lived experience of my "heart" provided a key to explaining what interiority is and how it develops. I finally began to understand, and not just accept, what the Christian tradition, starting with Jesus himself, meant by "the pure in heart"[6] and that "out of the abundance of the heart the mouth speaks."[7] He was talking about an inner center of energy that moves all the rest of the human person—thoughts, desires, decisions, convictions, achievements, fears—so that anything of real quality is done from the inside out, much more than from the outside in.

It would take several years for this new, cordial reality to take its central place among the elements of psychology that I had been taught, such as the intellect, will, imagination, sense perceptions and memory. A breakthrough came when I saw the heart's connection with the Beatitudes. The eight qualities that Jesus proclaims as characteristics of his kingdom—all centered around spiritual poverty—are qualities of the heart, his own heart in the first place, then that of his disciples. In other words, the spiritual quality of a person is measured by these features of Christian love, so that the heart, as the seat of love, is at the center of human interiority. What was happening was that I was beginning to put words onto what "interior life" means. Perhaps learning this experientially, as I was doing, is the only way to really learn it.

Another simple experience taught me how the heart is both transcendental and universal. I was walking in the rocky pasture outside the monastery one afternoon and must have been praying, because up from inside me came a movement which I can only describe as a prayer of universal offering. All the earth seemed to pass through me and up to the Father, offering itself in adoration to its Creator and Lord. It was an experience of the Christian priesthood of all the baptized: "Present your bodies as a living sacrifice, holy and acceptable to God, which is your spiritual worship."[8] I saw that my human body is not just mine; it is universal, catholic. It incarnates the universe and its worship

6. Mt 5:8.
7. Mt 12:34. See Ps 14(15):2.
8. Rom 12:1.

is meant to be a continual hymn of gratitude and joyful submission to the Father in the name of all creation.

At the same time that this process of broadening inner horizons was taking place in me, our little community was also deepening its internal growth. Father Alexander, the founding superior of La Dehesa, in Chile, had crossed the Andes in 1963 to become our superior, with Father Owen remaining with us for a few years to give us his moral support. Another important member was also added at that time in the person of Dom Edmund, the former abbot of Spencer, who had founded our monastery in the first place. At the age of 65, four years after his resignation as abbot and with the permission of his superiors, he decided to join our community permanently, never leaving it until he died 18 years later, when his last words were something like a battle cry that expressed the soul of his intense and difficult life: "I want heaven! I want Jesus!"

The new arrivals contributed so well to the life of our simple community that by 1967, two years after the Vatican Council ended, there were four young professed Argentine monks and three novices, plus the 13 or 14 founders from Spencer. The three novices, Juan, Gaspar and Omar, presented an interesting challenge, since they had all immigrated to Argentina from other countries—Belgium, Italy and Chile, respectively—several years before thinking of entering with us. The spiritual quality of their monastic lives has made them important members of the community throughout these 40 years.

Even before the Council ended I began to realize that a few texts of modern monastic literature would have to be brought up to date in some of their ascetical expressions and their approach to the reality of the Church. It was a question of how best to present the human search for God—and God's search for the human heart—in its true Christian context for the world of today and tomorrow. I had two texts especially in mind: much of Thomas Merton's 200-page essay on the monastic vows, and some of Dom Columba Marmion's approach to monastic obedience in his work, *Christ, the Ideal of the Monk*. Both of these excellent works deserved to be transmitted to our novices, but some pages needed to be rewritten. At first I had thought of translating certain sections of Merton's booklet for the sake of our novices, since there was nothing else dealing directly with monastic profession; but the Council's admonition to base such formation texts on the history of salvation made me see that translation alone was not adequate.

That was how I began what to date has been my only book, *Hacia Cristo*, the English title of which is *Centered on Christ*. It has gone through several revisions in these last 40 years, all of them to improve the communication of what it means to give one's life to Christ as a monk or nun in our rapidly changing world. It is still an imperfect work and I thought that someone would soon improve on it. Perhaps the most similar book is *Consider Your Call*, written in those same years by the English Benedictines, but this has the disadvantage of being a collective work, more informational than inspirational. In fact, I have been surprised how many Benedictines use my book, despite its many Cistercian overtones. Their acceptance of it is due in great part to the suggestions I received from Mother Cándida Cymbalista, of the Benedictine nuns outside of Buenos Aires, who supervised mimeographing the first revision of my original typewritten manuscript.

Communal Autonomy

My work with the novices came to an abrupt halt in 1967, when Abbot Thomas at Spencer advised Father Alexander, my immediate superior, to let me assist at a meeting of Cistercian choir directors to be held at Gethsemani Abbey that year, since I was responsible for our music, singing, and any translation of our Liturgy into Spanish. There was no time to lose, so I went personally to the cities of Buenos Aires and La Plata to arrange my travel documents and get my ticket. This turned out to be one of the most valuable parts of my whole trip, since it put me in contact for the first time with the daily life of the average Argentine city-dweller. I learned out of necessity how to find my way through subways, train stations, ticket offices and the infamous Buenos Aires *micros*, or city buses.

The persons I dealt with were kindness personified, an impression confirmed by many—though not all—visiting foreigners. The innate warmth, culture and goodness of the Argentine people touched me deeply, all the more so since they have a reputation for aloofness and self-sufficiency. But the latter is a superficial impression sometimes given when they are outside their own country, a shell or crust which can easily be cracked open to reveal the tender strength of an intelligent, faithful friend. For the first time, after over eight years in the country, I felt that my heart had become Argentine, a feeling that has lasted through these 40 years of social turmoil. I left the country sincerely eager to return.

The trip's immediate purpose—and that of the meeting I was to assist at—was to help our community make the shift from a liturgy almost exclusively in Latin, using traditional Gregorian chant, to one predominantly in Spanish, with much greater use of contemporary music or some kind of adaptation of Gregorian plainsong. Some communities had already experimented in this new domain and the meeting offered the chance to share our experiences and learn from each other's trials, errors and achievements under the direction of Father Chrysogonus Waddell, Gethsemani's well-known choir director.

Quite incidentally, the meeting gave me the opportunity to meet Thomas Merton briefly during a coffee break, only a year before he was accidentally electrocuted during an international monastic symposium held in Bangkok, Thailand. He was in a relaxed mood and the impression he made on me was surprisingly similar to what I had frequently experienced at Yale—and seldom since then—namely, a superficial sophistication expressed in urbane pleasantries. That was my unspoken interpretation of the short encounter, an interpretation that was itself undoubtedly superficial and probably influenced by his slight English accent, which also reminded me of Ivy League colleges.

The Gethsemani meeting meant my first return to the United States after over five years of absence. This in turn allowed me, before or after the choir directors' meeting, to visit my parents in their Princeton home, spend a few days at Spencer, and also represent our Azul community at one of the first regional meetings of American Trappist superiors, everything being crammed into a little over three weeks.

The three days at Princeton were especially poignant, since Daddy had suffered a severe stroke two years before and was cared for day and night by Mother, who also did the cooking and housework. They were both 79 years old and were going to celebrate their golden wedding anniversary the following year, which, in fact, they did. Daddy was clearly an old man, a housebound invalid, while Mother, though ageing, was still her cheerful, energetic self. She did not go with me to the local parish church for Mass, since she had to stay and take care of her husband. I was also able to visit my brother, Bill, now a 45-year-old executive living outside Philadelphia. He had become one of the vice-presidents of his large accounting firm, commuting daily to his downtown office like any respectable businessman.

A week after my return to Argentina, Father Thomas arrived for his usual pastoral visit and, halfway through it, announced that I would be the new superior, taking Father Alexander's place. It took us all by surprise, but I was grateful to God for having given me the preparation of my recent trip, particularly the meeting of American abbots and abbesses that had let me see from the inside some of the problems facing superiors at that time and how they can be met. The meeting had clarified for me what the Church expected of a monastery and its superior at the present moment, probably best summed up in the double movement described in the Council's decree on the renewal of religious life. This meant a dynamic tension involving the rediscovery of each Institute's spiritual heritage, together with the prudent adaptation of that heritage to the needs and capacities of the world today.

The transition required of the community by this change of superiors was made easier for everyone by Father Alexander, who accepted my request that he be our second superior. He has remained a dear friend and brother through all these years, despite the fact of becoming, ten years later, the founding superior of our monastery in Brazil, at which time he retook his baptismal name, Francis or, in South America, Francisco. With his help, Azul was able to become an autonomous priory within the next 18 months, which resulted in my being elected by the community as its titular prior. This, in turn, implied my representing us at the Order's general chapter of March, 1969, the first of my 14 successive general chapters. All of these meetings would be fundamentally for the purpose of reinterpreting the Cistercian charism, that is, the grace of the Holy Spirit needed to fulfill the spiritual mission entrusted to our Order as a whole, and to each monk or nun in particular, in behalf of the entire world. This purpose implies making our communities more convinced of the value of the Cistercian spiritual heritage, more sensitive to the deepest needs of modern men and women, and thus more discerning in their pastoral decisions.

Our monastery's autonomy from its founding house—except for some financial emergency—was not just a change of juridical status. Within the course of the next two years, three important events took place that were related to our autonomy and that deeply affected our community life. At first sight, they appeared to be independent from one another, but in God's providence they were deeply interrelated.

The first one was the most difficult, at least for me. It involved the increasing dissatisfaction of the young Argentine members of the community with our large building, especially the big church, and with our status as landholders in one of the best farming districts of the country. These younger brothers started to meet among themselves during the last few months of 1970 to discuss the situation and the possibilities of some radical changes, even that of abandoning our present location and going to what in Argentina is called a *chacra*, a small farm of between 60 and 100 acres located much closer to a populated area. This would permit selling most of our farm machinery, plus our cars, and developing some smaller industry, the products of which could easily be sold in the town, to which the monks would go by bicycle.

To understand such a project, it has to be seen in the light of three general tendencies that were particularly strong during the 1970s and 1980s: the adaptation of monastic life to Latin American culture, the strong emphasis given by the Second Vatican Council to poverty in the Church, and the latent resentment at the intrusion of the United States in Latin American countries, a resentment expressed by the slogan, "Yankee, go home!" The convergence of these three tendencies in the younger members, who represented the future of our small community, made the situation especially dramatic. What could I, a Yankee, do in such a context? I thought it best not to forbid the meetings of the group, which would have stimulated them all the more, but I expressed my doubts to some of the men and asked them to talk not only among themselves but also with the founders, for the sake of the unity of the community.

In such contradictory circumstances, when no plausible solution seems possible, I have learned to practice spiritually what I learned to do physically in my teenage years with the surf on the Atlantic coast of Nantucket Island. In the ups and downs of life in the monastery, especially in the obscurity of interior prayer or of almost impossible pastoral situations, I have found myself facing the obscure situation just as it is and "diving" into it by an interior act of faith in God, of trust in his wisdom and of personal surrender to his will, whatever it might be, getting "boiled" or riding in on top. So, as I faced the possibility of this young splinter group breaking off from the community, I simply prayed, "Listen, Lord, if you want this community, you will have to bring good out of this situation and fix it somehow. Show me what I should do."

That brings us to the second important event of those years, the visit of an outstanding charismatic Protestant minister, Juan Carlos Ortiz. He asked to come to our small guest quarters with another minister of his Evangelical church, to make a week's retreat between Christmas and New Year, 1971. Once here, he explained that the two of them had come to make the retreat fasting on water and orange juice, which they proceeded to do, dedicating much time to prayer in our big church. It was clear that they were sincerely dedicated men of God and men of prayer, so I asked Pastor Ortiz to speak to the community at the end of his retreat and share with us something of his own spiritual experience. He willingly accepted and, with all of us assembled in an informal circle, he began by explaining the nature of charismatic prayer as an expression of the power of the Holy Spirit and a tool in God's hands for the renewal of his Church. He ended by laying his hands on each of us, invoking with deep unction the Holy Spirit to come and renew us spiritually.

The encounter with Pastor Ortiz took place in the afternoon. That evening, after our usual prayer of Compline that ends with the solemn invocation of Mary, the Mother of Christ, the young Argentine members of the community met in a small chapel off the big church and, instead of their usual discussions, immediately began to pray in tongues, praising the Lord for what he was doing in his Church, thanking him for all he had given them, praying, too, for their older brothers from North America and begging the gift of unity for all our community. Gone with the divine Wind were the thoughts of a new type of monastery or, more precisely, a new foundation project on a more plebeian scale. What God wanted was for them to live in his presence, rejoice in his immense love and share that joy with the brothers.

The change in these men was breathtaking: instead of division, unity; instead of foundation projects, prayer and love. The grace of the Spirit overflowed also onto the older professed, the founders, many of whom experienced a new freedom in spontaneous praise of God and fraternal charity, as I myself did. The community, and I in particular, will never be grateful enough to Pastor Ortiz for letting himself be used as God's instrument in our behalf. John XXIII had talked about a new Pentecost and we had heard reports of the Catholic Pentecostal movement in the United States, but we never expected to experience it so soon, so intimately and with such beneficial results. The headaches and heartaches of the monastery's first twelve years were forgotten, consumed in a new love for each other and for our Cistercian vocation. That first generation of young men in formation were powerfully confirmed in God's action in their lives and, without knowing it at the time, we were all being interiorly prepared for two decades of steady growth in different dimensions, which constituted the third important community event of those years.

Only a few weeks after the visit of Pastor Ortiz, the first signs of this growth came from France. The large monastery of Trappistine nuns near the town of Ubexy, in the Vosges mountains of northeastern France, asked for advice about making a foundation in Latin America. An interesting offer of land had been made to them by a wealthy Mexican family, whose daughter was in a monastery in Spain, so the French sisters wanted to know whether Mexico was suited for a foundation, or perhaps Argentina or some other country. I wrote in reply, suggesting that they look at the Mexican property and then decide. Without saying so, I was of the opinion that our monastery of Azul was still too young to assume any responsibility for such a project. The French abbess saw the sense of my argument but asked if I could accompany her and another sister when they went to Mexico later that year, which I did.

That was the beginning of the expansion of Trappist life throughout Latin America. Within the course of the next two years, not only was the monastery of El Encuentro founded near Ciudad Hidalgo in Mexico, but the Italian Trappistines of Vitorchiano, in central Italy, would soon make a foundation much closer to us, an hour's drive from our monastery near the neighboring town of Hinojo. Within another ten years, four other houses would be established, of nuns in Chile and Venezuela, and of monks in Brazil and Mexico. As of this writing, there are fourteen monasteries of our Order in nine countries of Latin America, the last two of which—both of Trappistine nuns—were founded from the houses in Argentina and Chile.

The Cistercian Order

It was in this context that, over the next 30 years, I would repeatedly be asked to assist at regional meetings of superiors, give community retreats to our houses around the world, make pastoral visits and occasionally take part in different monastic symposiums. The topics ranged from the spirit and aims of the original founders of Cîteaux to such themes as the contemporary meaning of the Rule of Saint Benedict, the spirituality of Saint Bernard of Clairvaux, dialogue between Cistercian and Orthodox monks, and communion and community in monastic life. My retreats were exclusively to monastic communities, with one exception made for the Argentine Dominican Friars. These retreats have usually been based on a monastic reading of the New Testament or, what amounts to the same thing, the Gospel in monastic life today.

Despite the temporary absences that such meetings imply, I have repeatedly seen that they are part of God's plan for me, part of the personal mission he seems to have given me, which was the intuition I had even during my postulancy. But such trips can be abused, so I have followed a few personal guidelines for my absences and my travel. The first one is to discuss any invitation with the prior or—now that I am not the abbot—with the abbot, and do what he thinks best. The second guideline is to limit longer absences to one, or at most two, a year, preferably under a month each time. A third one is to give preference to monasteries in developing countries, since they are often isolated from visiting speakers. In fact, our Constitutions make the point that "superiors of the Order should provide help in the area of formation, especially for very remote monasteries,"[9] since "all the communities of the Order share a responsibility for young foundations, in particular those made in young Churches or in isolated regions."[10]

A fourth norm for these trips is not to go sightseeing or to visit this or that place without a solid reason to justify it, such as when the local abbot offers to drive you to a neighboring monastery or place of interest. This has given me the chance to see, for example, the specimens of Paleolithic art on the walls of the caves of Altamira near Viaceli, in Spain, or the home base of the millions of monarch butterflies high in the mountains of Michoacán, Mexico, not far from our monastery of El Encuentro. The policy, however, made me mortify my desire to return to Shanghai, even though it would have been easy to make a side trip before or after one of my visits to our monasteries in Japan. Similarly, and despite having gone twice around the world, I have never seen such beautiful places as Kyoto, Venice, Toledo, Niagara Falls or Bariloche, Argentina's vacation paradise, much

9. ST 69.1.C.
10. Statute on Formation (*Ratio Institutionis* OCSO, printed privately) 72.

less any of the several Disneylands around the world, despite having gone many times to the countries they are in.

Although it has been a privilege to come to know many monks and nuns around the world, and to see the inner beauty of their simple monastic spirit in very different circumstances, there were two results of my contacts with other monasteries that have been especially significant for me. The first one is the deeply cordial relationship I have continually experienced with Benedictine monks and nuns. On many occasions their dedication to God, the warmth of their welcome and the sincerity of their monastic life have been a source of admiration and inspiration for me. I only hope that I have assisted them in some small way, too. The relationship has been especially strong with the 17 Benedictine houses in what we call the *Cono Sur,* the southern triangle of Spanish-speaking South America: Argentina, Chile, Paraguay and Uruguay. Their friendship and support, especially in moments of difficulty, has been consistently fraternal and a witness to the unity of the monastic world.

The other fruit of my contacts with different communities has been the need to integrate the feminine presence into my life, both exteriorly and interiorly, that is, on the level of social, interpersonal relationships and on that of emotions and affection. This is not the classic field of monastic asceticism or spirituality, but life in the present-day world requires it, especially for monastic superiors who deal with other communities.

The geographical isolation of the Azul monastery, especially in the 1970s when there was no telephone and much less anything like the Internet, had kept us separated from most women, since our limited guest facilities were only for men. That type of separation suddenly changed, however, in the latter half of 1971 with the arrival of Mother Cristiana Piccardo, Trappistine abbess of the large Italian monastery of Vitorchiano near Viterbo in central Italy. I had met her and visited her community on the occasion of our general chapter that year in Rome. With over 80 sisters, many of them still under 40, they were looking seriously to making a foundation in South America and had thought of Argentina, partly because of the presence of our community, but also due to the large number of Italian immigrants in the country. After my visit, the sisters discussed the subject and voted in favor of such a project, which would be their first foundation outside of Italy. As it turned out, Vitorchiano would, in the following 40 years, make successive foundations in Chile, Venezuela, Indonesia, Philippines and the Czech Republic, besides sending three sisters as permanent members of an existing community in the Democratic Republic of the Congo.

Mother Cristiana talked several times to our community and personally explained not only the external aspects of the foundation project but also some of the desires and more feminine sensitivities of the sisters. She undoubtedly foresaw that I would be their father immediate and that I needed some introduction to the world of nuns, which was correct. I will always be grateful to her, not only for her personal transparency and feminine maturity, but even more for her witness of a lived and loving faith.

This was my first real contact with the vibrant quality of contemporary Catholicism in Italy and with one of its best representatives. Coming from a totally different background than mine, she confirmed me in seeing that the central element of the Christian monastic vocation is the living Body of Christ, the Church, the meeting place of the divine and the human in the world of our times, that it is a joy to be humble, and that obedience to the Church and her authorities is not at all an offense against the dignity of human freedom but rather a part of that dignity's fulfillment in Christ. The key to it all is divine love incarnated in the living Christ, his Body, a mysterious anticipation of heaven on earth—and sometimes of Purgatory—for those who have eyes to see and live it.

The Argentine foundation of nuns became a reality in early 1973 with the establishment of their monastery near Hinojo, a small country town about 50 miles from our monastery. The arrival of the seven foundresses was a key event of our community's first years of autonomy. Since the buildings of the Hinojo monastery were not yet completed, the sisters stayed a week in our guest quarters, during which we could see that they had imbued, each in her own way, the same spirit of faith and monastic simplicity that we had seen in their abbess. Their continued presence at Hinojo since then, with the steady entrance of younger Argentine sisters, has been an ongoing stimulus for us. In fact, less than 30 years after their own foundation they would establish a daughter house in Nicaragua.

On the basis of my contacts with a considerable number of monasteries, I have come to two practical conclusions about relationships between celibate men and women, the more general one being that these friendships are almost always healthy, wholesome and chaste. This does not mean without tension, misunderstandings or occasional slips into different types of sentimentality or even sensuality, but the segregated nature of monastic life easily remedies this type of sentimentality. The fact that both persons have been given a celibate vocation—especially when it is to the cloister—is a healthy influence over the natural attraction celibate persons can have for one another. Most celibate religious are very good people, independently from being especially pious or not. They tend to have a stronger than average personality and have sincerely given themselves to God's service.

A second conclusion concerns falling in love with a member of the opposite sex who is also celibate. Of itself, such an infatuation is a healthy part of the normal maturing process. But what is vital is to respect the dignity, conscience, celibate vocation and real holiness of the other person—male or female, lay, religious or priest—and to respect these qualities just as much in oneself. Falling in love is one thing, most likely a part of the passage from emotional immaturity to a deeper, more generous form of self-gift. Intimate physical contact, which can occur without really being in love, is something else and much more loaded with moral consequences.

There is also the important factor of avoiding anything that damages the internal unity of one's own community, and the need to give oneself more enthusiastically than ever to promoting such unity, as the fruit of deeper affective maturity. When that is done, as I have seen on several occasions, human love is integrated into divine love, *eros* into *agape*. A healthy intimacy is combined with a certain sobriety in the outward expressions of affection, and both persons involved come to a new, more self-sacrificing maturity in Christian living.

Growth in Prayer

The combined fact of being the superior of a young community, the father immediate of a new monastery of nuns, and more in demand by other houses of the Order, meant that the following ten years—from 1973 to 1983—were busy ones for me. The Church as a whole and the Trappists in particular were struggling with the adequate implementation of the decrees and spirit of Vatican II. The entire world was increasingly in danger from what was called the "Cold War," polarizing the world between Russia and the United States. The tensions ran especially high in the USA for other reasons: the failed Vietnam War, the Cultural Revolution that had started in 1968 among university students, the Black Liberation movement for racial equality, and the Watergate Scandal.

These same years were even more difficult in Argentina because of the circumstances involving the return of President Juan Domingo Perón, then his death, followed by years of military rule that provoked a civil war waged by urban guerilla groups and an equally bloody repression of their suspected sympathizers—including several innocent friends of our monastery—all of which culminated in the military invasion, then disaster, of the *Islas Malvinas*, the "Falkland War." The final result, clearly the fruit of prayer and innocent suffering, was Argentina's return to civilian rule with the restoration of democracy in the presidential elections of 1983.

During these ten years, our monastery passed from being half full of founders from Spencer, the other half having entered at Azul, to a state in which the clear majority was Argentine. This came about by the entrance of new men and the return to Spencer of two or three of those who had come to help with the construction. One brother returned, not to Spencer but to his heavenly homeland. He was Brother Roland Gendreau, one of the very first founders, an excellent carpenter from Chicopee, Massachusetts, who died of cerebral cancer in 1980, the first Trappist monk to be buried in one of our present Latin American houses. He had served as an army medical corpsman in Europe during the Second World War.

It was also during these years that our Brother Bernardo was ordained priest, became novice master and theology professor, then went to Rome for a year of further studies and returned to continue these services until his election as abbot in 1984. My own life was increasingly taken up by the needs of the community, being available for the brothers, preparing chapter talks and homilies, writing letters, and presiding at and coordinating the work of the different community councils, which included the one dealing with the renewal of our monastic liturgy.

Two components of this pastoral activity are worth mentioning because of their difficulty for me and doubtless for my brothers as well. The first one was, and still is, subtle and complex, involving the multifaceted wealth of the Latin personality—especially the Spanish or Italian varieties—compared to the more direct, matter of fact, prosaic qualities of my Anglo-Saxon heritage. I had real difficulties with the complex emotional forces at work underneath the surface of these often very likeable persons, forces which are synthesized in the word, *gana*, or its plural, *ganas*, usually translated as "desire, wish, or longing." In practice, it indicates a strong feeling, virtually equivalent to a willed decision to do something which appears attractive.

We all have these feelings, but my problem was twofold. I had been formed from childhood through my years in the monastery to be somewhat suspicious of these strong feelings, as impeding the fulfillment of one's duty of the moment. And secondly, the healthy, peaceful family life I had led, especially the steady example of my two parents, had not prepared me for the overtly emotional, more volatile quality active in and among Latins. I soon began to see that their strongly felt and expressed emotional life did not impede a keen use of their intelligence, which is often more acute and more developed than in Nordic countries, even among simple workers and farmhands. Some of my closer friends in the monastery, however, would gently point out that they felt I had not understood them, which was no doubt true. Others would wonder if I was really listening to them, since my attention to what they were saying was not accompanied by much emotional expression on my part.

In response to this difficulty, my pastoral responsibilities have forced me, over the years, to break down my northern reserves and be more demonstrative, even more emotional, which at first was psychologically awkward and difficult, but which I soon realized was much more Christ-like. The next step was to realize that Latin culture, which is sometimes made fun of in northern countries, is often more in keeping with Christian values than the subdued, efficient and orderly spirit of more one-dimensional societies. The United States itself is learning this healthy lesson now, through the influx of Hispanic workers.

A second pastoral difficulty I had was more common, but actually more irritating for me. It consisted in the repeated interruptions that would occur as I was trying to work at my desk writing letters or preparing some talk to the community. I tend to be methodical and thorough in what I do, sometimes excessively so, with the result that a momentary interruption, a knock on the door, especially repeated knocks followed by a question that was not really necessary, were hard for me to handle. Yet they are the daily bread of any religious superior, especially in a small community. Should I complain and send the man elsewhere, or should I try to show a smiling welcome as if I was delighted by his visit? Sometimes I managed to do the latter, but more often it was a simple, noncommittal invitation to come in and share whatever seemed to be necessary. It was a permanent ascetical exercise in self-control, usually against my *ganas* of the moment, but it gradually turned into a challenge to express Christian love in a simple, helpful way and, perhaps above all, to die to myself.

In April and May of 1976, at the suggestion of our father immediate, Father Thomas of Spencer, I made a full month's retreat in a little hermitage in the hills above our monastery of La Dehesa, in Chile. The view was majestic—at least in the mornings before the smog would set in—looking over the valley at the Andes Mountains, with some of the highest snowcapped peaks of the

Western Hemisphere, and it was my first experience of prolonged physical solitude. Since there was no manual work to be done and my meals were simple, my days were a continual alternation of reflective reading and prayer, either with the Psalms or in silence before the Lord in his Eucharist. I found that it took about ten days for my whole physical, emotional and nervous system to slow down into a steady, dry, peaceful rhythm in tune with the outside quiet around me.

The best part of the retreat was my early morning Mass, which lasted about two hours, because of prayer after the readings, the intercessions, and communion. My personal reading was centered on the Letters of Saint Paul, accompanied by a short introduction to the psychology of Carl Jung, which helped me reflect on my own life at that moment as I approached the precarious age of 45. As I often do, I started jotting down some notes on how monastic spirituality, when well lived, is a passage from a life dominated by self-achievement and self-fulfillment into increasing submission of body and soul to Christ through self-denial, humility, prayer, work and community life. The result is that finally faith, hope and love reign supreme.

This was not at all a new approach to monastic spirituality, since monastic authors have written similarly through the centuries, but I felt that the process needed a new formulation as an explanation of the three dimensions of monastic discipline, that of the body through the observances, the mind through *lectio* and prayer, and the heart through humility. This reformulation of monastic living became part of my book on monastic profession.

The long hours of prayer in solitude had deepened something in me, which probably can be described as "interiority," so that I came back from the month's retreat not totally changed, but much more at home with my personal history, my inner emotions and my vocation to the Lord of my life. I also came back, for the only time in my life, with a month's beard. The brothers at Azul took this in stride, but the sisters of Hinojo simply laughed. I was hoping that a beard would simplify my life and avoid my having to shave every day, but I discovered that, at least for me, it actually made me think more about myself and how I looked, plus the need to trim it regularly. So within six months I decided that it was really simpler to shave every day.

The year 1980 came and with it the 1500th anniversary of the birth of Saint Benedict. There were celebrations, study sessions and expositions throughout the monastic world, a simple one in Buenos Aires for the ten communities in the country that follow Benedict's Rule, and a much bigger one in Rome. The anniversary came shortly after the introduction into Argentina of Transcendental Meditation, which is an adaptation to western culture of Hindu meditation techniques. Several brothers of the community had heard about TM, as it was called, from our monasteries in the USA, and asked me if they could be initiated into it. I replied that they were free to do so but that it should not interfere with their daily monastic life. Personally, I could not accept performing the initial rite of kneeling before a picture of a Hindu guru and offering fruit or flowers as a sign of spiritual dependence, but if the brothers' conscience let them, they could do it.

The fact that this interest in Transcendental Meditation coincided with the anniversary of Saint Benedict triggered a need for me to clarify the nature and methods of prayer in a life according to the Rule of Saint Benedict. What do we as a Christian contemplative monastery have to offer on the level of prayer and contemplation? How can this be taught, and what can I as the superior say about prayer to my monks? Benedict does not seem to teach a way of prayer, but rather a way of life in which prayer is held in high esteem. But how does he think we should pray? How did *he* pray? It was hard to answer these questions and, as I went to Rome for the general chapter that year, I prayed to him for almost the first time in my life: "Saint Benedict, you are the father of monks. Give me the grace to see how God wants your spiritual sons to pray, so that I can explain it to them."

I expected that the theme of prayer would be addressed at the international symposium in Rome during the general chapter, since the leitmotiv of the celebration was *Rereading the Rule of Saint Benedict Today;* so I was disappointed to see that the central theme of listening to the Word of God was presented as vitally important, but with little said about meditating on it in personal prayer. In some way, this did not surprise me, because Benedictine and Cistercian spirituality does not emphasize silent personal prayer as does the Carmelite tradition. The usual attitude is one of, "Follow this way of life and prayer will take care of itself," or simply that, as Father Hilarion had told me during my first days at Spencer, "The most important thing in prayer is to be sincere."

An important factor in this seemingly nonchalant approach is the primacy of place given to the shared prayer of the community as a whole, that is, to the liturgy with its celebration of the Eucharist each day and of the Divine Office seven times a day, from predawn to bedtime. What is often left unsaid, however—as it was in the Roman symposium—is the need of making each liturgical act a personal prayer and not just an interlude of listening, singing and bowing, even though all is done in the name of the Church. As usual, Saint Benedict sums up the situation in a single pithy sentence: "Let us stand to sing the psalms in such a way that our minds are in harmony with our voices."[11]

I returned to Azul from Rome resigned not to having a clear answer to my request to know how to present Christian prayer to monks of the Benedictine-Cistercian tradition, but near the end of his anniversary year Saint Benedict suddenly and unexpectedly answered my prayer to him. One day while walking in Azul's cloister on the way to the novitiate, not thinking of anything in particular, I suddenly understood what Benedict had in mind for the prayer of his monks and why it had been so hard for me to identify it simply with the liturgy, *lectio divina* or mental prayer.

What Saint Benedict did was to organize and stabilize a life in which there are four different forms of prayer interacting among themselves, reinforcing each other and greatly enriching the life of each monk. These four types of prayer are liturgical prayer, *lectio divina*, continual prayer at any time or place, and what the charismatic movement calls "shared prayer," that is, occasional moments of spontaneous vocal prayer in the presence of others,

11. RB 19,7.

such as the spontaneous litanies of the prayer of the faithful at Mass or in the Liturgy of the Hours, and blessings for meals or at the beginning of community meetings. What has become known in recent centuries as "mental prayer" is, in monastic tradition, an integral part of *lectio divina*. However, the central type of prayer in monastic life is neither *lectio divina* nor even the liturgy, but continual prayer. That is the purpose of a monastery. *Lectio* and the Liturgy are schools where we gradually learn how "to pray always and not to lose heart."[12]

Saint Benedict had answered my prayer just at the end of his anniversary year, with the result that, from then on, I have felt much more at ease when talking about prayer, whether with monks and nuns or with laypersons. I saw that the art of prayer is twofold, as it was for Jesus himself. It means, on the one hand, learning to change gears from one type of prayer to another according to the activity at hand, shifting back and forth from Liturgy to *lectio*, continual prayer or some type of shared prayer, with each one of these prayer forms reinforcing the other ones. On a deeper level, however, all prayer forms mean having my mind agree with my actions and words—and my actions and words agree with my prayer!—that is, doing what one is doing to please the Lord from the inside, not just so that the choir sounds nice or to have my own activity of the moment function well.

This vision of monastic prayer has helped me appreciate, in particular, the connection between exterior monastic practices and interior prayer of the heart. In fact, it was a synthesis of these years in which I had been trying to form a new community in shifting circumstances. Without my knowing it at the time, God was using this experience to prepare me for what was to come, but I'll talk about that in my next letter to you.

12. Lk 18:1.

Letter 7

CALLED BACK

1983–1996

Dear Eddie,

The last letter I wrote you ended with a reference to the celebration in 1980 of the anniversary of Saint Benedict's birth. If you recall, I visited Spencer shortly after that, on the way to a meeting of abbots in Canada, and asked you if you would help us out in Argentina as temporary chaplain of the Trappistine nuns at Hinojo. You had been here before, could speak Spanish, and would work well with the Italian foundresses of the new monastery. I will always be grateful to you for accepting the request, especially since it coincided with the time when Father Thomas Keating was thinking of resigning after 20 years as abbot of Spencer.

Seeds of Change

Those 20 years had been marked by challenges of every kind for all our monasteries. Father Thomas had served Spencer's community admirably by his example and teaching, but he understandably needed a rest. The fact is that the Second Vatican Council had been an inspired watershed in the life of the Church, but that very fact brought with it a rethinking of what our life is all about. For monks, the question was, "Why a monastery?" Why follow these traditions? What is the relationship between a local, self-governing monastery and the central authority of the Order, or between Christian monasticism and its non-Christian counterparts? Can we accept non-Catholic candidates into our communities? Shouldn't we integrate the separate laybrother vocation more fully into the mainstream of the community? What kind of philosophy and theology should we teach? Should we perhaps begin to talk more freely among ourselves? Father Thomas had faced these and many other tensions in his large community for two decades and felt that it was time for a change.

An American abbot who visited Azul in 1981 explained Father Thomas's motives to me and said that I should get ready to be elected as his successor. Fortunately, that did not happen and the election went to an older man, Father Paschal Skutecky, whom I had known when he was a laybrother and long-standing companion of my brother, Bill, first at the monastery in Rhode Island, then at Spencer. He visited us in 1982 as our father immediate, but it was clear that his health was not strong enough to handle the stresses of leadership in a large community at that precise time of renewal and change. He himself had to resign in early 1983.

One morning several weeks later, you, Eddie, drove over from Hinojo and knocked on the door of my office. You caught me by surprise but explained that, since we had no telephone, someone at Spencer had phoned the sisters, asking you to get word to me that I should phone Spencer at once and ask to speak with their father immediate, Emmanuel Coutant, abbot of Bellefontaine in France, who needed to discuss something with me. You did not know anything more and were cautious in adding your own comments, but the circumstances pointed to a pastoral need at Spencer at this moment in which the community was looking for another abbot.

We talked together briefly about this, then you returned to Hinojo and I drove the 35 miles to the Azul post office, from where I could telephone to the United States. Father Emmanuel, speaking in French, slowly explained that the Spencer community had decided not to have an abbatial election at that time, but to have a temporary superior chosen by their father immediate, someone we call a superior *ad nutum*, meaning literally "at the nod," that is, at the beck and call of the father immediate. There were two reasons for thinking of such an arrangement. Above all, it would give the community a chance to dialogue with the new man and among themselves as to the best course to follow in the future, but it was also to see if an adequate person could be found to lead the community as its next abbot. In a second vote, the community had shown a slight preference for me over other persons mentioned, so Father Emmanuel asked me over the phone if I would resign as superior of Azul and assume this service at Spencer.

I had expected to receive a summons to an abbatial election in the near future, but not a request like this, so I answered without much hesitation that I could not accept his proposal at that time, because our community was not ready for a change of superior, which would imply one of the young Argentines. Then, without any premeditation, I said that I could accept being named apostolic administrator of Spencer, instead of its superior *ad nutum*, thus letting me remain for the time being as superior at Azul. An apostolic administrator, meaning someone named by the Vatican to act in the name of the Pope, can be superior of two communities at the same time, something not permitted as a usual course of action by either our Order's Constitutions or the Church's Code of Canon Law. In any case, I would present the situation to our men, see what they advised and phone back. Father Emmanuel agreed at once to such an arrangement, clearly relieved that I had not said a total "No." He would send such a request to our generalate in Rome, who would relay it to the Vatican. I replied that I would start discussing the problem with our community and phone again in two days.

Our first dialogue on the subject took place that afternoon, followed by two others the following day. It became increasingly clear that, despite the surprise of such a move, the community as a whole was open to it, seeing it as part of God's plan for us. Sooner or later, there must be a change of superiors to one from Argentina. It seemed that the time had come. Only one of the founders consistently opposed the change, saying that none of the younger men was ready to assume the community's leadership. For my part, I felt that God was advancing the timetable for our growth, as he had consistently done in my life from the beginning, but I did not want to push the community in any direction for fear of prejudicing its hard-won unity.

We took a secret vote at the end of our third dialogue, with all except one approving my departure for Spencer and recommending that I name Bernardo as my delegate, or "vicar superior," with all the rights and responsibilities of a full superior until my next visit. It was agreed that I could consult the community at any time by mail about how affairs were going and what seemed best for a more stable future. I had a right to do this anyway since, as apostolic administrator of Spencer, I would become Azul's father immediate. That very evening I drove again to Azul and made the final phone call to Dom Emmanuel, confirming all that we had proposed. Meanwhile, he had started the process of naming me apostolic administrator and said that the Vatican Congregation for Religious Institutes was open to such an arrangement.

It was hard to let go of my two Argentine communities, our own and that of Hinojo. They had both become very dear to me, as often happens when you have been with a community in its birth pangs. The day I left, we had an impromptu charismatic prayer meeting in the kitchen before the final *abrazo*, with all the brothers laying their hands over me and praying for this mission we knew would be long, difficult, and perhaps indefinite. It was winter in Argentina, the end of June, and I arrived at Spencer in time for the Fourth of July.

Poverty and Wealth

After a night's sleep in the abbot's "tower," as his living quarters are called, I started finding out what the situation at Spencer really was. The underlying problem had nothing to do with the community's finances, which were well managed, nor with any flagrant breach of monastic discipline, but was more the fruit of something not uncommon in religious communities at that time, namely, an accumulated lack of adequate intellectual and spiritual orientation in the turbulent wake of the upheavals of the 1960s and 70s. It took me six or seven months to reach this conclusion, months spent listening to this dynamic, intelligent group of over 70 men of all ages. After reading the minutes of their dialogues and, above all, seeing for myself the different groups and lifestyles into which the community was splintering, my impression was of an excessive emphasis among the brothers on undirected freedom of choice and the classic American cult of maximum liberty for all.

Another way of arriving at the same conclusion was to see the situation as the result of a one-sided interpretation of the documents of the Second Vatican Council, an interpretation in which its central theme—the Church in dialogue with the contemporary world—was being replaced by that of religious liberty. Such an approach was part of a more general and radical opinion that Vatican II wanted to break with the past and required a new beginning, with new structures and a new spirit. Applying this interpretation to monastic life would mean that a monk has the right to exercise his chosen plan of life even within a community following a specific rule, such as that of Saint Benedict, since the community exists for the good of its members.

What is left unsaid in such an approach is that the core elements of any Christian community must always be respected and cultivated. The Acts of the Apostles describes these essential qualities when it details the life of the first Jerusalem communities shortly after Christ's resurrection: "They devoted themselves to the apostles' teaching and fellowship, to the breaking of bread and the prayers. . . . All who believed were together and had all things in common."[1] When these unifying characteristics are present, a community will grow as a healthy school of Christian love, but when any one of them is seriously reduced—whether eagerness to be taught by the Church, a shared following of the poor Christ, the central place of the Eucharist or persevering prayer—a serious imbalance is introduced, which will tend to weaken the other elements of community life and, if the imbalance is not corrected in time, will lead to different forms of division and dispersal.

So it became clear that my task was, above all, to implement adequate intellectual and monastic formation. But how? I was not

1. Acts 2:42; 4:32.

at all prepared or capable of doing it alone, and I sensed that the brothers would understandably resent any more outside intrusion into their affairs, even in the name of renewal, since each person or subgroup understood renewal in a different way. So I did my best to work through the monastic councils. This meant weekly meetings of the abbot's large pastoral council, the smaller personnel committee responsible for the work assignments, and the formation team of the novice master, vocational director and dean of the simply professed monks. Over the course of the months and years, these group meetings provided a context for them to know me and for me to appreciate these key members of the Spencer community as we faced the shifting needs of our 70 dedicated brothers.

Renewal also required finding the right style for my chapter talks to the community as a whole. I started by alternating between doctrinal or liturgical themes and more pastoral or practical aspects of community life. But I gradually found that it was better to give a longer series of talks on a single general theme, such as Saint Benedict's degrees of humility, the different *Treatises and Sermons* of Saint Bernard of Clairvaux, the Servant Songs in Isaiah, the Eucharist or the new constitutions. Several members of the community correctly observed that I was better at giving homilies at Mass than longer talks in the chapter room. I think it was because I felt more at ease with the gospel texts than with subjects which I knew would not be well received by some of the brothers. This was a weakness on my part, probably triggered by an excessive desire to win over some of the more difficult members of the community. I will explain later how I eventually overcame this apprehension, or rather how God himself overcame it.

Vocational discernment was another important issue, as it is for any religious community. My 20 years at Azul had helped me in this art, which mixes intuition and rational analysis to produce a judgment concerning a person's call to follow in our particular form of life. Before going to Azul, I had had a minimum of experience in anything like vocational discernment, and the United States of the 1980s and 90s was very different from Latin America of the 1970s. In recent years, however, especially during my long retreat in Chile, I had read a little of Jungian psychology and a few of the postconciliar documents from Rome on formation for religious life and the priesthood, so I soon became acquainted with such tools as the Minnesota Personality Inventory, the Rohrschach inkblot test for emotional integration and the Myers-Briggs temperament analysis.

I found, however, that the most useful tool for evaluating a vocation was one that I had originally seen in a document on religious life coming from the Vatican. It expresses much accumulated experience and appeals to common sense enlightened by faith, saying that the judgment on a priestly or religious vocation is governed by three major factors, all of which are necessary, but in differing degrees of clarity and certitude according to the progressive stages of formation. The three criteria are the true desire of the candidates, their emotional and intellectual capacity to lead the life with ease and joy of heart, and their acceptance by the receiving community. This last factor seems self-evident, but it expresses the fact that a vocation in the Church is a dialogue between Jesus, who calls through his Spirit, and the young person who answers. It is the Church through the religious Institute, rather than the candidate, that makes the final discernment, since there can be factors that go beyond the desire and the qualities of the candidates themselves, such as the monastery's capacity to receive and form such a person or the greater needs of the universal Church.

Spencer had received some excellent vocations even during the difficult years after the Second Vatican Council, because it is an attractive, transparent and affectionate group of men, both old and young. Perhaps because its fieldstone buildings are so handsome and functional, and its sung liturgy often inspiring, it was inevitable that some young men had entered who were well-intentioned but drawn more by the beauty of the monastery than by a commitment to its demanding life of prayer, work and disinterested service to all. The presence of emotional immaturity is especially harmful in the cloister, since it easily leads to a self-centered use even of the best elements of monastic life. For this and other reasons, I decided, during my months as apostolic administrator, to ask several of the novices to leave, and I did not renew the vows of two or three simply professed. Some other younger men left spontaneously, so that during my first year at Spencer there were over fourteen departures.

More than one member of the community was troubled by this exodus. But one day Bishop Timothy Harrington of Worcester visited me precisely to reassure me: "Augustine, before you came, people were wondering what was going on at the monastery, but now they say that things are better and back to normal." I had not doubted that my vocational decisions had been correct, but I will always be grateful to Timothy for his understanding and support during this difficult period of readjustment to some of the intrinsic needs of healthy monastic living as summed up in the qualities of the first Christian community.

The fourteen men who left during my first year included several with whom the deciding factor was principally that of sexual orientation. When I arrived from Azul in 1983 I was surprised at the importance given to this debated subject, and it took me years to achieve a balanced view about it. There have been clear abuses and intolerance on both sides of the broad spectrum of this factor of human existence. I have come to know, appreciate and admire several homosexual religious and priests who have integrated their sexuality into their chaste love of Christ, just as heterosexuals must do. The homosexual's special sensitivity to friendship can be a positive contribution to community life.

However, his heightened sensitivities can also be a danger in two ways: through disordered, even secret, friendships on the part of the person himself, and through the formation of little cliques or buddy groups of like-minded—or like-feeling—companions, which can easily provoke a reaction by others both in the community and on the outside. These dangers combine with a special need to be affirmed by others, with the result that, as one monk put it, "homosexuals can have our vocation, but they need to be three times as good a monk as the rest of us in order to make it." I would tend to say, "four or five times as good"; but when this happens it is a beautiful triumph of God's love over our disordered human nature.

So Spencer's community progressed through its deep beauty and its purifying trials, its joys and its sorrows. I received more from the brothers than anything I gave them and am deeply grateful for their patience with my many weaknesses as their named superior for the first year and as their abbot for the following twelve. Certainly the most difficult moments were when, in the name of authenticity, I had to refuse requests for such things as personal trips, sensing that from then on my relationship with the brother involved would not be easy. On the other hand, many brothers supported and helped me with their prayer, personal fidelity and advice. These different visions of monastic living are not uncommon in our communities today, but they continue to remain a cause of concern, especially for the abbot or abbess, as they were for me during my years as abbot at Spencer.

It also took some time for me to be reeducated in the use of English in public prayer, not so much because it is different from Latin or Spanish, but because of the frequent use of the old Protestant hymns, with which I had been brought up as a child and then had abandoned during my second year in college. I would sing them now with gusto, like putting on an old pair of shoes, but I mentally criticized the pious, Old Testament self-centeredness of many of these hymns, which did not seem to bother the other monks. On the other hand, some of the newer hymns were truly moving reflections of the truths of faith, especially when set to a more vivacious type of melody than those of the 16th or 17th century.

Passages

My return to Spencer meant that I was closer to my family and old friends. Although I did not take the initiative to contact them, they heard that I had come back from far away and would occasionally visit me. I had not seen them since entering the monastery 30 years before, so these renewed contacts provided the unexpected opportunity for integrating my family roots more positively.

The most poignant of these experiences was the final period of my mother's life, spent in the Episcopal Nursing Home near

Wilmington, Delaware. I was able to drive her to the nearest parish for Mass and will never forget her expression of total self-gift as she knelt—almost ecstatic—at the communion rail, arms crossed over her breast, to receive her Lord and God. She was in her 90s and walked with much difficulty, but that seemed to enhance all the more the ardor of her spirit, intensely recollected and totally intent on this central act of Catholic life. I have given Holy Communion to thousands of monks, nuns and laity all over the world but have never seen anyone so intensely concentrated on the Lord as she was when receiving Communion. It could have been any minister. I, her son, had totally disappeared from her horizon and her blue eyes were blazing, as if looking at her most precious treasure, which indeed it was.

At the same time, she was still very much a mother and grandmother, surrounded by photos of her family. My sister Helen, who lived close by, watched over her until she breathed her last, nine months after my return to Spencer. I was able to preside at her funeral Mass at the nearby parish and at her burial the next day beside my father in the small cemetery of the Episcopal Church outside Princeton, New Jersey. Her life had been one of contemplation in action, with a fidelity to her divine Spouse that reveals the wonders God works among his people no matter who or where they are.

Mother's death, less than a year after my return to the United States, resulted in my being the only Catholic member of our immediate family, although Bill's wife, Maria, remains one, along with Jeannette, one of Edith's twelve children. As I mentioned before, Bill himself, after leaving the monastery and marrying Maria, was never able to accept any organized church or religion. Mother confided to me that she had been deeply distraught by Bill's rejection of any explicit Christian faith. She wondered if she should make some form of reparation for it, to which I replied that the best form of reparation was her own fidelity to the faith as she continued to serve her husband and children. She agreed and said that soon after Bill's civil marriage to Maria she was praying about this when she received the following interior message: "Leave him to me; I will take care of him," which understandably pacified her spirit in the midst of her distress.

After Mother's death, I saw Bill every year or two and would take a two- or three-hour walk with him on the roads, moors and cliffs of Nantucket Island, to which he had retired. As the two siblings most similar to each other physically and psychologically, although ten years apart in age, we felt comfortable in each other's presence and I think he appreciated the fact that I respected his personal convictions. On several occasions I described my life at Spencer and how the Catholic Church had evolved through the experience and teachings of the Second Vatican Council, but I sensed that Bill was really not interested in all that. His heart now lay in music, mathematics and social justice, and he repeatedly referred to his attraction to Buddhist cosmology and to the conclusions of quantum physics, both of which present a vision of universal harmony based on absorption of all beings into the cosmos.

On one such walk, we were on a dirt road not far from Sankaty Head Lighthouse overlooking the rolling waves of the Atlantic Ocean breaking on the beach below when Bill took his thought one step further: "I believe that after death we'll all be absorbed and become one in the cosmos. I guess you'd call it a type of pantheism."

It was my turn to become distressed at the thought that Bill had reached this point of religious despair. I answered as calmly as I could: "Doesn't the thought of meeting a loving Father and being embraced by members of a loving, universal family attract you?"

"No, it doesn't," he replied as we kept walking.

I did not reply, both to show respect and to give him time to ponder the seriousness of the subject, but I returned to Spencer sincerely concerned. My fear was basically theological. Would Bill, who underneath his goodness was fiercely independent and self-sufficient, not accept being saved by another person, even if that person be Christ the Lord? What will Bill say when he meets the Savior? Will it be "Oh, thanks!" or will it be, "No, thanks"? All I could do was pray.

Such was my concern during the last ten years of Bill's life. He had serious prostate cancer in his 70s, but was successfully operated on and recovered well. In his early 80s he developed a relatively rare form of cancer involving small tumors around his chest and back. After prolonged radiation treatment, he seemed to be recovering but suddenly began to decline, lost all energy and spent his last week in bed growing weaker and weaker but continually accompanied by his loving family.

Bill's daughter, Fatinha, told me the story of his last days. He was increasingly unable to speak and simply lay in bed, but on one occasion he suddenly sat straight up in bed, stretched out his arms and exclaimed, "Mother and Daddy are here!" Then he lay back and resumed his silence in peace, to pass away two or three days later, the morning of Easter Sunday. I was in Argentina at the time but telephoned later that morning, was told the news and was able to offer Mass for Bill's eternal rest in the Lord that same Easter morning.

Bill's sudden "visit" from Mother and Daddy is certainly open to different interpretations. Whether it was an objectively verifiable event or just a subjective projection of Bill's imagination does not really modify its positive influence on his belief system. Personally, I read the episode as an act of God's saving love in response to a mother's prayer for her son. Bill was in God's hands, God took care of him, and the specific way this occurred was a beautiful gesture of divine wisdom. Bill had expressed to me his skeptical indifference toward the possibility of being welcomed after death by a loving Father and a universal family, but he was never indifferent to his earthly family, especially not to his mother, who had stood by his side in his youth throughout his pacifistic duel with the US government and in each of his further expressions of self-reliance. Through Bill's earthly parents, the Father of us all visited him, embraced him and, I believe, convinced him that eternity was not absorption into the cosmos but a shared family resurrection into an everlasting Easter.

Constitutions

Along with these more personal concerns, my years as abbot at Spencer coincided with the preparation and approval of new Trappist Constitutions, rewritten in the light of the renewal inspired by the Second Vatican Council. All religious Congregations went through a similar process, but ours was especially significant for two major reasons: the worldwide extension of the Order and the fact that it is composed of both men and women. My international background and intercultural experiences had made me acutely sensitive to this process, which I was able to promote and to protect over the years.

The number of our houses had, by 1990, nearly doubled from what they were in 1953 when I entered, with the majority of the new foundations being made outside of the North Atlantic countries. Whereas in 1953 there were 8 Trappist monasteries in Asia, by 1990 there were 16, and in Africa the number had jumped from 2 to 16. Latin America had 11 houses in 1990, all established after Azul's foundation in 1958. In another ten years, by the year 2000, Asia would have 22 houses, Africa 18 and Latin America 13. Even more significant was the fact that in 1990 the 43 houses in these three regions, though they were less than 30% of the total number of our monasteries, already had more young monks and nuns in the process of formation than did all the North Atlantic houses combined. The future was clearly moving south and east, so that the challenge was now to incorporate in a healthy way this new plurality of cultures into the structured life of the Order as a whole. This also implied a greater participative role for Trappistine nuns.

For over a decade, through the 1970s and into the 80s, these and other elements of renewal were discussed. Finally the moment arrived to put such deliberations into a synthetic formulation and draw up a preliminary draft of new, postconciliar Constitutions. An Australian monk, Father Michael Casey of Tarrawarra Abbey outside Melbourne, was chosen to prepare such a text for presentation to the general chapter of 1984, the first in the Order's history—and so far the only one—to be held outside of Europe, at a conference center in Holyoke, Massachusetts, not far from Spencer.

From then on, it was a task of constantly revising and improving the details of Father Michael's text, so as to reflect the true life of our monasteries at that time and show its inner harmony with the Rule of Saint Benedict, the long Cistercian tradition, and the orientations of Vatican II. By the 1980s, there was a separate chapter of abbesses, which accepted the text of the abbots while modifying a few minor details for the nuns. In 1987 the two chapters of abbots and abbesses met together in Rome, finalized the two texts and presented them to the Vatican for its approval. Several small additions were suggested and the approved text was promulgated in 1990.

Ever since my first years as superior of Azul, I had been intensely involved in this tedious journey that had absorbed much attention on the part of most of the superiors of the Order. In fact, most of us were tired of so much continual discussion of pastoral orientations. By the time the Constitutions were finally approved and promulgated, most of us just wanted to shut up and live them. Thankfully, the approved text was a livable, often inspiring document.

Contacts

Along with the ongoing renewal of the community at Spencer and the work of finalizing the new Trappist Constitutions, there was an important third dimension to life as an American abbot in the 1980s and 90s, namely, the many contacts with persons outside the community itself. For me these contacts ranged from casual ones with guests or visitors to more important workshops on subjects such as affective maturity among celibates, vocational discernment, dialogue with the Orthodox Churches, Canon Law for Religious, helping Christians in China, and learning how to use computers and word processors.

It was a special privilege to acquire firsthand knowledge of Spencer's four daughter houses in the United States: Guadalupe in Oregon, Berryville in northern Virginia, Snowmass in Colorado and the nuns at Wrentham, Massachusetts. Since they were spread all over the country, each house had its special characteristics, problems and graces. Wrentham, with over 50 Trappistine nuns, was the largest of them, thanks in part to the unity of the community forged under the strong leadership of its abbess, Mother Angela Norton. Berryville and Snowmass were newer, smaller monasteries, struggling to establish their monastic identity in regions of the country where there were, in the 1980s, not many Catholics. Berryville's relative proximity to Spencer, its similarity in many respects to Azul, and perhaps also its general spirit, which reflected that of the eastern United States, made it easier for me to enter into its mentality and life rhythms.

In that regard, Guadalupe, in the far northwest corner of the country, was a special challenge. Two factors contributed to this, one being the differences that exist between the East Coast and the West Coast. Life in the West—at least in the 1980s—was both slower and more flexible than in the East. The other challenge was a keen interest present in some members of the community—starting with the abbot—for Zen Buddhist meditation practices. The monastery was something of a pioneer in this regard but was paying the price for its zeal by suffering a sharp internal division among its members. Most of my visits there were in an attempt to resolve this tension, but it took years before adequate internal unity was restored, thanks in large part to the prudence of a new abbot, Father Peter McCarthy.

On my first visit to the Oregon community, I asked the brothers if they had any questions to ask me. A younger monk spoke up, "What precisely is your basic religious message?"

I was caught by surprise and had to think fast, since I had never been asked that important question before. "I think I would call it 'The Living Christ,'" I replied. The young monk seemed satisfied, although I am not sure just what his own underlying motives were when he asked me about my basic religious message.

Thinking it over later, it seems to me that the phrase, "the living Christ," does indeed express what is most central to my whole existence as a monk, a Catholic, a Christian and a human being. It refers not only to Christ risen from the dead and ascended into Heaven also to Christ physically alive and active on earth in "his body, that is, the church,"[2] and in each of that body's human members. The living Christ is "The Eternal Galilean,"[3]

2. Col 1:24.
3. See *The Eternal Galilean*, by Fulton J. Sheen.

"this mystery, which is Christ in you, the hope of glory,"[4] the "one new humanity,"[5] the new first Man, Savior and now Father of the new human race, risen from the dead and reconciling all persons and all things in himself through his Holy Spirit. What more do we want? In fact, what else is there?

Soon after my arrival at Spencer, I was informed—then saw for myself—that one of the major needs of the monastery was for a new health care facility, or at least for a thoroughly renewed infirmary to take the place of the preexisting house for hired farmhands, hastily converted to a provisional infirmary in the 1950s. After considerable community discussion, a plan was agreed upon that involved totally renewing the present small building and adding an even larger two-storey wing, to be built in harmony with the style of the existing buildings and according to the building code for health-care facilities. It would cost over a million dollars, which meant that we ourselves could not finance it alone and would have to look for help.

Following the advice of several professional fund-raisers, we organized a three-year plan of soliciting financial aid from a few philanthropic foundations and from the community's many friends, benefactors, visitors and guests. It was an intense period of speaking personally with many persons, bringing them more into the life of the abbey, then showing how they could help us take adequate care of our older brothers. The project was worthwhile and our friends were generous, so we were able to complete the new building within two years.

For me in particular, it was my first real experience of the American business world, of the technical and juridical elements involved in any modern construction project, and of the precision necessary in the health-care industry as a whole. It was not what I had entered the monastery for, but it seemed to be God's will for me at that time and gave me the opportunity to know many truly remarkable laypersons who were striving to put the Gospel into practice in their daily lives.

4. Col 1:27.
5. Eph 2:15.

Another form of contact was even more poignant for me, since it involved dialoguing with ministers of different reformed Churches invited to Spencer every January during the annual celebration of the Church Unity Octave. On one occasion it was with my former companion at the Shanghai American School, Carl Scovel, and at another such meeting it was with the Episcopal Bishop of Western Massachusetts, whose wife had discovered that my father and hers had been classmates at the Cambridge Divinity School. Even closer to home was a visit from the Reverend Leslie Fairfield, a retired Episcopalian priest, and his wife, Mary, at whose marriage I had assisted in Shanghai 50 years before. He was clearly my father's "favorite son" among the younger Episcopalian missionaries at that time, so that these encounters brought me into contact with my Protestant roots in a way that not even my relations with my family members had done.

The sincerity of such devoted Christians is impressive, but my personal experience of the differences between Protestants and Catholics increased my sensitivity to the obstacles on the road to full Christian unity. The principal difficulty at present is not so much mistrust, as in former times, but a deeper disagreement concerning what Christian unity means. It seems to involve a clash of belief systems that can even exist within a single Christian Church or denomination. The differences are embodied in what is called the "Branch Theory," according to which the one Christian faith can and should be expressed differently in different cultures throughout the world, with each local or national Church recognizing and respecting the validity of the analogous expressions in the other regions.

Our yearly speakers on Christian unity, no matter what segment of the Reformation they represented, would consistently express their desire for unity in terms of this "Branch Theory," without ever mentioning the term, which uncritical Catholic ears would receive as the road to follow in achieving the unity Jesus prayed for at the Last Supper.[6] But I had become sensitive to the fallacies

6. See Jn 17:21-22.

in the branch theory, at least as it is commonly understood, starting with the fact that it only arose in the 16th century as a sophisticated application of the non-Christian principle, *cuius regio eius religio*: each region of the world is entitled to its own religion. My own father was following a variant of this principle when he replied to my question about his becoming a Catholic, "I believe that God's will is revealed in the situation in which he puts us. We should stay in the Church in which we were born and brought up."

Such an approach is simple enough, but it avoids the question of truth and the possibility that important elements of Christian revelation can become misinterpreted, either in theory or in practice, without a global, objectively unifying authority of Christian truth and morals. Ever since the first years of Christianity, Catholic tradition has consistently seen this to be the meaning of Christ's proclamation, "You are Peter, and on this rock I will build my church, and the gates of Hades will not prevail against it. I will give you the keys of the kingdom of heaven";[7] and later, "Simon, Simon, listen! Satan has demanded to sift all of you like wheat, but I have prayed for you that your own faith may not fail; and you, when once you have turned back, strengthen your brothers."[8] Holy Spirit of the risen Christ, enlighten us all to understand these words correctly, so that we work together for the good of your Churches and for the true joy of the entire world!

A somewhat similar, though more personal, situation arose in my ongoing dialogue with my oldest sister, Edith. A few years after moving to California, marrying and becoming the mother of the first three of her twelve children, she had a deep conversion experience, gave her life to Christ and became a fervent Evangelical Christian. Thirteen years my senior, she had assumed the classic role of older sister to almost all her siblings. So when she heard that I had become a Catholic monk, she scolded me by writing, in the name of the Gospel, "It will do you no good to be in a monastery. All your austerities are worthless. Only Jesus is the Savior!"

7. Mt 16:18-19.
8. Lk 22:31-32.

Her principle was excellent, but her conclusions were so fundamentally one-sided as to be ludicrous, so I simply replied that I was happy to be where I knew Jesus wanted me, in the monastery. Over the years I visited her twice and she visited me once. She had become more open to the Catholic Church, especially because of her ardent pro-life convictions, which resulted in meeting many dedicated lay Catholics in picket lines and demonstrations. On my last visit with her, she asked, "In the monastery, Bruce, what has been the most difficult moment for you?"

I reflected rapidly and replied, "The most difficult moment was when Bill left, got married and gave up the faith."

"Yes," she said, "that must have been difficult for you."

I realized that she was probably thinking that I, too, wanted to get married, so I hastily explained, "It was, but I never doubted about being called to the monastery and not getting married. After all, Jesus was not married."

"But Jesus was God!" she retorted at once.

I had decided to avoid any religious confrontation with her, so did not give the obvious reply, "Yes, he was God, but he was also man and, as man, he could have married but didn't." In any case, Edith confided at the end of my visit that it had been "like a visit from the risen Jesus." What more can you ask for from an older sister!

That final exchange with Edith, however, let me touch firsthand another key problem area of ecumenical dialogue, namely, the role that is played by 20 centuries of Christian tradition in interpreting who Jesus is and what he taught. An approach of "Scripture alone," or "only the first five Ecumenical Councils," puts an arbitrary time limit on the power of the Holy Spirit to "teach you everything, and remind you of all that I have said to you."[9] What is needed instead is someone among Christ's disciples with "the keys of the kingdom of heaven,"[10] that is, the charismatic service of making final decisions and unifying disputed interpretations of Scripture and tradition, at least the most

9. Jn 14:26.
10. Mt 16:19.

important ones, in the light of these 20 centuries of accumulated Christian wisdom.

The Clergy

Such reencounters with my Protestant roots coincided with a very different type of encounter, namely, my frequent contacts with Catholic priests, bishops and even cardinals. It is surprising what a difference of style exists between the Argentine priests and bishops whom I knew and their colleagues in the United States, a difference that can probably be traced to several cultural factors. One component of this difference is the relative simplicity of Argentine priests and bishops, the majority of whom are from Italian or Spanish families often living in small cities or towns, whereas the Catholic Church in the United States has been marked by the more urban Irish experience and its long-standing reverence for the priesthood. It is not at all that North American priests and bishops are unapproachable, but there is a dignified reserve among most of them that is replaced in Argentina by a more simple openness of heart. This difference is accentuated by the greater complexity of most North American dioceses with their large city parishes, tightly organized administration and increasing polarization of opinions.

In both countries, as well as in others I have visited, I have been impressed by the spiritual quality of the clergy in general, even with all their inevitable human failings. The more recent scandals given by a very few priests have only increased my esteem and affection for them, although these episodes have made it clear that any form of ecclesiastical cronyism—which will always be a danger when there is a spirit of "clan"—is a dangerous abuse of Church loyalty.

I confess that I have been tempted to dream of an "ideal priest or bishop" for the Americas, who would combine the fine qualities of the Church in North and South America, and thus be spectacularly competent and pastorally sensitive. God, however, seems to think differently. For him, spiritual diversity is "the Gift of the Spirit, whose secret joy will always be to establish communion and restore the likeness, playing with the differences," as Christian de Chergé, superior of the Trappist community in Algeria, wrote in 1993 in the context of that country's violent interreligious diversity.[11] In other words, human expertise remains human, whereas communion of imperfect persons in Christ reflects the inner life of God himself.

In this connection, my affection for my own father, an Episcopalian bishop, helped me to be at ease with bishops throughout the world, and I think this spontaneous trust was reciprocated. Quite unexpectedly, however, starting a few years after my arrival at Spencer, a serious problem arose that was perhaps due to my relations with several bishops. There was a growing rumor that I myself would be named bishop, or perhaps auxiliary bishop, of some neighboring diocese.

It is hard to trace the source of such gossip, but when several different persons mentioned it to me independently of one another I began to be worried. There will always be a need of capable, young bishops, but the reasons I was hearing seemed superficial, namely, the fact that my father had been a bishop and that I spoke Spanish at a time when there were very few Spanish-speaking bishops in the country.

My personal reaction was one of controlled fright, which I did my best to hide. I knew I lacked the important prerequisite of pastoral experience on the parish and diocesan level, since there is a world of difference between being the abbot of a monastic community and presiding over a diocese in 20th- and 21st-century America. An even stronger reason against such a possibility sprang from my intense, ongoing experience of a contemplative calling. This is the factor I mentioned to the only two persons whom I consulted on the subject: Dom Ambrose Southey, our abbot general, and Father John Eudes Bamberger, abbot of Genesee Abbey, near Rochester, New York. Dom Ambrose, with whom I spoke on the phone while he was in Rome, said that he would do what he could to block any such appointment, while

11. In his posthumous "Testament," in: B. Olivera, *How Far to Follow?*, CS 197 (Kalamazoo, Cistercian Publications, 1997) 127-129.

John Eudes urged me to trust in God, which fortunately I had learned to do.

The threat of an episcopal appointment hung over my head like the sword of Damocles for six or seven years and centered on two specific possibilities. The first one was that of being asked to be auxiliary bishop of Boston. I was told that Archbishop Pio Laghi, the papal pro-nuncio in Washington at the time, whom I had met when he had been nuncio in Argentina in the 1970s, had told someone that a Trappist abbot would soon be named bishop. A short time afterwards, at some function in Boston which I had been asked to attend, I found myself unexpectedly in the presence of both Cardinal Law and Archbishop Laghi. The Cardinal introduced me and then told the Nuncio, "I'll let you speak with him alone."

A strong feeling of discomfort rose up inside me, something similar to what I had experienced almost 40 years before when I was waiting to meet Sally Johnson outside the Northfield Auditorium. It was not personal, against either Cardinal Law or Archbishop Laghi, but rather against what my gut reaction read as a manipulation of my vocation.

"I am glad to meet you again, Archbishop," I said. "So am I," he replied. "How are you? Cardinal Law told me that you would be here." "Fine, thank you, but I'm really sorry. I have to leave. Good-bye." And I went straight out the door, got into my car and drove back to Spencer, embarrassed at what I had done to the Pope's representative, but not really sorry. Even from a purely human point of view, it was in harmony with my entire monastic life, although I had never thought of practicing so literally the ancient monastic saying, "Flee from women and from bishops!"

The Servant

In September 1990, only a few months after the incident with Archbishop Laghi, the Trappists held their general chapters in Rome, which happens every three years. The event brings together the abbots, abbesses and other superiors of the Order throughout the world, along with 20 or so regional delegates and members of the abbot general's council. It makes for a large group of 175 voting members, plus the 20 delegates and an equal number of secretaries, translators and staff. On important matters the abbots and abbesses vote separately, as would be the case on September 8th, when a new abbot general was going to be elected. Dom Ambrose had been the first English abbot general since the very first years of the Cistercian reform in the 12th century. He had been an exceptionally fine coordinator and animator of our monasteries during the 16 difficult years of trial, error and dialogue as we drew up our new Constitutions.

It was not at all clear who would or could replace Dom Ambrose. Various names were mentioned, among which were those of several European abbots, as well as that of Bernardo Olivera of Azul and my own. For over a year now, some people had been telling me that I would be elected, but I was not at all sure. There had never been a non-European abbot general and I knew that some persons were not ready to vote for anyone from the United States. Bernardo, however, was still young, in his 40s, and with only seven years of abbatial experience. On the other hand, a European monk might not be sufficiently sensitive to the special needs of the many growing communities in Africa, Asia and Latin America.

For my part, the situation at Spencer was crucial but difficult to discern. My recent reelection for a second term of six years as abbot had not been an easy one. There was only a small majority who voted for me, although no one else had come close to being elected. If I were elected as abbot general, who could take on the responsibility for unifying the community in its Cistercian calling? But if I were not elected and remained at Spencer, would I have any more success in uniting the community during the coming years than I had had until now? And I could at any moment be appointed bishop, thus leaving the community anyway. So my situation was obscure, with three possibilities opening up for me, none of which was particularly appealing:

- I could remain at Spencer as its abbot for another six years with a rather large minority passively objecting to my more classical monastic orientation.

- Or I could accept election as abbot general, which would be a liberation from the difficulties of Spencer but could be seen as leaving it with my mission only partially accomplished.
- Or I might be named a bishop, thus being plunged into a radically new situation that would require a radical change of attitude and lifestyle on my part, with very uncertain results at Spencer and in my own future ministry to the Church.

Of course, I offered these three possibilities to the Lord and asked him to do his will in all that was going to happen in the coming days, weeks and months, but it is not easy to function normally when you become aware that there is a tornado approaching your home. I was reminded of the opening scene in the movie, *The Mission*, which we had seen at Spencer, where a Jesuit missionary is tied to a wooden cross by the Indians he was trying to convert and cast into the river, where he floats downstream until he plunges, helplessly crucified, over the brink of the bottomless Iguazú cataracts. Yet I was at peace underneath the exterior events. Throughout my life I had avoided doing anything to push myself as a candidate for any position, instinctively following the advice of Saint Francis de Sales, "Ask for nothing special; refuse nothing that is offered."

The combined general chapters dedicated the final 18 hours before the election to prayer, asking for the light of the Holy Spirit. Several Spanish abbesses, hoping that Bernardo would be the first Spanish-speaking abbot general in the Order's history, managed to put an image of Our Lady of Guadalupe in the sanctuary of the chapel prior to the time of Adoration of the Blessed Sacrament. After Mass the next morning, the abbots and abbesses separated into different assembly halls to vote, with messengers carrying the results to the other group until, after several successive ballots, the two chapters, abbots and abbesses, agreed on the same person by separate majority votes. Bernardo was elected, although I received a considerable number of votes along with several others.

Before Bernardo was given a chance to accept or decline the election, while the abbots waited for the abbesses to join them for the occasion, I unexpectedly—even to myself—rose from my seat in the assembly hall, walked to where Bernardo was seated, embraced him in his chair, and whispered in Spanish, "Congratulations. We're all with you. Hope you'll accept," then walked back to my place.

As I was walking back, the abbots began to applaud, which was embarrassing, but I saw that the applause was basically for the gesture, as well as for Bernardo and me. A few seconds later, the abbesses walked in and began congratulating not only the new abbot general, but also me, probably because they knew we were from the same monastery and that I had been his novice master. Bernardo gave a short acceptance speech and I spent the next 48 hours describing verbally and in writing his life story and personality. Mother Martha Driscoll, the founding superior of the first Trappistine convent in Indonesia, was especially helpful to me at that time by her presence and encouragement, as she would be 19 years later in a somewhat analogous situation, a little like the younger sister I had never had, who intuits the needs of her slightly older brother.

As a result of the election, Bernardo's life underwent an abrupt change of style, mission and place of residence, while mine remained basically unaltered, with my future possibilities reduced to continuing as abbot at Spencer or being named bishop, both of them full of contradictions and probably doomed in the long run to failure. Yet I saw that I could do nothing about either of them, so that my task was to trust in God's loving and far-seeing wisdom, something I was still achieving only imperfectly.

As often happens to me, it was particularly during the celebration of the Eucharist that I became most sensitive to the existential situation in which I found myself, the human side and its divine interpretation. During two successive morning Eucharists soon after Bernardo's election—especially during the silent presentation of gifts before the consecration—I made an effort to offer myself to God along with his Beloved Son, but my mind and heart were full of gloomy foreboding about all that lay ahead. On the second such morning, while riding out the storm clouds by a type of silent adoration of God's darkness, I was suddenly filled, in fact overwhelmed, by the following very distinct words: *You are my servant.*

It was not exactly a voice, for the words *You are my servant* were not audible, but it was an overpowering message branded instantaneously into my consciousness as clearly as a clap of thunder. Perhaps even more than a message—since being God's servant was not a new concept for me—it was an intensely penetrating grace. Immediately, without any time lapse, there was a totally unprepared reply on my part that consisted of an inner movement of something below the heart, deep in my abdomen, that also expressed itself in words: "Lord, you know that I have never wanted anything else."

My first reaction to this remarkable inner dialogue should have been sheer gratitude for such a double gift of love, but gratitude was only my second reaction. The first one was almost a complaint: "This is typical of God. He consoles and enlightens, but still makes you live by faith, and does not say exactly what's going to happen in the future!" Then I realized how grateful I should be, what immense mercy the Lord had shown me, and almost at once I started silently and uncontrollably to weep.

The Mass continued and fortunately we, the many priest concelebrants, simply stayed at our places in the pews of the big church. At the embrace of peace before communion I turned to my neighbor and wished him the peace of the Lord as best I could. He was the young Irish abbot of Mount Melleray Abbey, County Cork, Eamon Fitzgerald, who would become Bernardo's successor as abbot general 18 years later.

I was awestruck at having been called by name by the Lord of Hosts, in fact by the same name that the Father used to point to his Only Son at Christ's Baptism and Transfiguration, but my tears were also, of course, the unleashing of much emotion suppressed during the previous days and weeks. As soon as Mass ended, I left the chapel by a side door, walked around outside in my alb and stole, and continued to sob without control for ten or fifteen minutes. As I recall my emotions at that moment, they constituted a bittersweet mixture of shock at God's mercy to me, of immense gratitude for these two gifts—my identity in his sight and my total acceptance of it—and of a renewed trust that the Lord of my life would strengthen me in whatever service would come my way on the road ahead. Slowly the sobbing subsided, I went inside, washed my face and walked into the large dining room late for breakfast. People were kind and did not pay any attention to me.

A few days later, Father Eamon met me as we crossed paths at a stair landing and said, "Augustine, how are you doing?"

It was obvious what he meant, so I had to give some explanation for my tears at Mass. But what could I say in 20 seconds? "Thanks. I'm fine. The election was hard for me. Many people had told me I would be elected." It was not untrue, just a miserable oversimplification.

18 years later, anticipating his own election as abbot general, I remarked to Eamon with a smile: "It was a big grace for me not to have been elected abbot general."

This time it was he who replied, "Thanks."

During the next few months I recounted the words I had received from the Lord to four different persons—to you, Eddie, as my confessor and spiritual companion, to the abbot general, to another abbot, and to an abbess—but to no one else until describing it here in detail. In fact, I hesitated before writing about it here, but any account of my life would be radically incomplete without it. The person involved in such an experience is not its best judge and the principal criteria for evaluating it will always be the fruits that have come from it.

At the same time, the message I received, and even the reply that sprang from underneath my heart, are not totally private. They are the Father's words to his Beloved Son, to all believers in Christ and, in a very real way, to all humanity, because "since Christ died for everyone, and since all are in fact called to one and the same destiny, which is divine, we must hold that the Holy Spirit offers to all the possibility . . . that, becoming sons and daughters in the Son, we may cry out in the Spirit: Abba, Father."[12] Through my poor, limited humanity it was all my brothers and sisters, from Iceland to the Fiji Islands, who

12. Vatican II, *Gaudium et Spes*, 22.

were responding to their divine vocation to love and serve their heavenly Father, crying out with me: "Lord, you know that I have never wanted anything else but to serve you in love."

With Bernardo's election as abbot general, the Trappist Order had made a remarkable leap of faith in its trust that this was the way God was leading us into the 21st century. It was a shared pilgrimage out of the North Atlantic countries into new territory, and a young, competent leader from these southern countries was, to the majority of the Order, a providential gift of divine wisdom. But it was not easy for everyone to see it this way, not even for some members of the two general chapters. To them the event seemed fraught with dangerous novelties, not the least of which was the unpredictable Spanish flair for thinking differently and acting passionately, a trait which I have learned not to fear but to value as a dynamic contribution to Western Civilization, to the spread of the Gospel and to the vitality of Christian spirituality.

One of the first trips that Bernardo made as abbot general was to the monasteries of the eastern United States, starting with Spencer. It was ostensibly to greet the brothers he had known during his few years there as a simply professed monk in formation, but it was also to support our ongoing work of community renewal. He would make two similar visits in the next few years, for all of which I am deeply grateful.

Africa

During these same years an unforeseen dimension began to open up in my life, a totally unexpected one. During a pastoral visit I had been asked to make to the flourishing community of Mont-des-Cats, in northern France, a young African monk from Kenya, Brother Charles Kawesi, who was finishing his theological studies at Mont-des-Cats, was ordained to the diaconate in the large abbey church. The Mass of ordination was presided over by Cardinal Francis Arinze of Nigeria, so that all the young African Trappists studying at our monasteries in Europe, perhaps a total of 8 or 10 of them, came together for the celebration. The words and style of Cardinal Arinze were solemn, dignified and to the point, as he usually is. Suddenly, during the silent pause for prayer and thanksgiving after Communion while I was seated in the sanctuary of the large church, I became aware of what sounded like a subway train passing underneath the floor of the church, similar to the underground rumble of an earthquake I once experienced in Chile. It kept increasing in volume during 10 or 15 seconds and I wondered how a subway could reach this far into the countryside.

Suddenly the rumbling thunder that was now filling the whole church turned into the spectacular, rhythmic duet of two deep African tom-toms, drumming triumphantly on either side of the church, celebrating the victory of the Risen Christ in one of the most powerful musical experiences I have ever shared in. I started to weep from emotion, as I seem increasingly to do in such circumstances.

At first I thought that these were tears of gratitude to God for the remarkable evangelization of Africa during the last one hundred years. That was one element, but further reflection told me that these drums represented something more, a level of being that goes deeper than the heart. It was the musical equivalent of my inner dialogue with the Lord only a short time before at the general chapter. There seems to be an inner center, a platform of human existence, that is sometimes pointed to by the word "guts," and more elegantly in Spanish as the *entrañas*, or in French, the *entrailles*,[13] where the most basic human emotions are rooted. They can be stubborn as an ox or valiant unto death, blindly cruel or tender as a mother's love. Here is the deepest ground of personal commitment to both inner integrity and transcendental reality, which often grow or wither together.

13. This inner dimension appears in the Hebrew Scriptures as "kidneys"; in the Latin Vulgate as *renes*, which is often equated with the heart; but my experience hints that they are different. In the New Testament the word appears twice (Lk 1:78 and Col 3:12) in the expression "bowels of mercy," usually rendered as something like "heartfelt compassion." It is interesting that modern Indonesian, which is strongly influenced by Arabic, a Semitic language like Hebrew, refers to the seat of love and mercy as the "liver" rather than the "heart."

These triumphant tom-toms at Mass were offering this inner sparkplug of human existence to the Lord of all life in the name of what we call the "Dark Continent." They were also giving a vibrant message to the drifting societies of Europe, Asia and America, while they expressed the immense gratitude of the entire Christian people to the thousands of missionaries—including our own monks and nuns—who have given their lives to the African Christ.

Such was my experience that morning at Mont-des-Cats. I described it to the men at Spencer when I returned home, but I did not realize at that time that a new door was opening up in my life. During the next fourteen years I would go to Africa on six different occasions to visit our monasteries in Uganda, Kenya, Benin, Nigeria, Cameroon, Democratic Republic of Congo and Madagascar. Even more significant is a process of cross-fertilization that began to occur between our houses on that continent and in South America. My visits were part of the process, but they have been followed by Bernardo's many trips there as abbot general, those of several local superiors going in both directions, and the even more intense communication between the only two Portuguese-speaking monasteries of Trappist monks in the world: Bela Vista in Angola and Novo Mundo in Brazil.

What Next?

The next few years at Spencer began a period of transition that was not entirely evident at first. Without making any precise plans about it, my experience at the general chapter had strengthened my sense of personal identity, of who I am before the Lord of my life. I am *his servant*, which in the Greek of the gospels (*paîs*) can also mean *child*, and my first responsibility is to serve my Master. All else is secondary, an attitude I found expressed to perfection in the words of Saint Augustine: "You owe your conscience to God. But to no one else do you owe anything more except that you love one another."[14] I realized that, in the name of

14. Saint Augustine, *Letter* 130,16.

what was probably a necessary pastoral prudence, to foster the unity of Spencer's splintered community, I had not shown my true self to my brothers enough. I had looked more at them than at the Lord. My first service as abbot was total service to the Lord.

I also began to realize that, in the name of pastoral prudence, I had been overly influenced by the strong emphasis on the human sciences—especially pastoral psychology, sociology and characterology—to the detriment of theological faith, hope and love. This relativizing of the divine dimension of all truly human activity, in the name of other human "needs," even in Trappist life, had been an inevitable danger in attempting to bring monastic spirituality, and Christian morality in general, into the post-conciliar world; but now it had to be newly subordinated to the Lord of all life. It all had to be more intensely re-evangelized, starting with myself.

So I felt an inner need to speak more freely in my chapter talks to the community, stressing the importance of the Church, her liturgy and her teaching office as the ordinary channels to us of God's grace and truth, and of ordinary monastic discipline as the necessary pathway—for us who are called to it—to healthy spiritual growth. There was no immediate reaction for or against this approach, perhaps because we were all thinking, "Let's wait and see what happens."

Two years after the general chapter of 1990, I made a month's retreat in the solitude of a house near our monastery at Snowmass, Colorado. It was a comfortable home belonging to a friend of the community who only used it during the summer months. The autumn colors of the deciduous trees on the slopes of the snow-capped Rocky Mountains made for a spectacular setting, and I could watch from my picture window as the deer and elk came warily into the open pasture for their last big meals before the winter snows. I knew what was in store for me during such a retreat, the third long one I had made in my life. The other ones, in 1977 and 1988, had been notoriously arid, though each retreat had been a moment of grace. My long hours of prayer here at Snowmass were no different. I tried as best I could to keep my mind from wandering, but there was very little sensible consolation involved.

Halfway through the retreat I celebrated my 60th birthday and, to celebrate the occasion, prepared for myself one of my favorite Chinese dishes, called in Shanghai *da tsaw va*, or in Mandarin *dan chau fan*, fried rice with chopped ham, raisins and peanuts, though for lack of ham I used canned tuna. Suddenly a car drove up, the door bell rang and Father Thomas Keating entered with a birthday cake, accompanied by Brother Paul Forster, plumber and water expert at Spencer, who was at Snowmass for a few weeks to help in his specialty. Thomas was now living permanently at Snowmass, deeply engaged in his outreach program of contemplative prayer for laypersons. Someone at Spencer had tipped him off about my birthday, so we were able to have a unique hour reminiscing about my novitiate almost 40 years before and discussing his plans for the extension of Christian contemplation in the world today.

During the final week of my retreat, it seemed natural to reflect on the meaning of my life and a little about my immediate future, asking the Holy Spirit to help me do this in whatever way he wanted to. As usual, there was no striking intuition as regards my future, since the repeated lessons to trust in God, keep at peace and embrace the normal signs of his will were beginning to take root in me, despite my desire to control everything.

I could see how God had used many successive external events in my life to steer me where he wanted me to go, each time giving me enough inner light and attractions of different kinds to help me follow the course of his wisdom. That seems the best way to explain how Bill's experience as a monk had triggered my Catholic faith and Trappist vocation, then how Spencer's foundation in Argentina had led to the unique experience of my 20 years there, and finally how the need for me to return to Spencer had—at one and the same time—brought me back to many of my roots and permitted Bernardo to become the first non-European abbot general in the eight centuries of Cistercian history.

But now what? Only the Lord knew. We were close to the halfway mark in my second six-year term as abbot of Spencer and another reelection might not be the best thing for the community, besides being difficult for me. The monks who wanted another type of leader, probably still only a large minority, would not change their opinion in the next few years, especially now that I felt more interiorly confident in expressing my own viewpoint. Their opposition continued despite the fact that the new abbot general, in the presence of the whole community, had just identified my approach with his own and with that of our newly approved Constitutions.

In other words, it seemed to me that the community, with all its fine human and spiritual qualities, was becoming and would increasingly become more divided, more polarized. Perhaps I was the problem myself, as some were saying, in which case a good discernment should be made before the next abbatial election. To make matters worse, however, it seemed as if the whole Catholic Church in the United States was becoming polarized in a similar way.

So, what to do? It seemed clear that God was asking me to give all I could to Spencer as long as I was abbot and to accept in faith whatever the outcome of the next election would be. If it should happen that I not be reelected, it seemed more in keeping with an attitude of service to stay on at Spencer in whatever capacity the new abbot would prefer, rather than to return to Azul, where they did not seem to need me.

This general stance, discerned during the second half of my retreat, continued to express my convictions on the subject although, as the time of the election approached, I decided that, in case I were not reelected at Spencer, I would submit my future—whether to remain at Spencer or return to Azul—to Bernardo's recommendation and do what he thought would be best. He knew me well, was aware of Spencer's situation and knew Azul's needs better than I did.

More positively, I saw that I should give more attention to preparing one or two men at Spencer as my possible successors in the abbatial service, either in the next few years or later. At that moment, there was no one person clearly in the running, but I had already seen that the best preparation for being an abbot is, first, a sincere life of prayer in the context of a normal monastic life, and secondly, several years of experience on the pastoral and financial councils of the community.

Such was my frame of mind as my retreat drew to an end and I returned to Spencer grateful for what had been given to me. As soon as I had settled in again, I learned that Timothy Harrington was resigning as our bishop and I was being mentioned as a possible successor. In fact, my name even appeared in the Worcester daily newspaper as one of the leading possibilities. This time my Spanish was not referred to, but rather the fact that I was "conservative and a good administrator."

In those very days I received an official letter from the papal pronuncio in Washington, who was now Archbishop, later Cardinal, Agostino Cacciavillan, asking for my opinion about who would be a good bishop for the Worcester diocese. I replied suggesting a few names—none of whom was chosen—and added that I would not at all recommend myself, even though my father had been an Episcopalian bishop, because I had never had the normal experience of life in a Catholic parish. I pointed out that the experience of being a Trappist abbot is not an adequate preparation for becoming a diocesan bishop. After another short wait, it was announced that our next bishop would be the Bishop of Norwich, Connecticut, Daniel Reilly. I breathed a sigh of relief with a renewed trust that I would not be thought of again in this connection. In fact, something else was going to happen, which I'll explain in another letter.

Letter 8

VIALE AFRICA

1996–2002

Dear Eddie,

One by-product of my retreat at Snowmass at the end of 1992 was to discuss more frequently with you my concrete situation at Spencer, especially since you lived at a discreet distance from the abbey in your hermitage at the edge of the woods. You probably remember that, early in 1996, I was away at the abbey of Our Lady of the Prairies, outside Winnipeg in Manitoba, Canada, where I had been asked to make the pastoral visitation.

Our Lady of the Prairies is the northernmost monastery in the Americas and the weather was bitterly cold in February, with the arctic wind continually blowing in from the north over the snow-covered farmland. Halfway through the visit Abbot Marcel handed me a fax in Spanish that had just arrived from the abbot general, Bernardo, who was in Rome at that moment:

> Dear Augustine, I have a request to make. There is an emergency at Aiguebelle and André Barbeau, my personal secretary, is the best person to become its new superior. This means that I must find a new secretary. As I was praying for light on whom to ask, the first name that came to me was yours. Would you accept becoming my secretary after your term of office at Spencer expires in June? I suggest that you tell the community at Spencer that you will not accept another re-election as their abbot, because my impression is that you will not be re-elected. Please let me know as soon as possible about your decision on this because, if you do not feel that you should do this, I will look for another secretary.

What to Do?

My absence from Spencer at that precise moment was providential, because I could reflect and pray about the situation with a greater degree of detachment. Of course, I mentioned nothing about the contents of this fax to Father Marcel, who very discreetly did not ask. I simply said that Bernardo wanted my advice on a problem he faces, then I continued speaking with the members of the Prairies community. But what was God telling me? What should I do?

I replied by fax the next day, telling Bernardo that I would need two or three weeks to reflect on his proposal and its consequences for me and for my community, that I was not closed to what he was suggesting—especially since it came from the abbot general—but that I should first consult Spencer's new father immediate, Etienne Baudrey, in France, and Thomas Davis, the abbot of our monastery in California, who was Father Etienne's chief American adviser and knew Spencer well. I added that I was hesitant to put the community of Spencer into a "lame duck" situation, in which the abbot, though still in office, is known to have only a few weeks or months remaining and the community is thrown into a confusing period of speculation and uncertainty.

A few days after replying this way to Bernardo, I decided to consult you as well, as my confessor living at Spencer with firsthand knowledge of the feelings of the community. So I immediately started to prepare a long memorandum in English for Etienne, Thomas and you, containing the English translations of Bernardo's request and of my reply to it, then asking your advice as to what my decision should be concerning this request to become the abbot general's secretary. I was able to send this out to the three of you before leaving Prairies.

Within ten days after my return to Spencer, I had received interesting replies from all of you. Etienne and Thomas both agreed with my hesitancy to anticipate the result of the election to be held in four months. They advised me to wait until after the election, whereas you immediately encouraged me to do as Bernardo had recommended and tell the community that I would not accept another reelection. These two different opinions actually reflected my own inner ambivalence about the options I had. My feelings tended to jump at Bernardo's invitation to join him in Rome at the service of all the communities of the Order, but my head—and my sense of duty to the pastoral charge I had accepted as abbot—told me that I should not anticipate the considered judgment of the community, which would only be made at the time of the election. Spencer had never experienced a normal, peaceful transition from one abbot to the next. I, its fourth abbot, should not continue this dysfunctional tradition and therefore I should finish my term of office as peacefully and as normally as possible.

Since the two abbots whom I had consulted agreed with this latter procedure, which I myself saw as the more pastorally prudent way of acting, I wrote Bernardo again to tell him that this was my decision. I have always felt that your different opinion was motivated by two factors: your basic agreement with Bernardo's judgment—which proved to be correct—that I would not be reelected, and your sympathy for me, which advised my taking advantage of this offer to help Bernardo and not prolong the agony of my last months as abbot of Spencer. Perhaps you also saw—I think correctly—that my personal gifts and experience lend themselves more to international, multilingual work at the service of a plurality of houses, than to acting as abbot in one particular community. I guess that, from force of circumstances, I had become something of a global monk.

In any case, in my letter to Bernardo I assured him that I was grateful for his invitation and, if I were not reelected, I would be happy to become his secretary, but that I understood perfectly if he wanted to keep looking for someone else who was more immediately available than I was. Bernardo replied to thank me and to say that he would wait for our election, even though it might be difficult to find another man in the three months between our June election and the September general chapter. From then on, without telling anyone else in the community about Bernardo's desire, I began suggesting personally and even in public that the community think of other men besides myself.

It is always delicate, even dangerous, for an abbot to anticipate in any way the outcome of an election in his own community.

Anything he says may be taken as campaigning for himself or for this or that other possible successor, who thus becomes known as "the abbot's man," usually in a detrimental way. Fortunately, there was no single person at Spencer who came easily to mind as my best or most likely successor, so the argument I used—which was objectively true—was that I, at 63, was already older than any of the community's previous abbots had been at the moment of their resignation and, besides, my short-term memory was beginning to falter, especially when recalling names or less important events. The brothers appreciated my frankness on this subject, although some replied that they hoped the abbot would forget many more items stored up in his memory.

Still without revealing the abbot general's suggestion, I talked seriously about our forthcoming election with my pastoral council, whose members I trusted and who represented a good cross section of the community. We all agreed that I should do what I could to avoid a meager majority of, say, 51% of the votes, even though the other 49% might be divided among three or four runners-up. When I mentioned this shared desire to a good friend of the community, Father Richard Lamoureux, who later became superior general of the Assumptionist Fathers, he suggested getting the help of a prudent Jesuit moderator from nearby Holy Cross College, in Worcester, Father Thomas Hamel. The pastoral council accepted this suggestion and Father Hamel agreed to come once a week during a month or two, to lead the community in a discernment process.

The peaceful, discreet direction of Father Hamel effectively channeled the latent politicking that can take place even in the best monastic communities before an important abbatial election. As the weeks passed, the field of possible choices became clearer and basically narrowed to three men: me and two younger possibilities, both members of the abbot's council, Father Dominic Whedbee, a former Dominican from their Western Province, and Father Damian Carr, the community's prior.

It was at this moment, at the end of May, that a major event shook the entire Catholic world, but especially the Trappist Order: the violent death of seven French monks held as hostages by one of the Moslem terrorist groups in Algeria, the G.I.A. (*Groupe Islamique Armé*). At first it was announced that they had had their throats cut and were beheaded as enemies of Islam, even though they had been pioneers of peaceful coexistence and dialogue with their many Moslem friends and neighbors. In later years, however, it has become clear that such an interpretation was very probably a politically motivated camouflage for their accidental death in an air attack by the Algerian Air Force against the guerilla band that held them captive. If this latter scenario is the true one, their lifeless bodies were just beheaded, then disposed of separately as part of the cover-up, while the seven heads were found in a bag left on the side of a country road.

The key element in the death of these seven brothers, however, was not its military or political implications, nor the details of their passing away, but their stirring witness of interreligious dialogue, monastic stability and Christian love unto death. It was a triumph of love over hatred and fear, especially since each one of them had foreseen the possibility of his death and had embraced it in anticipation, though sometimes with a certain trepidation. The posthumous *Testament* of the community's superior, Father Christian de Chergé, whom I had met briefly at the last two general chapters, is already a classic of contemporary religious literature, especially because of Christian's joyful anticipation of heaven and gratitude for his life given to the Moslem people he loved:

> This is what I shall be able to do, please God:
> immerse my gaze in that of the Father
> and contemplate with him His children of Islam
> just as he sees them, all shining with the glory of Christ,
> the fruit of His Passion, filled with the Gift of the Spirit
> whose secret joy will always be to establish communion
> and restore the likeness, playing with the differences.
> For this life lost, totally mine and totally theirs,
> I thank God, who seems to have willed it entirely
> for the sake of that JOY in everything
> and in spite of everything.
> In this THANK YOU, which is said
> for everything in my life from now on,

I certainly include you, friends of yesterday and today,
and you, my friends of this place,
along with my mother and father,
  my sisters and brothers and their families.
You are the hundredfold granted as was promised!
And it also includes you, my last-minute friend,
  who will not have known what you were doing:
Yes, I want this THANK YOU and this "A-DIEU"
  to be for you, too,
because in God's face I see yours.
May we meet again as happy thieves
in Paradise, if it please God, the Father of us both.
AMEN![1]

In the few days following the announcement of their death and the publication of Father Christian's *Testament*, several friends of the community, with whom I happened to meet, expressed their sincere grief for the monks' assassination, but also voiced their hope that their kidnappers would be punished as they deserved. But these well-intentioned friends had entirely missed Father Christian's message and the whole purpose of the brothers' death. It was clear that these seven men from very different backgrounds and personal histories had given their lives together precisely for the reconciliation of Moslems and Christians, for their unity in love, the fruit of Christ's Passion. How can we think of punishing someone for such a death? May we all meet them, together with those who killed them and beheaded them, as happy thieves in Paradise!

Our Spencer community was still under the inspiring mantle of our seven brothers' self-offering when we had a final meeting two days before our abbatial election. It was held in the presence of our father immediate, Etienne Baudrey, and of Father Thomas Davis, both of them accompanying us for a few days prior to the election. Following the procedure outlined by Father Hamel, we took a final straw vote, knowing that the three major possibilities

1. Full text in B. Olivera, *How Far to Follow?* CS 197 (Kalamazoo, Cistercian Publications, 1997) 127-129.

were Damian, Dominic and I. Out of the 60 or so voters, the result was something like 23 for Damian, 14 for Dominic and 20 for me, with the rest going to other men.

Although the other two abbots seemed to think that the votes for Dominic would swing towards me, I was sure that many, if not most, of them would shift to Damian. So the following day I asked Damian to come to my room, where we could talk at leisure. We had an excellent conversation for almost two hours, in which I explained everything to him, told him that I thought he would be elected—as indeed he was by a comfortable majority—and described to him the chief problems he would be facing as a new abbot, both at Spencer and in our daughter houses. He thanked me for my confidence in him, which was sincere, since I saw that he was not only popular with many in the community but also prudent and, above all, a man of prayer. Then we both waited to see what would happen. I think that I slept better that night than either Damian or our two visiting abbots.

Scourmont

The election the next day was a moment of grace for the community, for Damian and also for me. My future was not clear, but I was happy to have done what I could, and with seeming success, to implement a smooth transition to a younger generation of men at Spencer. As I told the visiting abbots, the members of the community who preferred to have someone other than me are happy and will probably live more peacefully because of the change, while those who voted for me are strong in their faith and will sincerely collaborate with the new representative of Christ in their midst. In fact, I have seldom received so many compliments and signs of gratitude as I did on that day!

That afternoon Bernardo phoned me personally from Rome to renew his request that I be his personal secretary for at least three years, starting at the end of the general chapter in September. Everything had fallen into place and I had no difficulty in accepting the invitation, especially since, when I had mentioned it to my new abbot, he had no objection. Bernardo and I agreed that I would look for a place in France which offered an intensive course in spoken and written French.

Within 36 hours, however, I received another phone call, this time from a good friend of mine, Father André Louf, the well-known abbot of Mont-des-Cats in northern France. He had received word of Spencer's election and wanted to know if I would be willing to become the appointed superior of the Abbey of Scourmont, in southern Belgium, of which André was the acting father immediate. Scourmont's abbot had resigned and was leaving the Order. The small surviving community was old and still fervent, but demoralized and with no one among its members who could assume the service of abbot. In fact, the departing abbot had himself come from another Belgian monastery.

I explained to Father André that I was already committed to becoming the secretary of the abbot general after the general chapter, so that I could not accept his request. Besides, I had already promised to take an intensive course in French during these ten weeks before the general chapter. André was somewhat taken aback but told me that I could be immersed in French at Scourmont itself, which is French-speaking. I replied that I would phone Bernardo to see if he agreed to my doing this until early September, at which time I would leave Scourmont and move to Rome.

Bernardo was hesitant, sensing André's desire that I stay at Scourmont and become its permanent abbot, but I assured Bernardo that I had no desire to do this and would turn down any such proposal. He had been good to wait for Spencer's election, and I would keep my commitment to him. In the back of my mind, it was not so much the thought of studying French which attracted me to Scourmont but the plight of this community clearly in need of help from someone with a certain degree of experience as abbot. This was combined with my ongoing gratitude to Anselme Le Bail, the former abbot of Scourmont, whose commentary on the Rule of Saint Benedict had been so meaningful to me during my novitiate years.

So, after a short retreat and a simple farewell supper with the community at Spencer, I flew to Belgium, arriving at Scourmont during the first days of July 1996. Father André introduced me to the brothers as their new superior, briefed me about the dynamics of the community and accompanied me in meeting the small financial commission (all of whose members were outside friends of the community) that was supervising its extremely prosperous economy based on the production, bottling and marketing of three high-class beers. The trade-name of these beers is *Chimay*, the small town close to Scourmont in which the single bottling plant is located.

The following two months were strange ones for all of us concerned with the future of this rich but struggling community. My heart went out to each of the 15 or so brothers, so loyal to their monastery and faithful to their religious duties, yet terribly alone in their daily life. It took me these entire eight weeks to uncover what had gone wrong, and why. Although my personal conversations and talks to the community were all in French, I spent little time studying it, since I needed to become at least superficially acquainted with the brothers, their daily life and their tightly organized financial administration. This last element was under the supervision not only of the small financial commission but also of a team of full-time professional bookkeepers. I would speak once a week with the coordinator of this group, and twice a week with the secretary, a dedicated laywoman, who was responsible, under the superior, for the distribution of the community's generous alms.

From what these persons and a few of the members of the community told me, I became increasingly convinced that there had been serious financial mismanagement during the final years of the recently resigned abbot's tenure in office. The money siphoned from the beer income into his personal bank accounts—and then into foreign banks—had been enough to let him establish a capital fund, which could support him for the rest of his life. There was even a plan to place almost all the monastery's financial holdings under the control of persons outside the community. Obviously, I demurred from giving my approval to such a financial restructuring, asked for more time to study the matter and submitted the whole situation to the abbot general, who in turn referred it to the highest authority in the Trappist Order, the general chapter and its pastoral commission.

On a broader level, I came to the conclusion that Scourmont's difficulties stemmed paradoxically from its golden age under Anselme Le Bail, its abbot for over 42 most difficult years, from 1913 to 1956. This man, a true pastor of souls and deeply committed to Cistercian monasticism, had formed—during the years between the two world wars—an outstanding group of humble monks, from whom he chose a dozen or so for higher studies and prepared them as brilliant leaders of the intellectual renewal of the entire Trappist Order.

He and they fulfilled this mission splendidly, but at a price, namely a lack of fraternal give and take. My impression was that Abbot Anselme's strong sense of spiritual fatherhood, combined with the more "monarchical" approach to Church authority at that time, had not seen the importance of the more communal dimension of Trappist life, thus keeping this otherwise remarkable group of men from fully entering into the renewal process after the Second Vatican Council until it was almost too late.

At the end of my final Sunday chapter talk, I told the now small community that I was sincerely sorry that I had to leave for my new work in Rome, but I was sure they would receive a new superior who would be better—and certainly more fluent in French—than I was. The subject of my talk had been the need to love each other as brothers, which they were, and that this would give them strength in the coming months and years. After my talk, just before I left for Rome, one of the younger members told me that it must have been the very first time that these men had heard any form of encouragement to love one another.

Within a few weeks, thanks to the action of the general chapter, the former abbot general, Ambrose Southey, was appointed as temporary superior of Scourmont. Apprised of the situation, he was able to sort out the intricacies of the community's financial management, restore order, begin to establish a healthy formation program for the few postulants who were presenting themselves, and prepare the community to elect a new abbot.

Roman Secretary

My two intense months at Scourmont had been an introduction to the European scene at the end of the 20th century. I was impressed by, and attracted to, the intelligent energy of the Belgian people. The sometimes difficult interaction between the French-speaking Walloons of southern Belgium, where Scourmont is located, and the Flemish North, reminded me of Canada, with its division between French-speaking Quebec and the English-speaking provinces, and also of the United States and Argentina, with their ongoing integration of a plurality of languages and cultural groups. There seems to be an energetic expansion of outlook that results from such a process. It can be aggressive, even chaotic, at times, but experience shows that it is more healthy, more broad-minded and "catholic," though more challenging, than the overwhelming predominance of one particular culture, a situation which, in any case, is increasingly archaic in the world of the 21st century.

At the same time, I realized that the importance and subtleties of Scourmont's financial organization required an abbot who was fluent enough in French to enter with ease into such a world. It was clear to me that at the age of 64 I would not be able to do that, whereas I would be able to contribute something in the line of what Bernardo was asking me to do, as his personal secretary. So it was with a peaceful conscience, though with a real concern for the situation of Scourmont's once flourishing community, that I arrived at our Roman generalate in mid-September 1996.

One of my first acts in Rome was to ask Bernardo's advice concerning a difficult choice I had to make. Should I remain a monk of Spencer, my original community though I no longer lived there, or should I revert to the community of Azul, which I had helped to establish and from where I had been taken to become Spencer's abbot? I had decided to follow the advice of Bernardo, who was now my abbot general and who knows me, Spencer and Azul very well, but personally I was inclined to remain a monk of Spencer for two reasons: to be faithful to that community despite the fact that I was no longer its abbot, and because, as I expressed it to Bernardo, "the last thing Azul needs at the present moment is the presence of another North American."

Bernardo disagreed with my reasons: "Azul needs you and does not think of you as a North American but as an Argentine. They elected you and reelected you twice as their superior, whereas Spencer has just chosen someone else as abbot instead of you."

I could see the logic of his arguments and in a way I felt relieved. My thought of remaining a monk of Spencer had been more out of a sense of duty, since my inner feelings had always been more in tune with the life of the Azul community. When I next met Azul's abbot, Eduardo, just before the general chapter, I renewed in his hands my vow of stability to that monastery.

"Generalate" does not appear in most English dictionaries. For English-speaking Trappists, however, it denotes what in Italian is the *Casa Generalizia*, or in French the *Maison Générale*, that is, the building in Rome used as the home base of the abbot general and the place where his permanent council and the central secretariat of the Order are located. It is presently situated on a quiet, residential side street, Viale Africa, in the same section of Rome, the EUR, where I had lived as a theology student 36 years before. In those intervening years, the number of students in residence had dropped from over 70 in 1960 to less than half a dozen, so that it was no longer chiefly a house of studies, but rather the coordinating center of the 170 Trappist monasteries spread over the five continents. During the six years in which I was at the generalate, there were usually five or six students present, chiefly from our African houses. The more permanent staff of the house was made up of between 10 and 12 members of the Order serving in different administrative or secretarial positions, making a total of 15 to 20, of whom four or five were nuns living on their separate floor.

Almost immediately after the general chapter concluded, Bernardo participated as an official observer at the special Synod of Bishops for the Church in the Americas. Each morning for almost a month I would drive him to the Vatican, park the car nearby, take the long walk and subway ride to the Piazza Bologna and the Dante Alighieri Italian School for classes in written and spoken Italian, then back to the Vatican in time to pick up Bernardo and return to Viale Africa for a late dinner. It was a crash course in Italian, but also in modern Roman traffic and commuting, as well as a superficial introduction to the special world of Vatican protocol, with which I would later become more familiar.

Since the Abbot general spends about a third of his time in Rome, living at the generalate, and two-thirds of it visiting the 170 communities of the Order, little of my secretarial work was done in Italian but rather spread more or less evenly among Spanish, French and English. The fact that Bernardo and I conversed in Spanish meant that a great deal of my work was translating his Spanish thought into written French or English, and occasionally Italian, at a rate of about seven or eight letters a day. For more important letters and documents, I would submit my efforts in French to one of the two French counselors, either Father Loÿs Samson, retired abbot of Cîteaux, or Mother Danièle Levrard, retired abbess of Les Gardes. Little by little I learned some of the correct phrases involved in normal French and Italian correspondence.

Another important part of my work was to take the steps needed to put Bernardo's travel plans into execution, contacting the houses he would decide to visit, programming the timetables and purchasing the tickets through a good local travel agent, Andrea Tatarelli, with whom I became very familiar. I began by speaking with him in French, but in my second year was able to shift to Italian. Once every six months or so, Bernardo would decide where he would be going in the near future, then would leave the details in my hands. At the same time, he was teaching me how to use e-mail and the Internet, something I had refrained from doing until then, despite the introduction of personal computers over ten years before. When I had left Spencer, the monastery's businesses were only just beginning to use the Internet and no monk had a personal mailbox. However, "time and tide wait for no man," and I soon sent out my first e-mails in the name of the abbot general through our dial-up connection, since broadband was still several years away. Two years later, I would redesign and administer the Order's website.

Traveling with Bernardo

Soon after the conclusion of the Bishops' Synod on the Church in the Americas, Bernardo and I made our first international trip together. It was to the Far East: Japan, where there are seven Trappist monasteries, and South Korea, where there is a single house of nuns. The present trip was chiefly to visit Tobetsu, usually called "Phare," Our Lady of the Lighthouse, on the northern island of Hokkaido, which was celebrating its first 100 years of existence, and the abbot general had been especially invited to be on hand. Until then, I was not aware that I had actually met, almost 50 years before in Shanghai, the first abbot of that monastery, Benoît Morvan, who had visited my parents' home as I mentioned in the first letter.

Our journey to the Far East was going to conclude with a long trip to our two monasteries on the island of Java, in Indonesia, but while we were at Sujong, our flourishing community of nuns in South Korea, word arrived by telephone that the Civil War in the Democratic Republic of the Congo, in central Africa, had reached our two monasteries of the eastern part of that country, La Clarté-Dieu and Mokoto. To make matters worse, their respective superiors had not been able to return to their communities after assisting at the general chapter six weeks before. They were stranded in other countries of Africa. After consulting the French counselor, Father Loÿs, in Rome, Bernardo decided to return at once to Rome, since the situation of both these African monasteries was desperate and could easily become tragic. This meant my contacting Indonesia, changing our plane reservations for the very next day, then going back to Rome, 3000 miles east, rather than 1500 miles south. Modern communication is remarkable in these circumstances and, with the Korean sisters' help, all was able to be arranged. Within 36 hours we were back at Viale, Africa.

Our forced return to Rome gave both the abbot general and his secretary an extra two weeks in which to catch up on letters and more common administrative tasks, and to have a peaceful Christmas in the simplicity of the Generalate's modest liturgical celebrations, which I appreciated from the very beginning. I quickly discovered that, whereas Bernardo was intensely active during his trips to the different monasteries, spending his days in continual dialogues and his early morning hours preparing for the talks and meetings of the next day, I had more time on my hands, precisely because the abbot general was not giving me work to do. But as soon as we would return to Rome, everything changed for both of us. He could relax, read his accumulated correspondence and either answer it himself, perhaps by e-mail, especially if it were in Spanish, or pass it on to me with some indication of how to reply.

The result was that my work intensified considerably once I returned to Rome, since I also had to start preparing everything for our next long trip. I soon found myself using the time we were traveling to write the chronicle of our visits to the houses we had seen on our previous trip, first in English, then translating them into Spanish and giving either the English or the Spanish version to someone who could make the French translation. Bernardo was careful to control them, since he realized that they would be publicly read in our communities and represented a meaningful bond of unity and information between him and the monasteries, and among all the houses themselves. He usually accepted what I wrote without too much comment.

Two months after our return from Korea we started a long six-week journey through France, Brazil, Mexico, the USA, Canada and back to Italy, visiting a total of nine communities. Then we spent Holy Week and Easter Week in Rome, followed by another six-week pilgrimage beginning in France and ending with our two communities in Madagascar, visiting three African houses on the way. Certainly the most touching moment of the trip was at its beginning, at the French monastery of Bellefontaine, where we celebrated the first anniversary of the violent death of the seven brothers of Tibhirine, in Algeria. The reason for doing so at Bellefontaine was not so much because three of the brothers had made their novitiate there, but rather because it was in central France and of relatively easy access for as many of the seven brothers' family members who could come. About 20 did, along with the Archbishop of Algiers, Monsignor Tessier, who dialogued at length with the group about the present situation of the monastery, his delicate mission in such a turbulent Moslem country, and what the future might hold. The center of attention, however, was the presence of two mothers, those of Christian de Chergé and Christophe Lebreton, the assassinated superior and novice master, respectively. The relationship between these two young men, one the son of a French army general, the other a young student in the 1968 cultural uprising, is part of the drama of their small Algerian community. The two mothers were clearly proud of their martyred sons, but sober and still subdued from the shock of their violent death. They would hold hands as they listened to the archbishop.

After returning from Madagascar, we had only ten days in Rome before a long trip north, this time in the abbot general's car, to visit a total of eight monasteries in Italy, France, Belgium and Holland, then a month away in central Spain, followed immediately by an intercontinental voyage to our five monasteries in the South Pacific: Philippines, New Caledonia, Australia and New Zealand. Reflecting back on those nine intense months of 1997, from January through September, with their five long trips and a much deeper acquaintance with the 34 houses we visited on five continents and 17 countries, I can only say that the whole experience was a gift from God. Each community and each member of the Order I met was and is a unique gift from the heart of Christ to the world and to the Church. This is not the place to go into any more detail, but simply to paraphrase the Books of Kings by saying that "the rest of the deeds of the abbot general and his secretary are written in the chronicles of the general's secretary."[2]

The same could be said of the first nine months of 1998, during which we stayed with 35 other communities in France, Spain, Belgium, England, Canada, Israel, China, Taiwan, Japan and Indonesia. Fortunately, Bernardo's and my health held up relatively well during these whirlwind months, which involved crossing over the Alps four times by car and the memorable celebration,

2. See 1 Kings 15:31; 16:20; 2 Kings 15:26,31.

with 700 monks and nuns present on March 21 at Cîteaux, of the 900th Anniversary of the foundation of this, the first Cistercian monastery. These months also included my first visit to China—Hong Kong—after leaving Shanghai 49 years before and, above all, a ten-day, once-in-a-lifetime visit to the Holy Land. I remain very grateful to God, and to Bernardo, his instrument in this regard, for granting me these deeply enriching experiences, which I tried to share as best I could with all the other monks and nuns of the Order.

Procurator General

I first heard rumors of a possible change in my situation during the meeting of the Central Commission in Israel, at our monastery of Latroun, halfway between Jerusalem and Tel Aviv. We were near the end of this meeting of some 30 representatives of the different parts of the Order, who come together between general chapters to prepare for the following one and review the needs of our 160 houses scattered over the five continents. I was an invited guest, since I was present only as the abbot general's secretary, but the fact of being a former abbot and member of this Commission made the members kind enough to think of inviting me to assist at their discussions.

Scourmont's unstable situation, with its prolonged need of an appointed superior, inevitably came up for discussion. No real solution was offered in the public discussions, but it was during that meeting that I first became aware that Father Armand Veilleux, the Canadian procurator general of the Order and acting superior of the Generalate in Rome, might resign his position in Rome and assume that important, delicate and challenging responsibility. In any case, nothing was clearly said to me at the time, but I felt something was in the air. When I returned to Rome, it became clear that such a change was going to take place and that Bernardo and his advisors were thinking of me to replace Armand on the abbot general's council. It became official when Bernardo informed me of Armand's decision and asked if I would be willing to fulfill his services, not only as a member of the council but also as procurator general. Father Loÿs of Cîteaux would be the superior of the house.

I had no difficulty in accepting such a request, since I could see that it was the simplest of several other possibilities, and I was glad to serve our houses in any way I could. The fact that I had recently visited so many far-flung communities and could speak the three major languages of the Order was clearly the chief reason for thinking of me, and it also made me feel more at ease in this new service. By November of that year, 1998, the change was made. Armand, who had helped to break me in as a member of the generalate, now explained what it means to be procurator general, something which I had never given much thought to before, being under the impression that it principally involved managing business and secretarial affairs.

By the time Armand took me to the offices of the Vatican's Congregation for Institutes of Consecrated Life and Societies of Apostolic Life, CIVCSVA for short, near Saint Peter's Square, and introduced me to its subsecretary, Father Jesús Torres, I could see that my new occupation would be both more important and more complex than what I had thought. "Procurator" is a title borrowed from the Roman Empire for someone entrusted with financial and administrative affairs as agent of a higher authority: Pontius Pilate was procurator of Judea! Our procurator general is a kind of general secretary of the Trappist Order and its official representative in the ordinary, routine relations of the Order with the Holy See. For anything really important, such as audiences with the pope or with cardinals, or if a monk of the Order is chosen as bishop, which happens perhaps once every 20 years, the abbot general acts in person, but when the abbot general is away on trips the procurator general takes his place at the Vatican.

During most of the following year, therefore, my life was spent at the generalate, either at my desk in the procurator's office or in meetings of the abbot general's council. I was, above all, a channel of communication for the specific needs of any Trappist superior, monk or nun, who was looking for administrative advice, information, permission or simply sharing, and who could not or did not wish to satisfy this need with local resources or the abbot general. With telephone and e-mail, this is easy to do today, so that the life of the procurator can be extremely busy, since he does not have a personal secretary. In a special, almost exclusive way, it involves receiving the official requests from local superiors for special permissions or dispensations corresponding to the particular pastoral problems they are facing.

The most common example of such situations is a request for what is called an "indult of exclaustration," that is, permission for a monk or nun to live outside any monastery for an extended period of time, perhaps two or three years. Other such permissions can be for the election of a superior with less than seven years of final profession, for appointing an apostolic administrator, or for selling property or buildings of more than ordinary value. For the Order as a whole, any major change in its legislation requires repeated visits to the Congregation for Institutes of Consecrated Life. Phone calls could arrive, however, at any time of the day or night about almost any subject, such as a lost or stolen passport, something important that has happened to some member of the Order, misunderstandings between communities or regional conferences, where the abbot general will be next month, or whether a specific situation needs a special permission or not.

Requests for information were usually easy to handle, but any type of permission from the Vatican meant discussing the situation at a meeting of the abbot general's council and then preparing a formal petition in writing to the Congregation. When this document was ready, I would take it personally to the Congregation, then wait about two weeks for it to be processed and the request to be granted, as usually happens when the reasons are well presented. Occasionally there is a refusal or more information is required, which must then be prepared and submitted.

By far the most difficult and disagreeable situations that arose during those years were those involving two different superiors of the Order—one soon after the other, but on opposite sides of the world—who refused to resign from their abbatial service. Both cases involved complex interventions of the Holy See in close collaboration with our Generalate, and Bernardo himself had to visit these communities more than once, since it gradually became clear that the two superiors were receiving poor advice from within the Order. In the more difficult case, the deposed superior made a final appeal to the *Signatura Apostolica*, the highest canonical authority in the Church, a kind of ecclesiastical supreme court that submitted the case to a minute examination in defense of the different parties involved, eventually deciding that the enforced resignation had been the correct decision. I made repeated trips to the Vatican about each of these two affairs, which provided me with the opportunity to see the more intimate workings of what often seems to be a mysterious, somewhat useless bureaucracy.

The fact is that the Vatican is constantly forced to deal with complex, sometimes strictly confidential situations, affecting not only members of the Catholic Church, but also many other persons in the religious, social and political spheres of the world today. To handle such affairs adequately, the successive bishops of Rome, the popes, have developed over the centuries a system of interrelated departments—congregations, secretariats and commissions—whose task is to investigate and promote "the truth in love, so that we grow up in every way into him who is the head, into Christ."[3]

It can and has been argued that an organization based on the Gospel and trying to promote the spiritual teachings of Christ should not have such a complex conglomerate of man-made institutions and structures. Many Catholics, even popes, have asked themselves similar questions and recent centuries have seen successive restructurings of the Roman Curia. But it is more important and profitable to ask the more general question, "How can all Christians implement, in the increasingly complex world of today and tomorrow, in a unified way and on a worldwide basis, 'the mystery of (God's) will, according to his good pleasure that he set forth in Christ, as a plan for the fullness of time, to gather up all things in him, things in heaven and things on earth'[4]?" This reordering and reorganization of all creation under the headship

3. Eph 4:15.
4. Eph 1:10.

of Christ cannot be just invisible, because it is human, and therefore sociologically verifiable and necessarily structured in some unified way according to its many functions.

My experience of the Roman Curia and its seeming complexity was a favorable one. Several sociological studies of multinational organizations have recently pointed out that the Catholic Church—it would be more exact to say the "Vatican" or the "Holy See"—is one of the most efficient and best run groups of its kind. My contacts there were not usually with the highest authorities, the archbishops and cardinals, but with those called "subsecretaries," since each group has a major secretary, who is usually an archbishop. I found these subsecretaries—there is now a growing number of women in such positions—to be dedicated, hardworking, intelligent and pastorally sensitive persons. Most of them realize that they will not become bishops, nor do they aspire to such titles. They have chosen to serve and they spend their days and nights doing so, in contact with the large and small problems of the Church and the world on all five continents, far beyond and deeper than anything published in newspapers or magazines.

I described, above, the two most disagreeable experiences I had in this regard, of two superiors who refused to resign their abbatial service. In each of these two cases and in every other one I had to deal with, I found that there is a great deal of respect in the Holy See for the rights and the conscience of the individual man or woman, no matter where he or she is living, often more respect than is present in those who criticize the Curia's workings. This, of course, does not mean that everything is perfect, much less infallible! There are real human shortcomings and a few petty attitudes on the part of one or two subordinate clerics who seemingly have difficulty finding other jobs to do.

In one particular case, an elderly Roman monsignor in one of the more important curial offices seemed to have misplaced or totally lost my original request in behalf of one of our larger monasteries. When I visited him for the third time about it, a subordinate official came into the office, saw my situation and immediately took it into his hands, found the original request and expedited the affair within 48 hours. It was then that I realized that the elderly subsecretary was in the first stages of Alzheimer's disease, and the authorities were in the process of negotiating a dignified retirement for him, probably with the enthusiastic cooperation of his whole staff.

This type of cordial, pastoral collaboration was what I found on all levels of the Holy See. I was surprised to see how the subsecretaries, archbishops and even cardinals with whom I spoke seemed happy to dedicate their precious time to listen to some request from the Trappists, whether it had to do with new foundations in Communist or Islamic countries, the change of a long-standing commitment to offer Masses for a specific intention, the wanderings of a cloistered nun, the transfer of a monastery from one diocese to another, the difficulties found in our dealings with another religious Institute, the reconciliation of a fallen-away priest, or the need to perform an exorcism in a monastery located in a diocese where the unworthy bishop opposed such a process.

On the level of our monasteries and their life, probably the most agreeable experience I had during these years was the role I could play in the change of the mother house of one of our houses in China. The original Japanese house, which had contributed greatly to this foundation, had a change of superiors, and the community asked that another abbey assume this important but difficult responsibility. Special qualities were needed on the part of any monastery that would assume a permanent pastoral role on mainland China, but we were able to locate one with a much less conflictual history in its relation with China than that of Japan. The change proved to be a most favorable turning point for the fast-growing, semi-underground Chinese house and a blessing for all concerned.

Troubleshooting

During my last three years as procurator in Rome, I was increasingly asked by the abbot general to help monasteries that had requested his presence but which he himself could not visit because of his other commitments. This was understandable, because

Bernardo had to plan his many trips at least six months in advance. Changing his plans would have meant depriving the original community of the pastoral visit they needed, and which he had promised. My trips were also multiplied because of the fact that I was the only native English-speaking member of the abbot general's council—the others being French, Dutch, Belgian, Spanish and Japanese—and the number of English-speaking monasteries is increasing, due especially to the expansion of the Order in Asia.

That is why I was often called upon when some type of emergency arose in an English-speaking house of the Order or to assist at a regional meeting when Bernardo could not do so. My trips had to be brief, back and forth from Rome, so as not to delay the normal work of procurator in behalf of the Order as a whole. So these few years saw me at the generalate for five or six weeks, especially when Bernardo was away on his pastoral visits, then flying to some other country for a week or ten days and returning to Rome for another five or six weeks. My passport became so full of visas and travel permits that I had to get another one, going to Nigeria twice, South Korea, Philippines, Indonesia, France, Spain, Ecuador, Canada, the USA, England, Scotland, Wales and Norway.

Two particularly poignant trips were to two countries I visited for the first and probably only time: Poland in late 1999 and Ireland 18 months later. The Polish trip was to a four-day conference on the Catholic Church in mainland China, organized by the Society of the Divine Word and held at a conference center outside the city of Gdansk. It was my first real contact with the missionary work of any Christian Church in China since I had left Shanghai over 50 years before. The purpose of assisting at the meeting was to help in my frequent relationships with our Asian monasteries, most especially in connection with the recent establishment of one or two little-known Trappist communities on the China mainland. The meeting more than served its purpose in that regard, since I met several Catholic missionaries—European priests and Chinese religious and laypersons—who explained how they were able to move about and function there.

An unexpected side trip was made by all the participants to Stutthof (Sztutowo in Polish), one of the former Nazi extermination camps not far from Gdansk, less than one-third the size of the infamous Auschwitz, in southern Poland. Approaching this abandoned camp with its barbed wire fences, dark barracks, central exercise compound and single gas chamber off to the side, dominated by its tall smokestack, is an unforgettably sobering experience. The pungent, disagreeable smell of burnt leather, that is, human skin, was still clearly perceptible. It becomes sickening when one realizes where it comes from. We were told that the people in the neighborhood during the Second World War did not know exactly what was there, but suspected the worst when they saw and smelled the smoky mist that hovered over the forest separating the camp from the main road.

Eight or ten months later, Bernardo advised me to see our six Irish monasteries, because he had only visited them once, seven or eight years before, and would not be able to go there again for some time. I did not need much encouragement to do so, since any American Catholic—by the very fact of being one—has close ties with the Emerald Isle. Spencer in particular is so full of the "F.B.I." (foreign-born Irish) that I knew I would feel right at home. And I was not mistaken.

I had heard so much about our Irish communities over the previous 45 years—and already knew a good number of their members—that each of them meant seeing something like a dream. For an American, at least, Ireland's rural counties lend themselves to this impression, a world full of hospitality, homey faith and brogued courtesy. In fact, there is so much history in Ireland, especially monastic history, that my two weeks of immersion in the monasteries, then being driven from one house to the next through the countryside and small towns from County Cork in the south up to and beyond Belfast in Northern Ireland, were like an in-depth course in Celtic lore.

So I passed from the stone watchtowers set up against Viking invaders, through the primitive Celtic hermitages, the battle sites of the Norman invasions, the ruins of the original Mellifont, the first Cistercian abbey there in the early 13th century, the triumphant emergence of the Church in the early 20th century after the catacomb years of the English occupation, up to the foundation in 1948 of Bethlehem Abbey in Portglenone, Northern Ireland. I was going to take a train from Belfast back to Dublin and the airport, but because of a bombing threat at the railroad station, the monks kindly drove me all the way to Dublin airport.

There was also a third reason for my successive trips, namely the fact that I had experience in giving retreats to monastic communities in English, Spanish and French. Although I would not ordinarily accept such a request, since other members of our Order were available for this service, sometimes a community was hard-pressed and needed their annual retreat on short notice, in which case, if they asked me, I would present their need to the abbot general and let him decide what I should do. The result was trips to such places as France, Cameroon in East Africa, Kenya in West Africa, Japan, Spain, Chile and New Zealand.

I can only thank God for the privilege of getting to know all these far-flung communities, many of them struggling with their particular difficulties, but each of them sincerely dedicated to growing in the love of God and service to his Church in their respective regions. Probably the major fruit that I personally gathered from these communities was the awareness of the underlying similarity of our shared problems, graces and desires, no matter on what continent we live or what our race, nationality or language might be.

I also saw for myself what I had heard others say, that the center of the Trappist Order—as of the Catholic Church as a whole—is no longer Europe, much less America, or any single country or continent. It is increasingly multicentered, or decentralized, but this fact makes it all the more important that there be some concrete, unifying point of reference, help and support at the service of such a worldwide network of communion. Catholic tradition, from the very beginning, has seen this necessary point of communion to be, in the words of the first-century martyr, Ignatius of Antioch, "the Church . . . that presides in the territory of the Romans, worthy of . . . praise for its integrity and presiding in charity over all those called together."[5]

5. St. Ignatius Martyr, *Letter to the Romans*, Preface. See Vatican II, Dogmatic Constitution *Lumen Gentium* 13: "The Chair of Peter . . . presides over

Among the Trappist monasteries of today, this hub of networked communion is no longer the community of Cîteaux, as in the 12th century, nor the general chapter, which now meets for only 20 days every three years, but seems increasingly to be—at least between general chapters—the generalate in Rome, that is, the abbot general with his council and secretariat. Although this was not the intention of the first abbots of the Order in either the 12th century or the 19th, it shows the constant need for a functional point of reference—which necessarily has to be a visible, personal representative of the entire group—if there is going to be a worldwide communion of monasteries, in a way that is analogous, though not at all identical, to what is meant to happen in the worldwide communion of Christian Churches.

Called Once More

The year 2002 was an especially intensive year for me, which I foresaw coming. After two pastorally delicate trips to different continents—both of them in an effort to improve the relationship between the superiors of neighboring monasteries—there was a four-day workshop in Rome for monastic formators from different countries, then regional meetings of superiors in the United States and Italy, plus pastoral visitations to be made in Canada and Spain. From May through September, however, the center of my attention was the general chapter that would take place in Rome that September, the preparation of which Bernardo had asked me to coordinate.

On August 6, the feast of the Transfiguration, I was in my office preparing to depart the next day for northern France to assist, in the name of the abbot general, at the general chapter of the Cistercian Nuns of Esquermes, whose congregation is affiliated to the Trappists. The chapter was being held in their central house near Lille. My phone rang. It was Father Eduardo of Azul, my

---

the whole assembly of charity and protects legitimate differences, while at the same time assuring that such differences do not hinder unity but rather contribute to it."

abbot. "Hi, Augustine. I have some good news for you," he said. "You've just been elected as our abbot."

I thought he was joking. I had completely forgotten that an abbatial election was scheduled at my own community, to which both Bernardo and I had been summoned. But we had written that our responsibilities in Rome kept us from making the long, expensive trip. Both Bernardo and I were convinced that the election would result in either the reelection of Eduardo or the election of some other member of the community. I asked Eduardo if he was kidding, but he assured me seriously that it was true. I asked to speak personally, in English, with Abbot Damian of Spencer, who had presided at the election. Damian clarified that I had been chosen in a peaceful, relatively short election from among the different possibilities.

"I don't see how I can accept now, since I have to be here for all of the general chapter and, in any case, I need to consult with Bernardo before deciding if I should accept the election or not."

"Fine, the community understands that you must stay in Rome through all the chapter. You could present your resignation as councilor and procurator to the chapter and return peacefully afterwards, in October."

"Look," I replied, "Bernardo is not here right now, so I have to phone him. Then I'll get back to you in less than an hour."

Fortunately, Bernardo was only in northern Italy, at the monastery of Boschi, and I reached him immediately on his cell phone. He was surprised that Azul had not chosen one of the brothers present there as superior, at least on a trial basis for six months or a year, and he wanted the community to consider this possibility. I relayed this to Abbot Damian, who at once consulted the voting members of the community about this recommendation from their abbot general. They rejected the idea, insisting that they wanted an abbot now and had elected me. So finally, after four hours of intercontinental telephone calls, I told Damian that I would have to pray and reflect in greater depth before being able to say either yes or no to my election at Azul, that I was leaving the next day for France and would phone him in three days from there with my final answer. He agreed.

"You'll be consoled to know," I told him, "that I'm beginning to sense that my ultimate decision will probably be to accept, but I need more time for a stronger inner confirmation and to begin to process all that this means for me and for my work here."

"I'll be waiting for your phone call," he replied.

As soon as I finished speaking with Damian, I phoned again to Bernardo, who assured me that he would accept whatever decision I made, but asked me to convoke his council that very evening, get their advice and relay it back to him. All the members of the council were present at the time—three monks and two nuns, four out of the five being retired abbots or abbesses—so we met after Compline that evening for 20 minutes, speaking in French. They were just as surprised as Bernardo and I had been, and for the same reason: that the community had elected a non-Argentine, even though I was a naturalized Argentine citizen. After their initial reaction, however, each one independently stated that he or she did not see any reason not to accept the election. The Spanish councilor was strongest: "If someone is elected abbot by his own community, he must accept it as God's will."

I thanked them for their help and advice, which I had not expected would be so clear and consistent, asked them to pray for me, then immediately phoned Bernardo again, who was waiting for my call. He, too, seemed surprised by their unanimous opinion and repeated that the decision was mine to make.

I kept my thoughts and prayers to myself during the general chapter of the Esquermes nuns. Even on my journey there, I had come to the conclusion that if, in the next two days, nothing stronger against my accepting the election presented itself, I should and would accept it, and trust that God would bring good out of it all.

Even before making the final phone calls, I began to see two converging reasons in favor of accepting the election, which I interpreted as the inner confirmation I needed. The first one had to do with the Trappist Order, and it answered a selfish scruple I had. I was thinking that it would be difficult to find another procurator general who could handle English, French and Spanish, as well as all the intricacies of the abbot general's council and of dealing with the Vatican, whereas it would be easy for Azul to elect someone else. I realized, however, that a procurator can be chosen from a wide array of competent people in the Order, whereas Azul's abbot can only be chosen—at least normally—from among its own half-dozen eligible priests.

The second reason for accepting was entirely personal and had to do with an image I had formed in thinking that I would continue my work in Rome—which I found to be stimulating, appreciated and meaningful—even beyond the usual time for retirement. But I now began to have a more realistic vision of my ministry in the Order. God had given me three different spheres of pastoral responsibility in my life: Azul, Spencer and Rome. It had been relatively easy to find my successor at Spencer, and it would not be so hard to find the person for Rome, but it seemed to be much more difficult to find someone else for Azul at this time. Moreover, I had spent many more years being pastorally responsible for Azul than I had at either Spencer or Rome, and the community at Azul had depended on me to a much greater extent than was the case in the other two places. Finally, and most importantly, at the Last Judgment the Lord will hold me responsible for the well-being of Azul, far more than for Spencer or for the Order as a whole.

With such growing convictions in mind, I had little hesitation in making the phone calls to Bernardo, then to Damian at Azul, and I finally wrote in longhand a fax in Spanish to the brothers of Azul, thanking them for their trust in me and promising them my best, once I arrived there ten weeks later, after our general chapter. As I slowly walked back to my guest cabin, I was suddenly flooded from within by the joy of triumphant music coming up from inside me. It was the vibrant march of Ralph Vaughn Williams's hymn:

For all the saints, who from their labors rest,
Who You by faith before the world confessed,
Your Name, O Jesus, be forever blessed!
You were their Rock, their Fortress and their Might;
You, Lord, their Captain in the well-fought fight;

You, in the darkness drear, their one true Light.
Alleluia![6]

What more could I want? After that, our own general chapter in September was something of an anticlimax, even though it was important in itself and complex for me as I tried to juggle my roles as organizer, procurator general, representative of the Azul community and secretary of the English-Japanese working commission. Ten days after the chapter ended, I flew to the United States for a final visit to Spencer and a talk with you, Eddie, before the long trip south to Buenos Aires and a new stage in my life, which I think will be the subject of my next and final letter to you.

6. The original words are by William W. Howe, *Hymns for Saints' Days, and Other Hymns* (London: Earl Nelson, 1864).

Letter 9

TAKEN

2002–2010

Dear Eddie,

My last letter ended with my trip from Rome back to Argentina. During the few days I spent in northern France, discerning whether it was God, or just men, who were calling me to return to Azul, the peaceful conviction grew in me that it was a paschal journey for me from one life to a higher one, under the condition that I die to myself. I mentioned this to Bernardo in my final phone call to him from France, informing him of my decision, and I think I did also to you when we talked about it during my short visit to Spencer en route to Argentina.

Kenosis and Integration

Humanly, my life at the Generalate as procurator had many "perks," as they say, many privileges and even honors attached to it. People, both in the Order and outside, think of the procurator general as the assistant abbot general, even though it is possible to be procurator without even having been a local abbot. He is not a major superior of any local monastery, but there is a mystique about working in and with the Vatican, which people falsely think involves having direct access to the Pope. Perhaps above all, there is the aura of having access to information that most people do not have and are curious about. To leave all that for common Trappist life in a remote monastery on the windswept Argentine pampas, 35 miles from the nearest town, is a real leap in faith, hope and, if done well, divine love.

In any case, I arrived in Buenos Aires in late October 2002 and the next day, en route to Azul, I stopped at the spiritual center of Argentina, the basilica of Our Lady of Luján, to commit, once again, all my life to Mary, especially this new period of service. Shortly after my arrival at Azul, a young Argentine woman, Claudia Mendoza, grasped my situation remarkably well. As a professor of Sacred Scripture at Buenos Aires's major seminary, she had come to the monastery to give us a three-day workshop on her specialty, the New Testament. When I introduced myself to her, I explained that I had just come from Rome, where I had served as procurator general. She looked at me and exclaimed with her feminine insight, "That must have been a kenotic experience!"

"What's that?" I asked, thinking that she had said, "kinetic," as in kinetic energy. But what was so *energizing* or *dynamic* about my experience of returning from Rome?

"A *kenotic* experience," she repeated. It was the first time that I had heard the expression, so I needed two seconds to realize that, coming from Claudia, "kenotic" was a reference to Saint Paul. It was the adjective of *kenosis*, which Webster's Dictionary defines as "the relinquishment of divine attributes by Jesus Christ in becoming human," the emptying of self described by Saint Paul when he says that Christ "emptied himself, taking the form of a slave, being born in human likeness."[1]

"Yes, I guess it was," I said, surprised, since I had never really thought of my return to Azul in those terms. "But it wasn't that bad," I added, and we both laughed.

But her woman's intuition had understood better than I had, and I began to see that my adult life, despite all my weaknesses, had really been a series of self-emptyings for the sake of Christ. That's what being his servant means, for me and for all who follow him. My experience had been one of passing from self-reliance to submission to his Church, from self-achievement to following him into a monastery, from attempts at self-justification to rejoicing in his merciful truth, from the more self-comforting life of a big monastery to the rocky beginnings of a distant foundation, from the warm satisfaction of a united group of men into

1. Phil 2:7.

a large, complex and often divided community, and now from a life of prestige to one of hidden simplicity.

At the same time, I can only thank God for having guided me through these progressive self-emptyings, for having been so patient and forgiving of my sins, hesitancies, resistances and occasional doubts. Somehow the Lord always made me shun human self-fulfillment and choose different forms of self-emptying, yet each truly kenotic experience turned into overflowing happiness and joy for myself and hopefully served others much better.

So my move from Rome might have been a humbling downgrade, but spiritually I could see that it would be good for me. What I did not foresee, however, was that my new life at Azul would be the occasion for bringing together many different strands of my life and, more specifically, coming to a fuller integration of mind and heart. It was a process that did not occur in neat compartments or laboratories, where each process occurs separately. On the contrary, the components were and are interwoven with each other, as all living things are, especially in their advanced stages. And, of course, it is still an ongoing process.

Past and Present

The first component of the process of integrating the past with the present was naturally my reinsertion into the community to which I had given myself entirely for over 20 years in the prime of my life and to which I was now returning at the age of 70. Much had happened during those intervening 20 years. All of us were older and—I was happy to see—more maturely rooted in our monastic service of the Lord. I myself had learned a lot from my years as abbot at Spencer and at Rome, so that becoming abbot of this community, even after an absence of almost 20 years, was not too difficult. The brothers received me warmly and, in the eight years that have passed since then, there has been a deepening of love and mutual esteem, both before and after my retirement as abbot at the age of 75.

During my years of absence, four of the founders had passed away and are buried in our little cemetery. They have been replaced by four younger men, all Argentines, so that the Argentine face of the community is much stronger now, especially after the return of Father Bernardo as our abbot at the end of his 18 years of service as abbot general. The community as a whole has achieved a good insertion into the life of the diocesan Church and is respected, even promoted, by the town government of Azul. The fact that all the local contacts are now made by Argentine members of the community has been a decisive factor in this.

Another new factor was the existence of a telephone. When I had left in 1983, there was no phone line available for either the monastery or our immediate neighbors, but now we have not only a wireless phone line to the outside but also a simple internal phone network for the house and another one for the farm. Computers, too, were new and since my return we increasingly use the Internet and e-mail for business and personal contacts, rather than letters or the telephone.

Since Argentina in general, and the region of Azul in particular, is so strongly influenced by its agricultural activity, our farm and ranch make us share the mainstream of the country's interests. Ours is a relatively small herd of beef cattle compared with many others, but it has been intensely developed by our brothers. Agriculture and cattle raising, however, have become much more complex in the technological world of the 21st century, so that it is increasingly difficult to integrate them into the contemplative nature of Trapppist life, but I found that the brothers working on the farm are keenly sensitive to their monastic commitments.

All things considered, the fact of living deep inside the Argentine farm country, the so-called *pampa húmeda*, the fertile farm and grazing land in contrast to the colder, drier Patagonia, has been and still is a positive factor, for us and for all who come to the monastery as guests or visitors. In fact the increase in the number of such guests and visitors is one of the most obvious changes in the last 20 years, thanks in part to a handsome, functional guest house built in the years of my absence with financial help from several houses of the Order and a few other benefactors.

Another new feature in the life of the community is its increased involvement in what is called the REMILA, the Latin

American Regional Conference of Trappist communities. When I left Azul in 1983, there were 8 Trappist communities in 5 countries south of the Rio Grande. Only 3 of these communities were autonomous priories and none was an abbey. Today there are 14 monasteries in 8 countries. 12 of these 14 communities are autonomous, and 5 are abbeys. In other words, Trappist life is firmly established in Central and South America, increasingly well integrated into the joys and sufferings of Latin American Catholicism, with the last two foundations—in Nicaragua and Brazil—made from within our own regional conference. The life of the regional conference is increasingly dominated by its native members, just as it is in the local communities.

On a more personal level, I was caught by surprise by the warm welcome I received from my old Benedictine friends, both monks and nuns. They, too, had matured over these 20 years and their young congregation of the *Cono Sur*, the southern cone of Uruguay, Paraguay, Argentina and Chile, was now well established and pastorally effective.

I experienced a change of service to the community in 2008 after my retirement as abbot and appointment once again as novice director, over 40 years after leaving that function to become a young superior. The change from abbot to novice master was not difficult for me, since everyone treated me most kindly and I was better prepared for the novices than I had been in the 1960s. What has changed, however, is the quantity and character of the young men who now ask to enter. In this connection, Argentina is no exception to the almost global process of technologized secularity with its consequences in family life and education. Religious and even moral formation is weaker than 40 years ago. Families are smaller and young persons usually require 10 or 15 more years of healthy social interaction before being able to make a serious vocational commitment. In this context, human, spiritual and doctrinal formation for monastic life is of paramount importance. I have found it a privilege, a renewed grace as well as a challenge, to work with the younger men in this area.

Besides my new insertion into the Azul community, these years since my return from Rome have included a more complete integration of my Chinese past. Quite providentially, the ten days between my departure from Rome and my arrival in Buenos Aires coincided with a two-day reunion of former classmates of the Shanghai American School that took place near Knoxville, Tennessee. During the general chapter I had received an emergency request to speak to this group of 50 or 60 former S.A.S. students on the subject of "International Relations after 9/11," since it was only a year after the destruction of the twin towers of New York's World Trade Center. They wanted me to talk on its worldwide repercussions, since they knew that I had done so much traveling in the year following that tragedy. I interpreted the coincidence of this request coming at a moment when I could assist at the reunion as a sign that God wanted this to be a certain closing of an important, though dormant, aspect of my life over 50 years after leaving Shanghai.

In my half-hour talk, I described the different reactions to 9/11 that I had observed around the world and stressed the growing emergence of six continental or intercontinental clusters of nations that will constitute the basic frame of reference for international relations during the next decade or so. These groups are the countries of Eastern and Western Europe; the alliance between the United States and England, which strongly influences Canada, Australia and New Zealand; the countries of the Arab League; those of Asia and the South Pacific, increasingly dominated by China; and the two weaker blocks of Africa and Latin America.

I emphasized that, of itself, the coalescence of these geographic and cultural groups of nations was a healthy, normal step in the long journey from city-states, then nations, towards a more worldwide organization such as the United Nations might become. The important task for us—especially the United States and China—is to be open to this intercontinental scenario and work as harmoniously as possible with the other groups of nations, not isolating ourselves or thinking we have all the answers. We must think globally while acting locally.

The short S.A.S. reunion was my first and last opportunity to see most of these men and women, who had shared some of my own personal history. I presented myself as a Catholic monk and priest but made an effort to avoid falling into religious arguments, especially since the group contained five or six Protestant clergy, men and women. I discovered that there were two other Catholics in the group, one of whom had become so after marrying a graduate of Notre Dame. It was also my last chance for a meeting with two former high school roommates at Mount Hermon, Bill Bishop and Tom Kepler, and with two of my closest friends through the years, Ben Gilson and Carl Scovel. Two of my adolescent crushes, Marybelle and Esther, with whom I had gone to different school dances, were also there, one a somewhat serious clergywoman, the other a happily married grandmother.

Toward the end of the dialogue following my talk on the state of the world today, the chief organizer of the meeting, a professional counselor one year younger than me, asked me what I personally planned to do in response to the challenges of the present world situation. I told him that it was a good question, pondered for two seconds, sent up a silent prayer to the Holy Spirit and replied: "Personally, I will keep trying to follow Jesus." Later, two of those present, good Protestants, told me how pleased they had been with my reply, which evidently impressed them more than my talk.

For six years after that, the Chinese strand in my life lay dormant, but it came to the surface unexpectedly again after my retirement as abbot, when my superiors agreed that I should accept a request by Mother Martha Driscoll to be temporary chaplain for three months to her community of Trappistine nuns at Gedono, on the island of Java in Indonesia. On my way there in April 2009, I made a ten-day pastoral visit to our sisters near Pusan, in South Korea. Mother Martha e-mailed me there, urging me to join her and two Chinese Trappistines in a short pilgrimage to the basilica of Our Lady of Sheshan, patroness of all China, outside Shanghai, then go with her to her monastery on Java. My abbot, Father Bernardo, was open to this. Thus, during an intense span of 36 hours, the four of us visited the two places where our family had lived while I was growing up and, above all, made pilgrimages to the Catholic cathedral, which I had often seen in my teens from the outside, and to the National Catholic Basilica of Our Lady of Sheshan. Here I joined with the hundred or so Chinese pilgrims to pray for the persecuted Church in this country that I still love. I received Holy Communion at a Mass in Chinese, just like the pilgrim I was. It was obvious that this return to Shanghai marked a real closure for me, the closing of an almost lifelong geographical and historical circle.

As it turned out, the short Shanghai visit was only a mysterious preparation for a much deeper and more significant closure, which is hard to describe because it is almost entirely spiritual. It took place during my ten weeks at Gedono, which were something like an extended retreat, although I was kept busy with the preparation of conferences in English for the sisters, and with work on Azul's Spanish Liturgy. During the sisters' long, predawn Vigils in Indonesian, I would pray silently, with the help of an English translation, the same Psalms the sisters were singing in Indonesian. Then I would read from Saint Bernard of Clairvaux's *Sermons on the Song of Songs*. These weeks of peaceful, more contemplative retreat, with my necessarily quiet participation in all the sisters' hours of liturgical or silent prayer, were the external context for a hidden work which only God can accomplish in the human heart and soul. My own experience was a combination of intense interior dryness with an intense desire that God's eternal kingdom come now to me and to the world "on earth as it is in heaven,"[2] just as Jesus taught us to pray.

During these ten weeks, I led the sisters in their community retreat in preparation for the feast of Pentecost, the coming of the Holy Spirit into the Church and into Christian life. This was also in preparation for the sisters' first foundation, on one of the islands of Macau, the former Portuguese colony near Hong Kong. This was the first time that I had given an entire retreat on the Holy Spirit and I was its primary beneficiary. The retreat turned out to be the immediate preparation for my celebration of 50 years as an ordained priest, which coincided that year with the

2. Mt 6:10.

Feast of the Sacred Heart and the beginning of an entire year dedicated throughout the universal Church to the beautiful vocation of the Catholic priesthood. The Golden Jubilee of Ordination was, of itself, simple enough. The local bishop, the present Archbishop of Jakarta, was thoughtful enough to come for the occasion, with the condition that I give a talk to his priests, which I did.

It was during the following months that I became aware that something had happened inside me. There was a less distracted prayer and a new agility or freedom of spirit that maintained body and soul at peace no matter what was happening. I remembered what Teresa of Avila wrote[3] about a stage in life when there is an unconquerable peace expressing itself in forgetfulness of self at the service of Christ, total availability to whatever divine providence offers, joy in persecution combined with inner and outer detachment. Perhaps I am somewhat nearer to that situation. When I returned to Azul, I mentioned all this to Bernardo, now my abbot. "The Lord finally took me," I said. "I don't know why it took him so long, but each person has his own rhythm." Bernardo could only agree.

"Glory of Thy People Israel"[4]

Another significant event that occurred after my return to Azul was totally unexpected, namely, a deep experience of person-to-person, Jewish-Christian dialogue. There was a certain preparation in my life for such a dialogue, thanks to having had a fine Jewish roommate, Joshua Dranoff, during my two years at Yale and later an even closer relationship during my 12 years as abbot at Spencer with an outstanding Jewish convert to Christianity, Bernard Bonowitz, the present Trappist abbot in Brazil. This preparation was completed by my firsthand experience in Israel during my two weeks there in 1998.

I was still surprised, though, by some remarkable persons who visited the monastery of Azul after I arrived there in 2002. Two of them were active rabbis. One of them had studied in a rabbinic

3. In her *Interior Castle*, Seventh Mansion.
4. Lk 2:32.

seminary in the United States; the other—now in Chile—had lost his wife in an Iranian-inspired terrorist attack on the large Synagogue and Jewish cultural center in Buenos Aires. He had not remarried and had contacted our monasteries to understand better the spiritual significance of his celibate condition. Both these rabbis saw the importance, especially in today's world, of Catholic-Jewish understanding, appreciation and collaboration. They spoke at different times to our community about this, which resulted in several other visits from Jewish men and women from Buenos Aires, with reciprocal visits by one or two of our monks.

For me, however, by far the most important event in this respect was a prolonged visit from a previously unknown young Jew from Israel whom, for the sake of prudence, I will call "Raphael." He had found our address on the Internet and wrote from Israel to ask if he could visit us to learn more about monasticism, since he had some friends in Buenos Aires. When he arrived in 2007, I dealt with him in English, since he did not speak Spanish. It became clear that his real interest was not so much the monastery but rather to learn more about Christian and Catholic doctrine in general. His monastic interests were a camouflage to cover up from his family and friends the nature of his intellectual unrest. He was, and I think still is, a lay teacher of the New Testament in its Hebrew translation in an unofficial Hebrew school in Israel, his students being the many young Jews who enroll—eagerly and often secretly—to learn more about the most famous of all Jews, Jesus of Nazareth, and what he taught. The school is unofficial, both to safeguard the students and also because it would only with difficulty be permitted by the Israeli authorities.

I spent hours during two intense weeks with this remarkable, audacious, intelligent young man, answering his questions about our faith, especially about Saint Paul and the teaching of the New Testament on the destiny of the Jewish people and religion. "God has not rejected his people, whom he foreknew," I assured him, quoting the Letter to the Romans,[5] and Jesus did not destroy

5. Rom 11:2.

the Law or the Prophets, but fulfilled them in himself and in his moral teachings,[6] which put the emphasis on human interiority and love for all persons, thus opening up the Jewish faith to the nations of the world, to catholicity. That was the reason why Christ and his disciples were rejected—thrown out—by the Jewish authorities, but neither Christ nor Paul rejected the Jews or the Jewish faith. They were convinced that they were fulfilling it and bringing it to its perfection, its divine destiny.

Raphael was impressed, and I explained that many Christians do not appreciate this clear teaching of the New Testament, so that the centuries have witnessed a vicious circle of mistrust, even hate and persecution, which does not reflect true Christianity. He left us to return to his country and to his teaching profession, saying that he had learned a lot and eagerly taking with him our only English copy of the new *Catechism of the Catholic Church*, which I gladly gave him. I will never forget him in my prayer, or God's goodness in offering me this unexpected vision of how the Holy Spirit is working among the youth of his chosen people today, so that they can see how Jesus, through his passion, death and resurrection, embodied their most glorious aspirations and those of all humanity. After several years of silence, Raphael has recently contacted me again, eager to continue our dialogue. He is doing advanced studies at a Hebrew university.

Two Popes

On two different occasions over 20 years—during the general chapters of 1980 and 2002—I had the opportunity to greet John Paul II as he spoke very briefly with the members of the chapter. Given the importance of his person in the life of the Church and the world of his time, I was expecting an imposing figure and was surprised to find him relatively short and stocky. In 1980 we were in a long reception line, so that as he passed by, he took my hand, looked at my name tag rather than my face, did not reply to my request that he bless my community and went on to the

6. See Mt 5:17.

next man. In 2002 he was greatly debilitated with what seemed to be Parkinson's disease, and he received us seated, almost collapsed, in his chair. The abbot general whispered my name in his ear, but the Pope's look and probably his mind were elsewhere. I said that we were praying for him, then got up from my kneeling position and left.

Three years later, after the general chapter of 2005, I stayed in Rome to assist at the usual Wednesday public audience of the new Pope, Benedict XVI, in Saint Peter's Square. A good friend of mine, Monsignor Francis Kelly, rector of the downtown residence for American priests doing graduate studies at the Roman universities, had given me a special ticket which would let me not only be close to the Holy Father, but greet him, as an abbot, along with the few bishops present. After convincing the chief usher that I really was an abbot, I ended up a few yards away from Pope Benedict during his talk, a commentary on one of the Psalms, then put myself at the end of the line of bishops and soon found myself standing before the Pope, dressed as I was in my monastic habit.

"A Cistercian!" he exclaimed in Italian, quite pleased. He tried to keep me from kissing his ring and immediately clasped my hands between both of his, gently but firmly.

"A Trappist," I clarified, since there are other Cistercians who are more well-known than the Trappists in Germany and Italy. "We have just finished our general chapter in Assisi."

"Yes, I know."

"We prayed for you there."

"Oh, thank you."

Then I shifted into English, which I knew he spoke well, and instead of explaining who I was, which I probably should have done, I told him very briefly about our monasteries in China and that two Chinese nuns were present at the audience.

"Really? Please tell them that I give them and their community my very special blessing."

"Thank you very much," I said, from the bottom of my heart, in reference not only to his blessing, but above all to the sincere cordiality with which he had welcomed me.

I knew my time was up. It had been an intense two minutes and had totally changed my image of Pope Benedict XVI. In fact I have very seldom met anyone as sincerely cordial and as totally present to the person being spoken to. I mentioned this to Monsignor Kelly, who said that many others have the same experience of him. Reflecting later about how much at home I had felt in his presence, I realized that he was the first pope I had met who was a Saxon by race, like me. John XXIII, Paul VI, John Paul II, each of whom I greatly admire, were either Latin or Slav. How beautiful it is that there can now be this alternation of papal personalities, to enrich the catholicity of us all!

My contact with the popes, however, did not end at Saint Peter's Square. When I returned to Azul from Rome, I was ready to put the past behind me. Soon, however, I started receiving letters complaining that people were trying to purchase more copies of my book on monastic profession, *Centered on Christ*, but found that it was out of print and that the editorial house, Saint Bede's Publications, seemed to have closed. I myself had no more copies and understood at once that I should prepare a third edition of the book, taking advantage of it to incorporate some of the doctrine on religious profession from John Paul II's exhortation on religious life, *Vita Consecrata*, which had appeared in 1996, several years after the publication of the last edition of my book.

So I began to reread *Vita Consecrata*, which I had only studied rapidly soon after it was published, and was startled at how much new, beautiful material was contained in it. Moreover, I realized that if I wanted to present the meaning of monastic profession and its vows to young people today, I would have to take into account what the Pope was saying, which would modify my own presentation in several ways. It took me over two years to accomplish this, but it was worth the effort.

The Pope's reflections on the beauty of life dedicated to the service of Christ and his Church clarified three essential points in the first editions of my book. The chief one concerns the origin and purpose of such a life, which I saw did not begin with the Desert Fathers in the third century, nor even with John the Baptizer in the desert of Judea, but rather at the moment when Jesus called his disciples to leave their life work and their families and to follow him physically and permanently as disciples, which meant to live with him as he was living: in celibacy, simplicity, community and prayerful dependence on the times established by his heavenly Father.

The first editions of my book had given very little attention to Jesus' life with his first disciples as the basis, the foundation, of religious and monastic profession. John Paul II, however, goes even one step further, by showing that this type of life is based on and reflects not only the human life of Christ but also the divine life of the Blessed Trinity, Father, Son and Holy Spirit, in their total self-gift to each other, so that it becomes a sort of embodiment of the social nature of eternal life as expressed, first of all, in the life of Jesus himself.

A secondary clarification, but one especially important for my book, was a new approach to what are called the "evangelical counsels," chastity, poverty and obedience. Catholic tradition had tended to stress the social and personal demands of these religious practices, which have their roots in the Gospel, seeing them especially as antidotes to "the desire of the flesh, the desire of the eyes, the pride in riches, (that) comes not from the Father but from the world."[7] John Paul, however, insists on the primacy of these counsels' mystical quality over their ascetical aspects. These practices constitute the essential characteristics of Christ's own lifestyle, which itself incarnates the inner life of the Divine Persons. They are, as he puts it, "the most radical way of living the Gospel on this earth, a way which may be called *divine*, for it was embraced by him, God and man, as the expression of his relationship as the Only Begotten Son with the Father and with the Holy Spirit."[8]

That was a powerful statement, and it was clear that I had considerable rethinking and rewriting to do for the new edition of my book on the meaning of religious and monastic profession. I also tried to explain an important change in my approach to the

7. 1 Jn 2:16.
8. *Vita Consecrata*, 18.

object of religious profession, a change which corrects what I had written in the previous editions and is a third new precision in my book. Thanks to Pope John Paul, I now saw that there is a clear difference between the essential act of religious or monastic profession, which is the gift of oneself to the total following of Christ in one's particular religious community, and the pronouncement of specific vows, which are only a partial specification of the total gift of self. In other words, the vows are not the primary element in religious or monastic profession. What is directly promised at profession is the total following of Christ in body and soul according to the grace, charism, and approved Constitutions of one's religious institute. On the other hand, we only vow a few important aspects or parts of this total following of Christ, the aspects that were specified over the course of centuries, especially during the Middle Ages.

Previously, I had thought that religious profession coincided with the vows, because of the phrase, "profession of the evangelical counsels,"[9] but now I saw that this phrase does not mention the vows, since there are other ways to profess the gospel counsels. This was the case with Saint Anthony of the Desert, who heard the invitation of Christ to follow him and immediately left his sister and friends, to live in detachment, good works, prayer, celibacy and solitude. It was a nonverbal profession of the total following of Christ, embracing all the evangelical counsels, and it led Anthony directly "to prefer nothing in the world to the love of Christ."[10]

I saw, therefore, that the real commitment of religious or monastic profession, its whole purpose, goes beyond the vows and includes such elements as prayer, common life, nonviolence and service to others, which are all part of how Jesus lived. This means that profession is historically anterior to any formal vow, as well as being theologically more significant and more all-embracing than vows are. Because of that, the act of religious profession, in whatever form it takes, is also more demanding

9. *Code of Canon Law*, 573.1. See LG 44.
10. *Life of Antony*, 15. See Also RB 4,21; 5,2 and 72,11.

than any vow, since it touches the heart in a way that the vows do not do but leads directly—not just indirectly—to "following the Lamb wherever he goes."[11] I wish that I had understood this much earlier in the first editions of my book, but better late than never.

Soon after finishing the new edition of my book, I was asked to give some conferences on another side of Pope John Paul's teaching on Christian life, his "theology of the body," based especially on a long series of talks he gave at his public audiences in the first years of his pontificate.[12] This subject filled a gap in my own formation, since I had never studied the origin, nature, and destiny of human beings apart from the considerable number of scientific books I had read as a high school and college student. Especially enlightening was the Pope's emphasis on two key elements of what he refers to as an "adequate anthropology,"[13] one of which is the foundation and the other, the fulfillment and crowning of everything that is essentially human. Both have played key roles in my life.

The foundational element is the *human capacity to know what is objectively true*, that is, what things really are, underneath the scientific data that reaches us through our five senses. This does not mean being especially "brainy," but just normally human and inquisitive about the truth. Doubt about this capacity was what I had wrestled with over 50 years before at Mount Hermon and then during my theological studies at Spencer. God's mercy resolved this fundamental question in my life, as I tried to describe in those first letters I wrote to you, Eddie. But only now did I understand how denial or doubt about the God-given capacity of the human spirit to know what is true—often referred to as "nominalism"—has radically undermined our Western Civilization during the last 600 years, often in people with good intentions.

11. Rev 14:4.

12. Available on the Internet at: http://www.vatican.va/holy_father/john_paul_ii/audiences/catechesis_genesis/ and in: *Man and Woman He Created Them* (Boston: Pauline Books, 2006).

13. *Man and Woman*, 132.

Nominalism expressed itself *religiously* in the one-sided fideism of the Reformation, *morally* in either an inhuman rigidity or an equally inhuman relativism, and *intellectually* in a widespread pragmatic, often agnostic mentality that denies any meaning to a transcendent human vocation, since it would not correspond to human nature as we know it through the experimental sciences. Such a mindset shows itself in Pilate's tragic question to Jesus, "What is truth?"[14] I did not share Pilate's methodological doubt, but I had personally experienced many other expressions of nominalism, not only in others but also in myself.

Jesus had already replied to Pilate's question at the Last Supper with a divine, symphonic answer, a theme with variations, which presupposes that the normal man or woman can know the truth. First he explained, "I am the way and the truth."[15] Then he added, "I will send . . . the Spirit of truth, . . . he will guide you into all the truth,"[16] and finally, in his prayer to the Father, "Your Word is truth."[17] So any serious renewal of human life at any time involves reinstalling trust in our capacity to know and rejoice in truth, objective spiritual reality, underneath and beyond feelings and appearances.

Spousal Love

The second key element of human existence is even more experiential than our knowledge of objective reality. It is *truth's consummation in faithful spousal love*, which is the fulfillment not only of marriage, but also of the celibate life. Spousal love is embodied, above all, by Christ on the Cross, reaching its fullness "in the resurrection (where) they neither marry nor are given in marriage."[18] It is as old as Adam and Eve.[19] The Hebrew prophets, then Jesus and the New Testament writers, used it as an image of how God loves

14. Jn 18:38.
15. Jn 14:6.
16. Jn 15:26; 16:13.
17. Jn 17:17.
18. Mt 22:30.
19. See Gen 2:23-25.

his people.[20] It seems to me to be the intense fusion of three other, less complete types of love that it brings to their maximum unity:

- *affectionate love*, characteristic of persons "in love," with emphasis on an all-encompassing desire to be with the beloved;
- *effective love*, that of devoted servants who put themselves at the active service of their beloved master in a union of wills;
- and *oblative or sacrificial love*, that of the truest friends, who go beyond feelings and service to give their entire life and existence to the person and projects of the beloved.[21]

This outpouring of the gift of self is how God loves his sons and daughters, which is what the life, death and resurrection of Jesus prove. In fact, Jesus' embodiment of spousal love is the guarantee that it has and will have the final word over human misery, concupiscence and sin. In us, it is one of the best expressions of what it means to have been made in the image and likeness of God. I realized that this was what I had first begun to experience as a fledgling postulant at Spencer many years ago.

My talks on this subject, to the Azul community and to several other groups, turned out to be an immediate preparation for two very different events, both occurring in 2008. The first one was the 50th anniversary of the arrival of our founding monks to establish here at Azul the first Trappist foundation in Central and South America. We had several public Eucharistic celebrations for this anniversary to accommodate our many friends, the largest one attracting almost 1000 persons.

20. For example, Hos 2:19-3:1; Is 61:10-62:5; Mk 2:19-20; Jn 3:29; Eph 5:25-28.

21. Spousal love seems to be what Saint Benedict, quoting 1 Jn 4:18, refers to as "that perfect love of God (*caritas Dei perfecta*) which casts out fear" (RB 7,67). Saint Bernard of Clairvaux calls it "love in all its fullness" (*plenitudo dilectionis*) in his remarkable summary of the steps in the Holy Spirit's action in our lives: "We need first of all compunction of heart; then, fervor of spirit; thirdly, the labor of penance; fourthly, works of charity; fifthly, zeal for prayer; sixthly, leisure for contemplation; seventhly, love in all its fullness. All these are the work of one and the same Spirit, accomplished by the process called infusion" (*Sermons on the Song of Songs*, 18:6).

The most intense celebration, however, was the one-day pilgrimage of all the brothers, ages 30 to 85, in a rented bus to the basilica of Our Lady of Luján, to thank Mary, the spiritual Mother of us all, for her personal protection over us and to reconsecrate our monastery's past, present and future to Jesus through her. We did this at the end of our shared Eucharist at the main altar of the basilica in the presence of the many other pilgrims. It was clear that our pilgrimage was a triple expression of spousal love: ours for Our Lady, ours also for this country of Argentina that so particularly belongs to her, and Mary's own love for her eternal divine Spouse and for us, his Body, the Church. The Eucharist itself was a fourth expression, since it embodies Jesus' own spousal love for us.

Almost immediately after our trip to Luján, we began celebrating the second important even in 2008, the year commemorating the 2000th anniversary of the birth of Saint Paul. Paul's inspired vision of all reality is, in fact, a splendid revelation of divine spousal love as the fulfillment of every vocation and desire of the human heart. The Pauline texts are true love letters to the first Christian believers, and I remember listening enthralled, even as a young adolescent, to Paul's several hymns to the love of Christ.[22] He saw that Christ Jesus, himself human, had loved us so much that he took our place as sinner and criminal, and suffered what we deserved, but his total self-gift, which is what spousal love is, communicated Christ's own life to those who believe in him, and so turned Jesus on the Cross into the new Adam, the new Father of a renewed human race.[23]

My conviction that creation itself had been changed by God's becoming man in Christ had recently become much stronger. Paul calls it a "new creation":[24] God the Father re-created the world on the Cross, starting with a New Man, the new Father of all humanity. The first creation had ended with Adam, who immediately went astray and twisted creation out of shape, so the new

22. See Rom 8:33-39, 1 Cor 13:1-13, Eph 1:3-12.

23. See Saint Paul's different proclamations of this divine plan, especially in Eph 2:13-22, Col 1:13-22 and 1 Tim 2:4-7.

24. 2 Cor 5:17; Gal 6:15.

creation began with a new Adam, whose resurrection is the BIG BANG, the explosion—this time an infinitely peaceful one—that re-creates heaven and earth by reorienting the universe under its true and permanent head, the Lord Jesus Christ. Exteriorly, the world seems—at least for now—to be the same, but Christian faith is convinced that this Resurrected Man, who was and remains God on earth, is an eternally living Magnet, reordering the universe under himself through an ongoing salvation of the tortuous course of human history. It is a winding journey, as all our lives are, since it amazingly respects and integrates human freedom and human culture into the reordered universe.

Jesus himself was talking about this when he prophesied, "I, when I am lifted up from the earth, will draw all people to myself."[25] What has been created—fully in the Risen Christ and progressively in redeemed humanity—is total communion among free human beings in his redeeming, transforming, spousal love. I had always implicitly believed this, of course; in fact, I had given my whole life to God so that this communion could be a reality in me and in others! There are meant to be no more divisions, but harmonic unity of all in the Body of Christ, which is the Church of those who believe in him. Every human person now has access (which must be willing, voluntary and believing) to the same Father in the same Holy Spirit and through the same Christ, the "one teacher, . . . one instructor, the Messiah."[26]

The heart of the real universe, therefore, is the spousal love of the heart of Jesus Christ. It has become the superhighway between God and every man or woman on the planet Earth, communicating the gifts and fruits of his Spirit to all humanity and thus forming the Body of Christ on earth and in heaven. This is the process we are all caught up in, to which our human nature demands that we say "Yes" or "No" in time and in eternity.

It was also thanks to Pope John Paul's intuitions that I saw how monastic life, with the total gift of self that it continually fosters, leads to a radical fulfillment of what is most noble, most

25. Jn 12:32.
26. Mt 23:8-10.

transcendent and beautiful, in human existence. It is what he continually taught, citing Vatican II: "The human person can fully find personal identity only through a sincere gift of self,"[27] and as Jesus himself said on more than one occasion, "Those who try to make their life secure will lose it, but those who lose their life will keep it."[28] I think it is what I discovered in a new way inside me—even though still imperfectly—during my ten weeks of retreat at Gedono, in Indonesia, that coincided with the end of the Pauline Year and my 50th anniversary of ordination to the ministerial priesthood. I gave myself and God took me.

I have seen many examples of spousal love, especially among persons who have been consistently generous in their service of the Lord, since this intensity of love—which is both fully human and a mirror of divine life—presupposes a solid grounding in chastity and patience. Spousal love is an experience and, at the same time, a more permanent state of soul and heart varying from person to person. One brother I knew, a priest who had seen active service in the US Marine Corps during World War II and was a deeply faithful monk for over 40 years, came to experience an almost constant physical joy in being united with his divine Spouse, but that is not so common, especially among men. My own experience is that of a much more conscious and constant attention to God's loving presence in everything and everyone, starting with myself. Its two main expressions seem to be greater liberty and deeper intensity in serving God and others.

This sounds wonderful, and it is, but it immediately produces—in fact it essentially requires—a new level of deep self-renunciation, both in human relations and in prayer, in chastity and in patience. My task is to say "Yes!" to this new level of self-denial and launch out into the deep, not with fear but with total trust that this is where God's love—the love of the Heart of Christ—can be expressed in my poor service and prayer. Both my service and my prayer are poor, and getting more so, but they are probably purer now, that is, more full of love.

27. GS 24.
28. Lk 17:33.

Prayer, in particular, seems now to be a consuming desire for something that goes far beyond any imagination. Desire for what? I really have no idea, nor do I pray with ideas. It is a longing for everything, yet nothing in particular, but an intuition of trusting faith tells me that what I desire is the Beloved, the Bridegroom. I find some satisfaction of the tension that this deeply pregnant void implies by expressing it with the silent word "You," or one of its derivates: "Just you. Your kingdom. Your mercy. Mercy on your people. Glorify your name. Your will." My reduced distractions make this simple prayer of longing come more spontaneously, but it is not at all a sensible joy or even a quiet consolation. On the contrary, it means persevering in what is sometimes called "the human person's ontological desire for God," which is the central, eternal element of any and all human existence. Despite its intense dryness, I do not look for anything else, because love is its own reward. I totally trust the Beloved to fulfill it when and how he knows best, for me and for others.

One particular example of spousal love stays with me in a special way, perhaps because it embodies in its simplicity the best of monastic life and every person's deepest calling, since spousal love is meant for all. It will serve as a conclusion to this series of letters, which have turned out to be rather long and can end here on the theme of spousal love, just as spousal love seems to be the final discovery, the consummation, rather than the beginning, of one's life journey. At least for me it has been.

The episode I am referring to took place suddenly during a conversation on one of my trips to Africa. I was giving their annual retreat to the community of monks at the Abbey of Our Lady of Victory, in the mountain highlands of western Kenya, some 50 miles from Lake Victoria and 15 miles from the nearest town, Kipkelion. Toward the end of my visit Father Conrad came to see me. He was a faithful, simple monk who had entered Tilburg, in Holland, shortly before the Second World War and had volunteered to help found this pioneer monastery in the heart of Africa in the 1950s. Now, 40 years later, he was in his early 80s and the only white man left in the community. He explained how all the Dutch founders of the monastery had been invited, even encouraged, to return to their mother house when the Kenyan foundation had grown enough to become an autonomous community and had been able to elect its own African abbot. Tilburg, on the other hand, was going down in numbers.

"But I can't return," Father Conrad told me very simply. "I love the Africans. I don't mind being the only white man here."

I was touched by the gentle, resigned voice and meekly humble attitude of this hidden lover of the human race. "Well, Father," I said, "it seems that God wants you to offer everything up to him—the community he has given to you, all of Africa, the whole world and your own life—in an act of worship and love."

"That's what I do all the time!" he exclaimed with a wonderfully peaceful, penetrating conviction.

What would happen, I thought—what would *not* happen!—if we all could do something like that all the time? Here in the middle of Africa I had found a treasure, the gospel's pearl of great value, spousal love flowing from God himself into the heart of Christ and into the heart of his Spouse, the Church. It is humanity transfigured, what every monk and monastery is meant to be: a brilliant, live jewel, blue with the mantle of our Lady, Mother of us all.

And I saw the holy city, the new Jerusalem,
coming down out of heaven from God, prepared as a bride
adorned for her husband.
And I heard a loud voice from the throne saying,
"See, the home of God is among mortals.
He will dwell with them; they will be his people
and God himself will be with them.
He will wipe every tear from their eyes. Death will be no more;
mourning and crying and pain will be no more,
for the first things have passed away."
And the one who was seated on the throne said,
"See, I am making all things new."[29]

Thanks so much, Eddie, for reading all this and living it with me. Your brother, Augustine.

29. Rev 21:2-5.

Appendix I

Text by
DOROTHY ROBERTS
1950

This account of my mother's conversion was written by her—seemingly in considerable haste—a year after she had been received into the Roman Catholic Church, very soon before she and my father left Shanghai permanently. It was probably in response to a request for her story made by one of the French missionaries there, since I have been told that it was published in French in the 1950s, either in a missionary magazine or in a collection of conversion stories. She gave me her original typewritten manuscript in the 1970s, a few years after the death of my father. Before then, I was unaware of almost all that is described here, just as she did not know—nor ask about—most of the details that led to my own entry into the Church a year after this chronicle was written. She passed away peacefully in 1984 at the age of 95. The text respects her spelling and punctuation, unless clearly a typo. It also incorporates her few handwritten corrections and additions. My own occasional explanations are in the footnotes.

It Took Sixty Years

It seemed to begin with a letter from our son, Bill, giving the astounding news that he was living in a Trappist Monastery,—The Cistercian Order of Strict Observance,—in Rhode Island, U.S.A. and hoping to be received into the Roman Catholic Church and into the Order. He had been a Conscientious Objector during the war, and in prison for most of four years,—1941 to 1945—coming out on parole for part of a year to work as orderly in a hospital, and then back in prison again to serve out his term. During the time in prison he lost his belief in organized churches and almost his Faith in God. He wrote that it was like knocking on a door and hearing a voice saying, "No one is here." He read books when allowed, and one was "The Story of St. Thérèse de Lisieux." He was impressed by this but added a postscript to say, "But don't think that I shall ever become a Roman Catholic!" After coming out of prison he lived and worked hard on a farm in Vermont where a few men who had met in prison,—C.O.s, all of them,—tried to live as a community and express their ideas in work. Bill was not satisfied and built himself a shack on the hillside where he lived alone with his self made "peasant pipe"—a sort of flute—, the Bible and his thoughts. A note came to us saying that he had left the farm and the shack and was going on a sort of pilgrimage. He closed with the words, "It is a wonderful and fearful thing to be in the hands of the Living God." After wandering about and going to see his sister in Boston he was passing the gate of the Trappist Monastery in Valley Falls, R.I., toward evening and he "was told to turn and enter." He went on a bit and then had to come back and at the gate ask for a night's lodging. That evening he found himself asking Our Lady to show him Her Son and his prayer was answered. After a few weeks in the guest house he was received for instruction before entering the Church and as a novice in the Order. That was more than two years ago and he has taken his simple vows with every intention of taking final vows in three more years. He is now Brother Luke.

His father and I have been missionaries in China, sent out by the Protestant Episcopal Church of the U.S.A. We were living in Shanghai when this happened and his father was the Bishop of the Jiangsu Diocese. My father was an Episcopal minister, my grandparents were all Congregationalists, so that I was brought up in the best of New England Protestant thought. My father was extremely liberal and from Y.W.C.A. work in Wellesley College and all sorts of interchurch connections in America and in China I had grown up feeling that tolerance was almost the greatest of Christian virtues. Definiteness of Faith seemed to me the mark of a narrow minded person and rather childish.

Was the beginning of my "conversion" when our son entered the Church? We know so little of how God is preparing us for the great events of our lives that we look back with amazement and see that chance words or incidents are really the touch of His Hand and the whisper of His Loving Will. For two years,—1912 to 1914—I was living in the Italian District of Boston, in a tenement where we were doing an informal sort of social work. Two of our neighbors were the Giancola girls, Millie and Helena. Millie was described by her sister as "an awful holy girl," and it was she who asked me to go to the churches on Holy Thursday, after she finished her work in the candy factory, and Helena went along too. The picture of the lighted churches, the throngs of devout worshippers,—newly arrived immigrants from Italy and rather sophisticated Americanized boys and girls, all kinds and all ages,—has always stayed in my mind, as also the silent, almost empty church in Paul Revere Square where I used to slip in and spend a quiet five minutes now and then. I didn't really go for prayer but I liked to watch the men and women kneeling before the statues or in the pews always with devout eyes fixed on the tabernacle before they left. I tried once or twice going into one of the Episcopal Churches but it didn't seem the same. Now I know why. When I came out to China for the first time in 1914, a friend asked me to call on Miss Dowling in San Francisco, who had just entered the Catholic Church from the Episcopal, and as my friend said, "Must be very lonely." She took me into the Church,—I wish I knew which one,—and she explained to me that one of her reasons for her entering the Church was the knowledge that wherever she saw the light burning Our Lord was there in a Real and Special way. She has died and, I believe, knows that I have followed her and I thank her for her help. We have had friends staying with us who have been so anti-Catholic that I found myself defending the Faith and then wondering why I did it, and wanting to find the truth. They helped me into the Church!

We all grow up, more than we realize, with a background of the Mother Church. Art, poetry, prayers, hymns and Lives of the Saints. Yet we are trained as were these Italian boys and girls to feel that we have outgrown our inheritance and are independent in a new land. It took me sixty years to find the Way Home. When we first heard about our son our friends wanted to comfort us and assured us that it was "just a phase." Our first dismay over, we felt relief that he had found a firm faith with his wanderings over, for he sounded too sure and too joyous to wish him quickly out of it. Could this be our son who was writing on every page, "God is so Good!" and "I do believe that the Bread and Wine is changed into His Body and Blood, Soul and Divinity"? I knew that he meant what he said and that his faith was the result of deep thought and humility of mind and heart and the Grace of the Holy Spirit. My first impulse was to try to follow him,—not to enter the Church,—but to understand more of his experience. He seemed to have stepped into a new country. So when he asked us to read a few books, The Life of St. Bernard and of The Little Flower and Msgr. Sheen's, "The Mystical Body," I resolved to go on a pilgrimage also and try to find them.

Siccawei[1] is, perhaps, the best known Catholic Center in Shanghai. Non-Catholics know its observatory and weather reports, its industrial work,—brass work and beautiful embroidery,—the two pointed spires that stand at the end of Hung Shan Road, seen down a long vista of the long avenue. So my pilgrimage took me there first. It was like a different world and as I timidly went through the Convent gate I felt very strange, yet unexplainably at home. I found that most of the nuns whom I met talked French or a different Chinese dialect, so that I couldn't possibly explain to them what I wanted. I wandered into a lovely enclosed garden but hastily withdrew when an amused looking Sister told me by means of gestures and French that it was their private garden. She led me to the Chapel, restful and hushed after the busy, noisy market crowd through which I had come, out on the street—and I found myself standing near a statue of Our Lady. Only then I would have called her "Their Lady," if I named her at all. "Found myself" is the way it seemed, for I felt urged on by some inner Power. I looked up into the face of Mary and thought,—"If I could kneel here and feel that she is praying with me," for Bill (I had not learned to call him Br. Luke) and for our other four children, each with his or her very special needs which at such a distance we could only vaguely

1. Transliterated since the 1970s as *Xujiahui*.

pray about. And again I found myself kneeling there, and saying, "Even though for sixty years I have never spoken to you before, won't you please help us now."—And I looked about the church and felt the Presence of Our Lord, as never before. And I moved over to the rail in front of the Altar and knew that He was there. The sense of His Presence would have been overpowering if His Mother had not been praying with me. I felt small and timid as a little child, realizing how much I had to learn and how little I knew, but soon I found my whole being centered on Him and I had my first lesson in adoration. "And I came out to where the old world shone white" (G. K. Chesterton) and there were the market crowds, the rickshaws, the voices,—and a Voice.

Next came a trip to St. Joseph's Church on So. Szechuen Road, near the Bund and to the Convent opposite. The Sisters there, at the orphanage, directed me to The Church of Christ the King on Chang Lo Lu,[2] where a Jesuit Father Gatz came down the stairs to the hall, asking me in English, "Is there anything that I can do for you?" I stammered something about books, and he took me into the study and asked questions and I asked him questions,—foolish sounding questions full of life time prejudices. He had probably heard the same questions many, many times before but he answered them thoughtfully and I knew that they were not the personal opinions of one man, but the answers which The Church of Christ received from Him and has given all through the ages,—a bulwark of Faith and Hope and Love for Her seeking and needy children. Fr. Gatz found the books and brought them to our house, a few days after that. When I returned the books we talked again and he taught me to kneel in the Church for a few moments each time that I went there. I marvel now as I look back upon it, at the calm way he left it to God's Spirit to urge me on. Fr. Gatz never urged or even suggested that I come back again, but left the initiative to me. Of course he knew that the Holy Spirit was the Initiator. I found my way into other Churches, light and beautiful, old and new, tawdry and artistic

2. That is, Chang Lo Road.

and learned to stop saying, "I don't like—" but to find Our Lord there in the Tabernacle, and to realize that some of what did not appeal to me, was the devout expression of worshipping Christians of other times and other temperaments and were pleasing to Him. All the time I was being made more humble and more centered in God, and God was teaching me many lessons:—that tolerance and charity are not synonymous; that the Church tries to keep strong and clear the teaching of Christ, even at the cost of seeming intolerance, but has infinite sympathy and love for all human beings and through the Confessional knows the frailty of man and the Mercy of God; that the "I do not believe" of the Protestant must be changed to "I believe, even though I do not understand;" that within the generous framework of Catholic Faith there is plenty of room for thought and investigation; that instead of the One Church of which our Lord spoke being for the far distant future, we have it now, the One, Catholic and Apostolic Church, in which we believe; that the Creeds are alive and real, every single article of belief being beyond our finite understanding but a challenge for growth, through Grace, toward the fullness of understanding that we may approach as we grow in Grace and in the knowledge of Our Lord and Saviour, Jesus Christ; that Love of God comes first, above all things, and that the love of our neighbor does not mean an easy, pleasant attempt to please him but a willing of his highest good, remembering that Our Lord loves him as much as He loves me; that the break in the Body of Christ is a great tragedy,—greater even than the sins or errors of some members of His Church.

Attending Mass and praying it with the Priest was another step ahead and I began to go every Sunday, at the same time keeping up attendance at the Anglican or Episcopal Churches. In China they are called the Sheng Kung Hwei. At the Mass I had such a vivid sense of Adoration and Offering that a new sense of the Divine-Human encounter stayed with me long after it was over. Father Gatz explained the meaning of the Rosary and gave me one which I have tried to use every day since. The Devotion to The Sacred Heart of Jesus took possession of my heart and mind, even though I wished that the pictures would not be so anatomical. In both of these devotions I had a joyful sense of being one with Christ's followers of all ages and all nations; I learned that it is far better to be a disciple than a critic; the words, the meaning, the dramatic action of the Liturgy of the Church, especially the Consecration, the Transubstantiation,—all seemed like the rushing of a mighty wind,—and the still, small voice.

"You are doing a very dangerous thing," said the Father one day. And then began the agony of spirit, the conflict of loyalties that must come to every convert. My spirit had been soaring and I had been saying happily, "It is good for me to be here." Now I must face the difficulties and know whether or not I could pay the price and ask it of those closest to me.

The Episcopal Church (Anglican) had nurtured me and sent me to the Mission Field, for I had first come as a teacher in a school for girls, up the Yangtse River in Wuchang. As the wife of a greatly loved Episcopal Bishop, I would be withdrawing from many obligations. Could it be the will of God, when apparently my service to others would be greatly limited and they would be confused by my action? Never had we felt so keenly the tragedy of the break in the Christian Church, and we were being asked to pay the price. Could that price be paid best by my husband from whom I must separate in many of our interests and Church services, (we could not take Communion together), or best paid by my relinquishing my own conviction and turning away from this clear call from Our Lord? My talks with Mother Fitzgerald at the Convent of the Sacred Heart, and one talk with Fr. Marin, at Maison Chaminade in Peking were a great help. They both said simply and confidently, "Pray for the Light. The Light will come." During that summer our youngest son and I visited Peking, where I went to Mass at an old and poorly attended church, and Kuling, where I found a lovely church, nestled in a valley, with mountains all around. I met there a young French acquaintance, who looked surprised to see me at Mass, and said, "Why, I didn't know that you were a Catholic!" "I am not but I hope to be," I replied and I knew then that this was the prayer from my heart. There was a statue of St. Thérèse in that church, and I was glad to find her there.

The next fall I started regular instruction and did a good deal of reading. Benediction always dispelled my doubts and more and more, my prayer was in the beautiful words of Our Lady who was close to me through this struggle,—"Behold the handmaid of the Lord. Be it unto me according to Thy word." My husband knew that this conflict was going on and was generous and wise enough to stand by and leave the outcome to me and to the Spirit. For some time I tried to be both an Episcopalian and a Roman Catholic, and I kept up my connection with various interdenominational[3] groups in Shanghai. But it was a strain and soon began to seem dishonest. For there was no doubt in my own mind that I belonged in the Catholic Church, which is The Church of Christ as is no other. Yet one can not give up the close associations of sixty years without a wrench, and I knew that this stab at the heart, this suffering, would always be there. Yet every time that I asked myself whether this longing to stay with my friends, with my family (Br. Luke is the only Catholic), came from God, I had to acknowledge that it was human fellowship that drew me back. The picture by Hoffman, of Christ and the Rich Young Man, is hanging in our living room, and he seemed to say to me, "One thing I asked of this young man, that he give up his possessions. One thing I ask of you,—that you give up the approval of most of your friends and family, which you have treasured above all else, your popularity which made everything so easy for you, that you learn to really suffer for Me and My Church." If I refused to listen and took the easier way, I knew that He would always look sorrowfully after me.

Then, too, I must be sure that it was not because of Bill—Br. Luke—that I was entering the Church, that even if he should renounce it, I would keep on.

I did not talk with many others at this time,—only with my husband and Fr. Gatz. With such a background of the Episcopal Church, I knew pretty well what most of my friends would say. "Why can't you find it all in the Catholic Branch of your

3. That is, among the different Protestant denominations.

own church?" Observances, yes,—even Sacraments,—but unity through Obedience, no. One of my friends wrote me, "Do you realize that they call us heretics?" I replied that I did not spend much time in calling others heretics, but that I had come to feel that I myself was a heretic. The hardest was when people said, "Have you any right to think of your own soul and spiritual growth,—when it means not sharing in your husband's work and worship? Are you not entirely selfish,—or else out of your senses?" My great desire has always been to share everything with him. Could our affection stand the strain? Thanks to his greatness and with the Grace of God—I felt that it could. Oh,—the peace of the moment when we take a leap, trustingly, into the arms of God!

The Church received me into its fold on May 30, 1949, at a short ceremony before Benediction, in the Church of Christ the King. My baptism as an infant was recognized and I received my First Holy Communion the next morning, May 31, the Feast of Our Lady Mediatrix of All Graces and Our Lady of China. The General Confession preceding this, and every Confession, was a blending of joy and suffering, which has characterized this whole experience and always will. Pondering Our Lady's Mysteries in the Rosary and the Seven Dolors has made me realize how true this is of all of our deepest experiences, as it was true of hers. To the person who is the only Catholic among most of her friends and family, who has to suffer the pain of hurting those most dear, there is much of this double quality producing tension. But the daily Act of Faith, Hope and Love is a great steadier. If we love God above all, we are on the Way of the Cross and Resurrection and Eternal Joy.

Those last days of May were exciting ones for the whole city of Shanghai, for the Communist Armies (The People's Liberation Army) marched into the western area where we lived on May 23rd, and for two nights and two days stray shots were flying about and we had to stay off the streets, but by the morning of Ascension Day, my bicycle and I were speeding through deserted but quiet streets for early Mass. Soldiers with uniforms the shade of mustard pickles had taken the place of the traffic police, and groups of them were patrolling the streets. They were well behaved so that it was soon possible to move about with a good deal of freedom.

In all this time my "Catholic Bicycle" helped greatly,—so called because on it I was able to get across the city to the Church of Christ the King, less expensively and more easily than by bus or pedicab.[4] It took about fifteen minutes and always will the early morning trips through the streets, remain very clearly in my mind. Sleepy apprentice boys taking down the boards that close up the shops at night; women fanning the smoky flames of the little charcoal braziers; the "traveling restaurants" carried about on a pole over the shoulder of the seller were set down by the side of the road to give bean curd milk[5] and fried cakes to the early morning workers. By the time that Mass was over the world was astir and the shop keepers calling their wares. And for every one of the thousands of people swarming through the streets Our Lord Jesus Christ lived and died on the Cross and lives again, if they but knew where to find Him. When I was called to the Mission Field as a Student Volunteer in Wellesley College, I thought it was that I might help to win the Chinese people to Christ. But actually it was in order that, out here in Shanghai, forty years later, I might be called into His Church.

Deo Gratias

By way of giving thanks to God and to those Priests and Sisters and friends whom he has used to help me greatly in this first year of life in the Catholic Church, I want to state some observations and convictions—all probably taken for granted by life-long Catholics, that is, some slowly dawning on this infant mind, others bursting with a flash of Truth, what, I suppose, is meant by Spiritual Understanding. This is only a small beginning of what is to be learned in this life and the next.

4. A three-wheeled bicycle with seat, pedals, and handlebars in front for the operator and a cab in back for the passenger. It is the equivalent of a bicycle-powered rickshaw, or *jinriksha*.

5. That is, soybean juice.

At first it seemed a lonely road, but the welcome I have received from the Sisters of the Good Shepherd Convent with generous spiritual advice, books lent and prayers said before Our Lord in their Chapel, and with "Our Lady of Peace," standing nearby has been a constant help and inspiration; as has the Sodality, with its monthly Mass and other meetings at the Convent of the Sacred Heart, and Mother St. Aiden and others of the Helpers of The Holy Souls at Siccawei. The devotion and singleness of purpose with a breadth of human sympathy and Divine Love of the Fathers at the Church of Christ the King, as well as others in Shanghai have shown what the Priesthood is, and have made me understand how they are set apart for instruments, through the Sacraments, for God's Grace. The different nationalities and races worshipping together in the Shanghai Churches,—Portuguese, Chinese, Japanese, Americans, Koreans, British, Russians and others,—rich and poor and "everyday" people, old and young (the little children, kneeling before the Manger at Christmas or being held up to touch the Holy Water, or watching the Priest at Mass) shows forth the Catholicity of the One Church.

From feeling that Sacraments, while valuable, were mostly subjective, an affirmation of a truth—I have come to know that through them God works. He does use the material or the action as channels or instruments for His Grace to come to us. Through them He reaches us and we mysteriously but truly share in His Divine Life.

Creeds had always bothered me because I felt that they were not really believed, and I tried omitting phrases, really wishing to drop them entirely. Now I can joyously say "I believe—," not understanding, but knowing that they are true because the Church teaches them and God has revealed the Truth. Both tradition and the Bible take on an undeniable voice of interpretation in order to penetrate the confusion,—to see Our Lord and to hear Him and to come to God through Him. Through this year the richness of life and the nearness of Heaven has been made vivid by increased devotion to the Saints, to my special St. Thérèse, the little Flower, who so greatly and simply loved God and made Him Loved, and above all to the Greatest of the Saints, Mary, the Mother of

Our Lord, Our Mother and the Mother of His Mystical Body, the Church. I begin to see the unending value of the Liturgy of the Church, if we follow year after year the cycle as offered to us, and of special devotions,—the Rosary, the Sacred Heart and others, appealing to such a wide variety of temperament. I realize that we can not observe all or assimilate all the richness that is there, but we can all find some that express what we would express and as time goes on grow into an understanding of others that perhaps do not now seem to meet our need, always remembering that into the treasury of devotion has been poured and is still being poured the love and devotion and expressed adoration of all races and types and temperaments. Were it not so the Church would not be Catholic.

As I said before, during much of my life I have felt that tolerance is the same as charity and that for unity we must pare down our Christian Faith to the lowest common denominator. Now I know that tolerance and charity are not synonymous, and that the Church preserves and guards the Faith which is the Incarnation, Jesus Christ, true God and true Man, all He lived and taught; the Sacraments He instituted in order that He might be with us always; the Faith once delivered and constantly delivered, even at the cost of intolerance. But that She is as wide in Her sympathy and charity as the Master whom She incarnates. Tolerance may be indifference to Truth. "There are many roads to heaven and it doesn't matter which we choose," forgetting that the Divine Teacher whom we follow showed us His Way, which leads to life everlasting, and it does matter whether we follow His Way. But we must all strive for Unity on the basis of Charity. "Love one another as I have loved you," all the time praying that in God's Way and no other, we all may be one. We go to Christ to learn of Him and change our lives (let Him change our lives) not to find out how much of what we think or do agrees with what He seems to have said, dismissing as impracticable what does not agree with our way. The Bible is true and this Church, which is supposed to have the closed Bible, is really preserving the Bible as true and God given and to be believed and followed more than any other.

Converts have difficulties that are not granted to those brought up in the Church, but with God's help, these very difficulties are a privilege and a cause for thankfulness. I pray that our home may in some way be a meeting place of Catholics and non-Catholics so that in meeting many prejudices may disappear and understanding hearts may be born.

Our time of departure from China is near. To leave the Church of Christ the King, and especially my first "Father in God" and Spiritual Director who has so wisely directed my faltering footsteps through this first year in the Catholic Church, is not easy. But the One Church is in the United States, as She is all over the world. He who has called me into His Church will guide us in the years to come and will accept my imperfect offerings. May all be done for His Praise and His Service and His Glory.

This photograph of my parents was taken by a professional photographer in Shanghai in 1949, when they were 61. It was only a few weeks after the Communist army had taken control of the city and my mother had been received into the Catholic Church. The picture was sent to all the members of the family to show that, despite these two events, my parents were in good health and living together in peace. My mother's chronicle, above, was written a few months later. As a complement to it, the following poem by my father, evidently written during his last years, was found by my mother among his papers in 1981. It had a small paper clipped to it saying, "Dorothy."

On the Way Out

When evening shadows round us fall
And life ebbs like the sea,
We hear our Heavenly Father's call,
"Return, my child, to me."

So Christ our Lord, when called to bear
The pains of Calvary,
Found strength and comfort in the prayer,
"Father, I come to Thee."

We, too, in our declining years
May cheered and brightened be
To know, as our departure nears,
We come, O Lord, to Thee;

To Thee and to that honored host
That crowds Eternity:
Fulfillment to the uttermost
Of human destiny.

Appendix II

Text on
CHURCH UNITY
1990

This somewhat autobiographical reflection on unity was written at Spencer in 1990, shortly before my reelection as abbot there. It was in preparation for an ecumenical meeting, but I decided to archive it, since it might have been interpreted by some members of the community as a personal declaration in view of the abbatial election. I forgot about it and only unearthed it 20 years later, after completing these letters to Father Eddie.

Searched for by Unity

Why unity? For many years I couldn't figure out why Church persons, spiritual writers and even Jesus Himself wrote or talked so much about this strange reality. Or was it a reality?

What bothered me most in the talk about unity was the relativity it seemed to imply: the backing off from one's sincerely held convictions for the sake of someone else's point of view. Did anyone really have the right to impinge on my freedom of conscience like this? And could I in conscience renounce a plan of action which I judged to be right, just for the sake of keeping "united" to those with whom I disagreed? It seemed so inauthentic, so superficial! Perhaps unity is important, but truth and faithfulness to one's conscience are even more important. An emphasis on unity could easily get in the way of these higher values, so I thought.

I suspect that I am not the only person who has had this difficulty in coming to grips with Jesus' prayer, "That all may be one." Perhaps I can share with you the steps I was interiorly dragged through in order to arrive at following Jesus—and the Church—in praying for a unity based on that which reigns between the Father and the Son.

First came faith. I could not escape the supreme importance of the priestly prayer of Christ at the Last Supper, "Father, . . . may they be one just as you and I are one: I in them and you in me, so that they may be completely one, in order that the world may know that you sent me."[1] Although my moralistic difficulties with unity still remained, I began to see that Jesus had higher goals in mind. Maybe there are degrees of truth. And maybe my degree, though real, is not up to the degree of truth that Jesus wants in the world and which seems to be linked to unity among his followers. He clearly wants us to be united—and very united.

With a deeper faith in these key words of the Lord, there came a second step in unity: a tolerance for the opposition, even in matters of religious belief. This was hard for me. I had broken with most of my family and friends in order to become a Roman Catholic, so was I now going to become tolerant of what I had rejected at such a price? It took time. Little by little many words of the gospel took on an ecumenical meaning: "Blessed are the peacemakers, for they will be called children of God";[2] "Whoever is not against us is for us";[3] "Lord, do you want us to call down fire from heaven to consume them? Jesus turned and rebuked them";[4] "Sir, leave it for this year also, and I shall cultivate the ground around it and fertilize it; it may bear fruit in the future";[5] and many others. Tolerance gradually grew into respect for the other's truth precisely as not mine.

A third step towards unity opened up to me quite unexpectedly: the reality of interior grace. This is really the key to everything else. There is a spiritual river which flows underneath the surface of a divided Church, springing up in the hearts of the

1. Jn 17:21.
2. Mk 5:9.
3. Mk 9:40.
4. Lk 9:54-55.
5. Lk 13:8-9.

faithful. "The waters of a river give joy to God's city."[6] Healing comes from this river, as Ezekiel prophesied,[7] since it flows from God's Temple, the crucified and risen Body of Christ. What does this hidden river contain? Somehow I realized that this underground stream which had touched me was a life deeper and richer than my own: a life of divine love and a channel of truth. The heart melts when it knows itself truly loved, and by a God! Somehow the mind enters into the heart, and the heart into the mind. An inner unification takes place. Love and truth have to embrace in the soul before anyone can really be an instrument of either love or truth in the Church. This essential lesson in ecumenism can only be learned from within, as a gift from the Lord of all unity.

There still remains putting this into practice, and this is the fourth step. Perhaps there is a fifth one: when Christ's prayer is fulfilled. Meanwhile it seems to me of paramount importance to live by both truth and love. We have to follow our conscience, but the latter has to let itself be wounded by wisdom: by what is true and by how to love. Love without truth is not real and becomes anti-love. Truth without love is not a divine truth and is a counter-witness to Jesus, since our conscience can be false. Love does not deny the problems and real differences which separate the followers of Christ, but it jumps over them, as it were, to create a new climate in which our hearts will be more disposed to agree on this or that meaning of the Gospel message. "When that day comes you will not question me about anything, . . . but I will tell you clearly about the Father."[8] That day will certainly come, because Jesus has prayed for it. It is the object of our prayer, too, as we let ourselves be searched for by unity.

---

6. Ps 45(46): 5.
7. Ez 47:12.
8. Jn 16:23-27.

The surviving founders of the community of Azul with the abbot of the founding house, on the occasion of Azul's 50th anniversary in 2008. From left: Br. Thomas Ringwood, Fr. Paul Mary Heide, Abbot Damian Carr of Spencer, Fr. Augustine Roberts, and Br. Martin Crahan.